D1601214

My Turn to Weep

My Turn to Weep

Salvadoran Refugee Women in Costa Rica

ROBIN ORMES QUIZAR

BERGIN & GARVEY
Westport, Connecticut • London

Library of Congress Cataloging-in-Publication Data

Quizar, Robin Ormes, 1942–
   My turn to weep : Salvadoran refugee women in Costa Rica / Robin
Ormes Quizar.
      p.   cm.
   Includes bibliographical references (p.   ) and index.
   ISBN 0-89789-540-1 (alk. paper)
   1. Women refugees—Costa Rica—Interviews.   2. Refugees,
Political—Costa Rica—Interviews.   3. Refugees, Political—El
Salvador—Interviews.   4. Salvadorans—Costa Rica—Interviews.
5. Child care workers—Costa Rica—Interviews.   6. Feminism—Costa
Rica.   7. El Salvador—History—1979–1992.   I. Title.
JV7413.Q59   1998
325′.21′082097284—dc21   97–40996

British Library Cataloguing in Publication Data is available.

Library of Congress Catalog Card Number: 97–40996
ISBN: 0-89789-540-1

First published in 1998

Bergin & Garvey, 88 Post Road West, Westport, CT 06881
An imprint of Greenwood Publishing Group, Inc.

Printed in the United States of America

The paper used in this book complies with the
Permanent Paper Standard issued by the National
Information Standards Organization (Z39.48–1984).

10 9 8 7 6 5 4 3 2 1

This book is dedicated to the Salvadoran refugee women who gave me the honor of listening to their stories.

Contents

Acknowledgments   ix

Introduction   xi

Part I: The Women Alone   1

  1   María   "Three soldiers raped me . . . and I was eight
             months pregnant."   3

  2   Rita   "They invaded all the resettlement groups."   17

  3   Carmen   "It is my turn to weep."   37

  4   Mirabela   "We, as women, . . . cannot remain with our
             arms crossed."   51

  5   Alicia   "My entire family fell apart."   67

  6   Ligia   "Exile has been a kind of school."   83

Part II: The Women Together   93

  7   Carmen   "This is the way we can collaborate for now."   95

  8   Rita   "I only wanted to cry and cry."   109

  9   Alicia   "So we go on alone."   117

10   Mirabela   "Robin, when will you let me talk with
                you again?"   131

11   María   "'Lady, I thought you were stupid.'"   139

12   Rina   "My husband abandoned me . . . just when
              I needed him most."   145

13   Carolina   "Feeling much stronger because we
                  were together . . . "   153

14   Ligia   "There are limits as to what you can do."   159

15   Alicia   "For the sake of our cause . . . "   167

Epilogue   "That is the way life is."   175

Works Cited   183

Index   187

Acknowledgments

The writing of this book has been a collaborative effort involving many people, only a few of who I will be able to mention here. For those of you not named, I thank you for your support, friendship, and many wonderful suggestions.

I wish to thank Margaret Datz for her special help in my getting a Fulbright to Costa Rica and then her encouragement as a friend and a writer once I embarked on this project. My thanks go to Gail Nystrom for introducing me to the refugee community and to Judit Tomcsányi for her sensitivity and linguistic skills in the transcribing of the taped *testimonios*.

I am grateful to two friends and members of my writing group who read portions of my early draft: Ann Scarboro who kept gently pushing me onward and Susan Boucher who gave me many valuable comments on my writing.

Thanks also go to two readers of much later drafts, Paula Palmer and Payson Sheets, both of whose understanding of the history and culture of Central America helped significantly to guide my efforts.

I wish to thank my colleagues in the English Department as well as in the administration at the Metropolitan State College of Denver for their encouragement and financial support in the final stages of writing this book.

Finally special thanks go to the Salvadoran refugees who made this project possible and to my daughter Jessi who cheerfully put up with me during the process and who never doubted that I could do it.

Introduction

The assumption underlying mainstream feminist theory in the United States is that women everywhere experience oppression primarily from the gender roles that are culturally assigned to them. As Cott (1987:9) puts it, "feminism aims to alter power relationships between men and women," historically advocating, among other things, the rights of women to vote, to receive equal pay for equal work, and to own property. U.S. feminists have generally stood in "opposition to ranking one sex as inferior or superior" to the other and in "opposition to one sex's categorical control of the rights and opportunities of the other" (Cott 1987:4).

This mainstream view of feminism remains skewed towards those who can easily ignore their other status markers, such as race, class, religion, culture, or political opinion, and who can focus first and foremost on their gender status, on their status vis-à-vis men. Women of color in the United States, for whom some of these non-gender status markers remain paramount, have often been critical of the feminist movement as being too simplistic and even as being irrelevant (Westwood and Radcliffe 1993:5). Latin American feminists have had similar criticisms of mainstream U.S. feminism, though they have been much freer to develop their own brand of feminist thought, suitable to their own political and cultural situation. Many Latin American women's groups have arisen out of socioeconomic movements that cut across class lines rather than gender lines; for example, urban women fighting for lower consumer prices or demanding schools and medical clinics in their neighborhoods. Other groups have developed under repressive regimes, protesting the imprisonment and disappearance of people, mostly men, who were allegedly involved in subversive political activities. Middle-class professional women in Latin America have typically aligned themselves with these other two groups, providing help to the victims of repression and advocating social change in favor of poorer urban women (Jaquette 1989:3–5). Latin American women's movements have thus tended to support a conservative view of the family, quite distinct from the view purported by mainstream U.S. feminism. Their concerns are progressive primarily in their focus on the leveling of class distinctions; their goals are the reduction of poverty and the extension of education, medical services, and basic human rights.

Of course, each Latin American country has a distinct political and socioeconomic climate, which results in differing forms of advocacy for and by women. The present study, about a group of Salvadoran refugee women running a daycare center for their children in Costa Rica, illustrates the multidimensionality of Latin American feminism in its complex situations of power, subordination, and exploitation. The women in this study have experienced two sets of circumstances: one, their refugee status in Costa Rica, and the other, their lives back in El Salvador, where they lived through a civil war. This study shows them through the words of their *testimonios* [personal stories of the witnessing of political oppression], as well as through the perspective of them that arises from my interactions with them at the daycare center.

In the late 1970s and early 1980s, when the women were still in El Salvador, their country was dominated by a small wealthy U.S.-backed group (the so-called Fourteen Families), who controlled the land, the export industry, and much of the government and local industry. The great majority of the Salvadoran people were peasants living in abject poverty, either as wage earners bound to other people's land or as the struggling owners of their own tiny plots of land. The women who ended up as refugees at the daycare center tended to fall between these two extremes; most of them had enough money to flee to Costa Rica but not enough money or power to remain safe from pursuit by the military in their own country. All were associated with occupational or socioeconomic classes that were looked upon with suspicion by the Salvadoran government—peasants, union members, teachers, students, and liberation-theology Catholics. This is not to say that any of these women were guerrillas, or "subversives," as their government claimed; they were merely associated with groups that had potential reasons for resenting the status quo.

During these same years in El Salvador, both men and women were subject to exploitation by a higher class elite, and in the context of the civil war, both were subject to torture and death. However, there was a gender differential in the types of degradation involved. Women found themselves seduced and raped by their employers at work (and then tossed back onto the street when they got pregnant), or violently gang raped by groups of soldiers during a raid on their home (often in front of the entire family, including their husbands). Men were more likely to be accused of "subversive" activities than women and thus were more often imprisoned, tortured, killed, or "disappeared." Men were also more likely to find themselves exploited at work, both through physical or mental abuse and through extremely low wages, although women who worked outside the home were also subject to similar abuses.

Though El Salvador historically has had racial and ethnic groups who experienced severe discrimination, these groups have blended together so that the distinctions are almost invisible. As in other Latin American nations, miscegenation among descendants of Spanish colonists, black slaves, and indigenous peoples has caused a "whitening" of the society such that no clear racial markers remain (Westwood and Radcliffe 1993:6; White 1973:54). Suppression of ethnic divisions in El Salvador has additionally developed out of the voluntary or forced acculturation of ethnic groups, as well as systematic eliminations of these groups by military or paramilitary forces (Anderson 1971; North 1985:22). Thus, though there may be distinctions in racial or ethnic background among Salvadorans, discrimination on the basis of these factors is more historical than current.

Latin American feminism, with its focus on socioeconomic differences rather than gender distinctions, was closely aligned with the revolutionary politics of El Salvador during the 1970s and 1980s. Although the U.S. government tended to propagandize the Salvadoran revolution as being part of the global struggle for communism, that perspective was seen as fanatical by the refugee women at the daycare center. Their concerns were much more down-to-earth: poverty, malnutrition, education, health care, and human rights. Revolutionary politics had similar goals, even though the rhetoric of the revolution was often couched in Marxist terms.

Political activism in El Salvador during the civil conflict took the extreme form of guerrilla warfare against the military-backed government. A less violent form of activity was propagandizing, either by writing and distributing political literature, painting political messages on walls, or holding meetings and lectures centered on open political discussion. Another form of propagandizing was participating in demonstrations that were focused on particular issues, such as demanding justice for the "disappeared." Any union activity devoted to raising salaries, increasing workers' benefits, or improving working conditions was also considered political propagandizing. Both violent and nonviolent means of protest were viewed as "subversive" by the Salvadoran government, and those involved were labeled "communists." Such labels were convenient for pointing out enemies of the state, in addition to being part of the effective government rhetoric for gaining U.S. military aid during the civil war.

As the *testimonios* of the refugee women illustrate, Salvadoran citizens were under suspicion in their country even if they showed only the potential for political activism. The daughter of a progressive farmer who distributed fertilizer to the peasants was in as much danger from persecution as the wife of a union leader who held clandestine meetings at their home. A woman was considered "guilty by association" with certain men, whether she was aware of the men's activities or not. All the women in a family—the mother, the wife, the sisters, the daughters, the aunts—came under pressure from the authorities if a member of the extended family was murdered or became one of the "disappeared." Such women often felt obliged to go into hiding or to flee their homeland.

For most of the women at the daycare center, becoming politically active back home had not been a viable option. Two women took part in street demonstrations, and though their participation was minimal, they knew they were taking risks. Only one woman admitted to becoming involved in all kinds of dangerous activities, including joining the Committee of Mothers when it was still only a small group protesting the killings and "disappearances" of the men. Now, however, all the women at the Center were motivated into activity after being forced into exile, most of them through tragic circumstances. They operated together, in "collaboration" with one another as they put it, keenly aware of their potential influence as a group. Nevertheless, their political action fell well within their traditional roles as women. For one thing, they viewed their work at the Center as a practical expression of their political opinions. Their daily work involved cooking, cleaning, and childcare, though on a higher plane they promoted themselves as the nurturers of an improved Salvadoran culture through their ways of raising the children. In addition, cooperative behavior at the Center (regarding duties, scheduling, and decision-making) was touted by the women as a superior mode of operation, even though the daycare staff did not always achieve this ideal.

Cooperative group behavior was obviously a political asset to the women; they would have feared to speak out alone. Cooperation was an asset in other ways, as well. When the women arrived in Costa Rica, they were initially given short-term emergency funds by international relief organizations, which they applied for and received as individuals. Although they often participated in co-housing projects and helped each other out with cooking and childcare, they viewed this behavior as temporary—a step toward living and working on their own. Dutch and Swedish funding agencies built on this cooperative behavior, however, and provided financial backing for groups of refugees who were willing to develop grass roots projects that promised eventually to become self-supporting. The daycare center was one of these cooperative projects. Although it never became financially profitable, as other grass roots projects did, the Center was an obvious benefit to the refugee community. Not only did the children receive the advantage of good care, the women gained valuable work experience, economic support for their families, and increased self-respect.

When I arrived in 1988 and asked to conduct research among the group, the women immediately saw an opportunity to express their political opinions through my work. They started by insisting that I listen to and then disseminate their *testimonios* of persecution, in hopes of having some influence on world opinion of their plight. Like their work at the daycare center, the oral expression of their personal experiences was a form of political activity that fit easily into their traditional patterns of behavior. Storytelling and impromptu drama are a significant aspect of their culture, and women are expected to participate in such activities. At the same time, they knew that I would be putting their *testimonios* into written form, which was the necessary format for gaining the respect and attention of the outside world. They not only hoped that I would do this, they insisted on it.

By the time of my research, the refugees had considerable experience with using their *testimonios* to achieve control over their own lives. They had first been required to tell their stories in order to receive legal documentation in Costa Rica. They then needed the stories to acquire relief aid in the form of housing, food, and medicine. Later, the refugees used them to get sympathy from reporters and to obtain financial support from international agencies. The women were now prepared to build on this experience and use the *testimonios* collectively for political leverage, with my research as the conduit for their message.

This book describes only a small group of women refugees from El Salvador and therefore cannot claim to be representative of all refugees, or even of all Salvadoran refugees who came to Costa Rica in the late 1970s and early 1980s. It is clear, for example, from the limited data I gathered on the male refugees in Costa Rica, that the men had very different problems from the women. Moreover, not all refugees were lucky enough to get a project funded by an international agency, as these women had. Nevertheless, the women at the daycare center fit well into the image presented by the literature on Latin American feminism, and for that reason, the group provides a significant perspective. As individuals, the women are resilient and assertive, yet they remain "feminine" in a traditional sense. They work collaboratively toward their political goals, they encourage other people and organizations to fight their more complicated political battles for them, and they strive toward their own more easily attainable goals at the daycare center. They are obviously less concerned with breaking away from historical gender role patterns than with struggling against inequities in a socioeconomic system that causes them and their families to live in poverty.

Although I am making the claim that the refugee women's lives represent a contrast to the struggles of U.S. feminists, I will make little reference to feminist theory within the text. This is due to my focus on the women's own orientation to their problems. Since they do not view themselves as "feminists," I feel I cannot represent them as such. Instead, I attempt to describe them in the context of their world—within their own cultural and historical background—so that the reader can understand where the women get their strength, in spite of the violent oppression they have experienced.

Part I focuses on the Salvadoran refugee women as individuals, with each chapter centered on a specific theme relevant to the woman's story. María's *testimonio* of rape and murder provides a sharp contrast between the perils of life in El Salvador during the civil war and the peaceful existence at the daycare center in Costa Rica. Rita's personal story of the confiscation of her family's farmland is interwoven against the history of rural settlement and land displacement in El Salvador. The losses of her family members are placed in the context of a country where military control has traditionally been exercised over the peasantry. Carmen's story is that of a young teacher being sent out into a rural community to work and illustrates the growing middle-class awareness of the widespread poverty and unrest in El Salvador. Mirabela's story is a direct political statement, on the one hand condemning those she considers responsible for maintaining socioeconomic inequities in El Salvador and on the other hand praising those she perceives as martyrs for justice. Mirabela's chapter also deals with U.S. involvement in El Salvador. Alicia's story of finding her husband's body in a cemetery and of the consequences of this loss to her family illustrates how a young woman uses her intelligence to outwit the authorities and escape from El Salvador. Ligia's story of an upper-class woman who reluctantly left her aristocratic family in El Salvador to join her more liberal-minded physician husband in exile demonstrates the general migration to Costa Rica, the "Switzerland of the Americas."

Part II focuses on the women as members of the refugee community and emphasizes the problems of adaptation. Carmen explains some of the early experiences of the refugees as they entered Costa Rica, while her husband Federico provides a contrast to the female perspective. Rita focuses on the psychological wounds experienced by the refugees. Alicia's story of adaptation and her social interactions with me as an ethnographer demonstrate the strength of her personality. Her storytelling talent and the competitiveness of her behavior are seen as a threat to the welfare of the refugee community and serve to illustrate a major conflict among the women at the daycare center. Mirabela demonstrates the significance of the *testimonios* in refugee life. María shows some of the difficulties that refugees had in getting emergency aid for their families and also the emotional trauma of remaining dependent on outside help. Rina's story illustrates the strength and hope of the refugee women in the face of violence and persecution. Carolina's story touches on the interrelationships among socioeconomic classes in El Salvador, especially patterns of authority between a *patrón* [protector and donor] and his underlings, and shows how this affects the behavior of the refugees in Costa Rica. Ligia focuses on her attempts to keep the daycare center viable despite decreasing international funds and increasing personal conflicts at the Center. Alicia's interactions at the daycare center provide further insight into the tensions among the refugee women at the same time that they indicate the political cohesiveness of the group. This chapter also shows the final stages of my year of research. The epilogue describes my subsequent contacts with the women through letters and a return trip to Costa Rica, demonstrating the success of the refugee experience as a transition towards a better life.

Part I

The Women Alone

1

María

"Three soldiers raped me . . . and I was eight months pregnant."

María wakes up early to get her three children off to school. Her eldest daughter, twelve-year-old Francesca, is already out of bed and dressed, helping in the preparations by wrapping the mid-morning snacks of *pupusas* [tortillas stuffed with beans or cheese, a typical Salvadoran food] into small plastic bags, one for each child. Her son Manuel, who always takes a long time to wake up, sits sleepily on the edge of the bed he shares with his uncle. Outside by the *pila* [large cement sink] the younger daughter Elisa splashes her face with cold water.

This is the time of day when the little house seems most crowded. Actually, María's place hardly qualifies as a "house," even though she pays monthly rent for the family to stay there. Consisting of boards for walls and a piece of laminated metal for the roof, it is more like a lean-to shack that is connected to the back of someone else's house. The lean-to started out as a single room, but María's brother and some of their Salvadoran friends partitioned it into four tiny cubbyholes. This new arrangement allows for the privacy of two separate bedrooms and two serviceable family rooms.

María stands at the electric stove warming up the tortillas and beans for breakfast and breathing in the welcome aroma of coffee. It smells wonderful. The pain in her neck that always disturbs her sleep has subsided somewhat. She looks forward to the warmth and fullness of breakfast, feeling lucky. It is still early in the month, and there is no thought yet of skimping on the morning meal. The children will be comfortable at school, and she herself will not have to spend several hours waiting impatiently for lunch.

Manuel emerges from the bedroom. His uncle is still sleeping, being the only one in the house with no place to go today. Manuel pulls

the curtain shut to shield the bedroom from the morning clatter. He sits
down in a chair to wait for his plateful of tortillas and beans, taking noisy
sips from the steaming cup of coffee already set before him on the table.
María dishes out Manuel's breakfast first and then serves the two girls
who have joined him at the table. Finally, María takes a bite or two for
herself, sitting on a low bench by the stove. She is already tired from the
morning's exertions.

Later in the day María will be at the daycare center up on the
hill, where her duties are to take care of the smallest babies. She is one
of a small group of Salvadoran refugees, mostly women, who run the
Center for their children in a large Costa Rican town. The Center is
housed in a middle-class dwelling in a quiet neighborhood. Apart from
the exuberant sound of young voices coming from the building, there is
little to indicate that this house is any different from the others on the
same street; a passerby will see no sign on the door to advertise the
activities inside.

A person walking by between seven and eight in the morning
might observe the arrival of children accompanied by an older sibling
dressed in a school uniform or by a parent on the way to work. The
children do not come in cars; they arrive on foot or by the public bus
system. The only child that is brought here in a car is the son of a well-
known Salvadoran singer. His family's car is at least a decade old, but
a sure sign of his mother's artistic success. The women at the Center are
proud to count this little boy among their charges.

One of the mothers arrives very early, rushing her four-year-old
daughter into the back room by the kitchen and quickly washing the little
girl's hair in the *pila*. Mother and daughter come to town by bus from
up in the hills. They are afraid to wash the child's hair at home before
they leave in the morning because of the drafty ride on the bus. Their
house does not have running water in the evenings, due to a scarcity of
water and the antiquated water system in their rural community.

María sits on the bench watching the children play and holding
on her lap a baby who seems to be about three months old. María looks
up at me and smiles absently as I come over to greet her. I take a seat
beside her on the bench, and for a few minutes we watch the children
together in silence. I recall the *testimonio* she gave me a few days
earlier.

María: Well, our life in El Salvador was working in the fields. But we
lived this way . . . in the country, in a small village. Our work was farming. And
me, I enjoyed selling religious objects. But when . . . but because we had photos
of Monseñor Romero . . . the . . . the soldiers came . . . since our neighbors had
pointed us out. . . .
And we worked there only planting and harvesting corn and beans,

because with this—the crop that we got out, after we sold it—this is what we lived on. We didn't pay rent there on our house, though. You worked out in the fields, and you got your living from that, from the crop that you harvested.

But when the soldiers noticed that you, well, that you were a Catholic, then they went around persecuting you. When they arrived at our house . . . and it was when . . . well, really, they took out my fourteen-year-old daughter, and they took me and my father out, and my father was . . . they murdered him, and my daughter, too. They raped her in a church, and me . . . I was eight months pregnant, and they raped me, too . . . and they said, well, that they had murdered me, because they had stabbed me in the back and here on the chest and neck, and right in front of me they set out to drink my father's blood. And they said to us that we . . . they said that we were helping the guerrillas. . . .

And it was not true, because we spent all our days at work, and it was . . . I do not know . . . because some people had come, people who work in such things, in the fields, they had come to bring fertilizer to our house. Because what my father did was to give fertilizer to all the farmers. And this was why, the motive really, the soldiers had done this, why they had been ordered to cause a massacre there at our house.

Three soldiers raped me . . . and I was eight months pregnant. . . .

And then the soldiers said that they had murdered my father and my daughter, and they tied a strip of rubber over my mouth so that I could not say anything, and with a long knife they gave it to me in the back, and they said that . . . now . . . or rather . . . that now they would kill everybody with this, since we had photographs of Monseñor Romero and everything. . . .

But you plead to God so . . . I said, "I pray. . . ."

That is how I was able to get up from where they had thrown me. They had even put tree branches on top of me. I said, "If I stay alive, I will go to another country, I will denounce everything that they do to people." I said, "Because they do such things that people are no longer able to say anything . . . and I will denounce them." I said to myself, "Because . . ." because I, being eight months pregnant, and the others, my other two children, who remained in the house. . . . My niece and nephew that had been left orphans, they said to the soldiers, "Don't you do anything to my aunt." They said this to the soldiers, but the men did not . . . they did not . . . well, I really don't know if they were under drugs . . . they didn't pay attention to anything. They only paid attention to the colonel, the one that . . . because he gave the orders.

Where . . . the colonel kept saying to them, "Do the job well, *cabrones* [male goats; cuckolds]," he told them . . . because soldiers talk badly that way, "Do your job well. If you don't do your job well, you will all die too."

This is why I say that . . . I do not blame the soldiers that much, really, because . . . because they are . . . since he . . . well, they have someone, a boss, who orders them around, and they have to do things in order not to die, but . . . I am thankful to God that . . . I am alive, and . . .

I walked sixteen kilometers from where I lived because there were no buses, and well, wounded in the back and pregnant and raped, so that I could hardly walk. But I succeeded in getting to a hospital. Some journalists took me there, who saw, really, the state I was in. . . . They took me to be cured, and some woman in . . . in the Sacred Family, some nurses took me to a refugee

center in San Salvador and . . . there they cured me. And the baby boy that I
carried, had . . . the one that I carried in my arms like this . . . or rather, the one
I had with me when I was pregnant and stabbed . . . the nine-month-old boy that
I carried in my arms . . . the one that the soldiers had kicked, and a little nine-year-
old girl that I brought, the one that I still have, that . . .

I return to the present, focusing once again on the María I see
sitting beside me in the patio. The baby on her lap begins to fuss, so she
shifts him around to face her. When he still refuses to quiet down, María
raises herself up slowly from the bench and takes him off into the
toddler's room.
I sit there thinking. It is hard to reconcile my peaceful picture of
María's life at the Center surrounded by babies with her incredible story
of rape and murder and violence. I am not even sure that I have
understood her words correctly. María's story is replete with unfinished
sentences and scattered thoughts. Maybe I have misinterpreted the
Spanish. Or maybe I have imagined it all. Later, however, after the
story has been carefully transcribed from the tape recording, I realize that
María has actually said what I have heard her to say.

In February of 1988 I went to Costa Rica on a Fulbright
lectureship to teach linguistics at the National University in Heredia. I
was interested in conducting cultural research, alongside my teaching, but
my decision as to what specific project I would do had been postponed
during the initial hectic weeks after my arrival. First, I had to find an
apartment, buy a used car, prepare for my classes, and get my young
daughter into school.
I learned about the daycare center from an American woman
named Gail. Gail had worked on and off with the Salvadoran refugees
ever since their mass entry into Costa Rica in 1979–1981. Her work had
officially involved educational programs to help the refugees, but she had
also lived among them, putting her in a unique position to help me
contact the different groups.
Gail initially took me to an experimental refugee farm in the hills
outside of San José. A large tract of land had been granted on a five-
year lease to a small number of Salvadoran farmers in the hopes that they
could make a go of it on their own, thus freeing them from reliance on
handouts from international relief organizations. There was considerable
hope that this grass roots project was working, but the lease was about to
expire. The farmers were discussing plans for renewing the lease and
were even looking for ways to buy the land.
Gail told me before we visited the farm that the families might
be reluctant to have me work with them. During the early years of the
project, the farmers had allowed reporters and relief workers in to study

the farm, but as far as the farmers could see now, there had never been any positive, tangible results from the studies. It appeared that the researchers were interested primarily in furthering their own careers, rather than in helping the refugees. The refugees had thus come to feel a general resentment towards outsiders.

Gail took me to the home of Martín, who was her closest contact among the men of the project. Martín was pleasant but distant when I spoke with him about the possibility of doing a study of the farm. He himself was willing to let me conduct research there, he said, though not prepared to convince any of the others to work with me. A noisy television set was running in the small dark room where we were talking, distracting Martín and complicating our conversation. Finally, when I had allowed sufficient time to pass, I thanked Martín for his time and his kind offer, and I left.

As the car wound back down through the lush, hilly countryside to town, I remarked to Gail that I thought I should find a project closer to home. I wanted to be able to drop in on a casual basis so that I could establish a more trusting relationship. Gail had a fresh idea immediately. She drove me down a quiet side street in town, stopping in front of the building that housed the Salvadoran daycare center. Since it was Sunday no one was around, so Gail and I sat in the car as she told me what she knew about the Center. Even though she had not worked on this project, she was acquainted with some of the women. They had lived through amazing experiences, she said, and their stories ought to be told. I was intrigued, but after my brief encounter with the refugees at the farm, not confident that the women would even talk to me.

The following day I dropped by the Center. It was only a few blocks from my apartment, and I could walk there easily. How convenient it would be! At the front gate of the house, I greeted a woman who had a child clinging to her hand. I told her that I was an anthropologist looking for a group of Salvadoran refugees to study and that my friend Gail had recommended the daycare center as a possibility. The suggestion sounded a bit crass to my own ears, but the mention of Gail brought an immediate smile to the woman's lips. She asked that I please come again tomorrow when the director, Doña Ligia, would be there. I was encouraged by the woman's attitude—so unlike that of Martín's at the farm—and I promised to come by again.

A few days later I returned to the Center. Doña Ligia, having heard about my previous visit, was ready to receive me. I was ushered into her office and welcomed as "Gail's friend." There were women and children everywhere, it seemed, so it took a few minutes to clear the office so that we could talk. A small dish of tropical fruits appeared for each of us. Finally, as we ate, I gave Doña Ligia a general explanation of the type of research I was hoping to do. I wished to study a group of

Salvadorans: to analyze why they had left their homeland, what type of disruption the move had made in their lives, and how they had managed to adapt to their exile in Costa Rica. Because of my teaching position at the university, I would be conducting this research on a part-time basis, but I would be happy to help out at the Center as some kind of assistant if they liked.

Doña Ligia clearly wanted to "collaborate" with me, as she put it. She seemed to feel that the Center staff could gain from my doing research with them. I could tell she wanted outsiders to hear some of the stories of the women. In addition, she spoke of my helping with translating letters and other written materials from English, as well as the possibility of my acting as a liaison between the Center and some of the parents. Doña Ligia was obviously aware that I would gain something from my study. She understood my need for a research project and saw no immediate contradiction between my research requirements and her own goals for the Center. A staff meeting for the following week was arranged, where my research plans could be presented to the group and discussed. If everyone seemed willing to cooperate, a schedule of interviews with the staff members at the Center would be set up for me.

When I arrived at the Center for the staff meeting, I was brought into the kitchen where the workers were already gathered. Except for one young male teacher, they were all women. I was invited to sit on a low bench while two of the women washed and dried the lunch dishes and the rest of the workers stood leaning on the kitchen counters.

As Ligia introduced me, I was again struck by the warmth of the welcome I received as "Gail's friend." Suddenly everyone was talking all at once, not allowing me to follow much of their rapid Spanish. As the talk died down, though, Ligia broke in and gave them all a brief summary of my plans. Her version was that I hoped to study the people in the daycare center and that I would be interested in interviewing each of the workers. Then she turned the meeting over to me. I embellished on Ligia's statement only slightly, feeling it best to avoid a specific research proposal, if possible.

Luckily, no one seemed very concerned about my vagueness, except in a few matters. Someone wanted to know if I would use a tape recorder for my interviews. I replied that I would unless anyone objected. No objections were raised. We discussed the idea of protecting the identity of the interviewees, should any of their information put them or other people in a compromising position. Because of the political nature of the stories, I assured everyone that pseudonyms would be used in any publications. A few of the women later gave me the names they wanted me to use, while others asked me to choose their pseudonyms. One interviewee requested that I use her real name, but I declined to do so with my apologies, telling her that her association with some of the other women might put someone else in danger.

The most crucial issue brought up at this meeting, however, was that if I studied these particular refugees, then I was under a strict obligation to make their stories known to people in my own country. Although I promised to do my best, I realized only later that their expectations of me along this line were vastly more extended than my own. The women seemed to feel that I had a direct line of access to the President of the United States—then Ronald Reagan—and could make him listen to me talk about their problems as refugees. (Actually, I discovered that this is not such an unreasonable expectation in a small country. It was relatively easy to get an audience with the Costa Rican president—then Óscar Arias—assuming he believed you to have some political influence.) Nevertheless, I fervently hoped that I could write something that would help the Salvadoran refugees.

"Come into my office," says Doña Ligia. "We will set up a schedule for the interviews." It is a few days after my first meeting at the daycare center, where we agreed on the general conditions of my research. I have not expected things to move this quickly. My original plan was to become acquainted with everyone gradually and then arrange interviews for specific individuals when I felt they were ready. I have a whole year ahead of me, after all. But at Doña Ligia's proposal that we hold the interviews immediately, I do not hesitate. We sit down together to work out a schedule. I let her decide whom I should meet with and when, because she needs to make the arrangements according to the duties of the workers and the times they can most easily be spared.

I could see some obvious advantages in having Doña Ligia arrange the interviews. First of all, it was a quick and easy way to establish a personal relationship with each of the refugees. After telling me their life stories, the women would probably feel as if they knew me, and I would certainly feel as if I knew them. Another advantage was that I would not have to worry about the complications of accommodating everyone's family, should the interviews be held in people's homes. I wanted the taped sessions to be as free from interruption as possible. The Center would provide me with an empty room and as much time as I needed with each of the staff members.

However, there were problems with this approach that I did not anticipate. One significant issue involved Doña Ligia's choreographing of the *testimonios*. She knew—as I certainly did not—which of the women's stories would be most dramatic and compelling. She also knew which women were most anxious to talk. These were the interviews she scheduled first, a fact which had a profound impact on my research. My initial impressions of the women were filled with an emotional intensity that remained with me throughout the entire year.

Another problem centered on the controlling rights over my taped sessions with the women. These initial formal interviews, which were all conducted during my first month of fieldwork, included stories from all the full-time staff at the Center, with the exception of one young woman who declined to be interviewed, saying that her mother had already given me their family story. Most of the sessions were taped at the daycare center in the privacy of a separate room. Only three of the first set of interviews were conducted outside the Center, one at my home (with the woman's niece listening from the next room) and the other two with individuals in their own homes. The decision to hold these interviews outside the Center arose because Ligia wanted to put the tapes on file for future use, presumably to raise money for the Center. She felt she had the right to do this, since the interviews were being held with Center personnel during working hours, but not everyone was comfortable with that procedure. To avoid conflict over the rights to the tapes, Ligia and I ultimately agreed that I should hold any subsequent formal interviews away from the Center.

A third issue involved the women themselves and their individual control over the data I received. The term *testimonio*, as used by the refugees, refers to any story of the personal witnessing of political oppression. The refugee community was already well acquainted with this rapidly growing genre of politically-oriented oral stories when I arrived among them. Reporters, relief workers, and human rights activists had circulated among the various refugee groups, especially during the early 1980s, asking similar types of questions. A few Center staff members had obviously told their stories a number of times in a variety of situations. Since *testimonios* are normally used to persuade outsiders of the enormity of their plight, the staff undoubtedly had certain expectations both about the nature of these interviews I was conducting and about the possibilities for their future utilization. In some ways these expectations helped my research. Most of the refugees were comfortable with the situation and were able to give their stories without much prompting from me. I received a lot of data in a very short time. But in other ways these expectations about my work were a hindrance. The refugees controlled the data to an extent I had not expected. They were selective about the information they gave me, as if they were on show for an international community of listeners far beyond just me. This control over the substance and presentation in the *testimonios* meant that one of my subsequent tasks would be to get behind the *testimonio* to the motivations of the individual refugee.

I arranged for one of my linguistics students at the university to transcribe the tapes in Spanish for me. (The translations into English from Spanish are mine.) In 1988, Judít was in her final year of the doctoral program and was experienced in transcribing tapes from Bribri and other Indian languages. She is Hungarian, not a native speaker of

Spanish, but her precise attention to detail and her natural linguistic abilities made her a real asset to my research. Moreover, Judít took the problems of the refugees very much to heart and obviously sympathized with the women, both politically and personally. Even though she never met any of the refugees while I was there, she talked about individuals as if she knew them, helping me occasionally to interpret what they were trying to tell me. Judít was not a political refugee herself—she had come to Central America as the wife of a Costa Rican; however, she had many of the same desires and fears about returning home, in her case, to a communist-dominated land and a twin sister she had left behind. Moreover, she was no stranger to abuse and appeared to experience a therapeutic effect in transcribing the tapes of the refugees for me.

The request by the women to spread their stories guided my initial research. I was truly interested in hearing the *testimonios*, and I knew these stories would give me plenty of ideas for further investigation. After I let them tell me what was on their minds, I could ask the questions that concerned me most.

In any case, my potential obligations to the refugees were of constant concern to me during those early days of research. For instance, their acceptance of me within their group depended largely upon my association with Gail. Using Gail's name had worked like magic in my gaining access to the women. However, I did not yet understand Gail's relationship to the Center. She herself had only claimed a minimal acquaintance with one or two of the people on the staff. Doña Ligia and her assistant Carmen sat me down during one of my early visits and requested that I call Gail about helping to get donations for educational materials for the Center. The women told me that Gail had arranged for them to have a party the previous Christmas with presents of clothes, toys, and learning materials donated by U.S. Embassy wives, and now that the Center's Swedish sponsor was cutting back on funds for educational materials, the staff was looking for other means of support. I promised to call Gail and see what she could do about getting materials for the children.

A few days after I called Gail, she appeared on my doorstep with two bags full of toys. The things had been given to her by one of the Embassy wives who was now getting ready to leave Costa Rica. Gail asked if I would deliver them to the Center, which I did. However, even though I was careful to stress to Doña Ligia that the toys had come from Gail, and not from me, I soon realized that I was being perceived as the donor, a role that did not make me feel particularly comfortable. For one thing, it laid upon me numerous obligations that I was not sure I could fulfill. And for another, I sensed from the beginning a resentful attitude among the refugees towards the role of *patrón*, based on their experiences in a paternalistic society back home.

Luckily for me, at just about this time I became acquainted with a woman named Tina. Tina was a "Swallow," which is the Swedish equivalent of a Peace Corps Volunteer. She was a journalist by profession, assigned to help Salvadoran refugees in Costa Rica create a newsletter of their own. Tina was a novice as a Swallow, but her training had been extensive with regard to the "dos" and "don'ts" of overseas relief work. During those early weeks I discussed my research project with her often. I expressed my concern over being put in the position of benefactor, along with Gail. I told Tina I felt guilty about not spending more time and effort giving practical help to the refugees. The women had talked to me about their needs for raising funds to support the daycare center and for finding toys and other materials for the children. I knew that they were telling me such things because they hoped that I would help. At the same time, as I told Tina, I was not sure that I could get actively involved in fundraising for the Center and still have the time and energy to conduct my research. My role as advocate had to be limited to a more symbolic one, centered around the telling of these women's stories, as I had promised to do.

Tina was very firm with me. Her training had taught her to live with the guilt brought on by the refugee situation without allowing it to take over her life. She claimed that no matter how much I helped these people, the feelings of guilt would never go away. Their needs were so enormous, I would never be able to satisfy them. Having established this rather bleak approach as a premise, Tina went on to discuss what I could reasonably do to help the refugees within the confines of my research. We both felt that the research itself had potential long-term benefits, by focusing attention on the plight of the refugees. Based on her training, Tina recommended against my going out and raising funds or rounding up materials for the Center. The Swedish sponsors of the daycare center were gradually reducing their funding in the hopes that the refugees could learn how to raise the money themselves. If I interfered in the process, I would only be making it more difficult for the refugees later, when I would no longer be around to help. I could perhaps encourage them or offer suggestions, but I should not do the work myself.

María's story haunted all the women at the Center. Their worst fears were epitomized by her experience. An attack by Salvadoran soldiers had been a potential, and often very real, threat to each of them. Because so many of their lives centered around their families, they feared not only for themselves but for their children, their parents, their husbands, and their sisters and brothers. The women probably felt especially vulnerable because they had never been taught to fight back. Their only recourse had been to run away.

But why should the women have felt threatened by the soldiers?

Were these soldiers not of their own people? Surely the massacre of María's family was only a random act of terror. None of the women thought that this act was random, though. There was some reason, however erratic, for what happened at María's family home that night.

María tried to explain it to me. She said that she was caught selling photos of Archbishop Romero, the religious leader who was assassinated in March 1980 for his political convictions. María sold his photo to make a little money. Romero's photo was among her photos of other religious dignitaries and saints, which she also sold, along with candles, incense, rosary beads, and images of Christ on the cross. Her little business had gotten her into trouble.

María also talked about her father. He was a well-respected farmer in the village where they lived. Although he was a landowner who occasionally hired workers to help him on his farm, he was not a wealthy man. Apparently, however, he had progressive thoughts. In the late 1970s he was approached by an outside agricultural advisor (María called him a *gringo*, by which she meant he was a North American, though the term seems to refer to Europeans as well). This man encouraged her father to become a village leader in the modernization of farming techniques in the area. He was to be the distributor of fertilizer to his more indigent neighbors. His progressive attitude had gotten him into trouble.

The two offenses committed by María and her father seem far too innocent to provoke such a violent attack by the army, but they are the only explanations María could offer. It appears that such activities were viewed as evidence of undesirable cooperation among the peasantry. It is also possible that envious neighbors spawned the attack. The refugees often spoke of the army's method of paying villagers to spy on one another. A family in need of money could even fabricate incriminating information, if necessary.

Even so, this doesn't begin to explain the viciousness of the attack against María's family. Nor does it explain its diabolical nature. The soldiers arrived under cover of evening, but they made no attempt to hide their actions. In fact, they were putting on a display of horror for the villagers. The attack was a symbolic statement, both sanctioned and reinforced by the cultural ideals of *machismo* and *marianismo*.

Under the military regimes of Latin America, as documented for Argentina, Chile, and other countries of South America, gang rape of women is institutionalized as part of the general reign of terror (Bunster-Burotto 1986:297–325). Female political prisoners undergo systematic psychological and physical torture, designed to extract information from the victim, as well as humiliate her. Attacks against women include mutilation of the sexual organs, forced observation of the abuse of other women and children, and mass rape. *Machismo* sanctions this violent expression of the superiority of males in the name of military and political security.

Degradation of women, and thereby of the men with whom they are associated, is central to the message in such sexual attacks. The strength of such degradation is intensified by the cultural ideal of *marianismo*, or the belief that women are spiritually superior, even saintly. In a culture where virginity is idolized and where women are seen as semi-divine because of their seemingly infinite capacity for patience and self-sacrifice, such political violence directed at a woman has the subtle psychological effect of debasing her morally. Raping a woman in front of the image of the Virgin Mary is a way of stripping her of her purity, or as Bunster-Burotto puts it, of turning her from madonna into whore (298–99). The violation of a pregnant woman—seven or eight months along in the pregnancy—or the torture of her children are both part of the systematic attempt by the military regime to destroy a woman's self-esteem, which centers around her motherhood and her family. The attack on María thus had far-reaching implications, beyond the cruel personal humiliation, physical injuries, and loss of her daughter and father. It was the spiritual torture of a deeply spiritual woman.

Although the torture of women may be less systematic in El Salvador, occurring spontaneously as part of the general massacre of a village or an extended family as in the case of María, the message is similar. Its effect is perhaps even more dramatic, because it is witnessed by so many people and because it seems to have a special message for the peasantry. Dragging María and her daughter off to the church to be raped degrades both the women and the Church; after all, it is the Church from which María and her family have received their "subversive" influence. Drinking or pretending to drink the blood of a human being has demonic overtones that are incalculable in the context of a religion where drinking the blood of Christ is a sacred symbolic ritual. Piling branches over María's body, after hacking her almost to death with a machete, is a way of burying her so that she can remain on view as a message for the other villagers: "Behave yourselves or the same thing will happen to you."

Such actions, of course, succeeded in putting fear into the hearts of others. Totally innocent people who had never before been concerned about politics or the army suddenly found themselves analyzing their own lives. They looked in desperation for actions that might incriminate them. Do my teenaged sons gather together with friends? Have I invited the wrong person over to drink coffee? Does my daughter own a typewriter? Unfortunately, some people waited too long to review their lives and take appropriate action, and they paid for it. Like María, they paid dearly.

I puzzled over María's story for weeks. Maybe she really was a political activist, a "subversive" as the government would call it. But I found this hard to believe. María was far too naive and soft-hearted; within the context of her culture, she was the ideal self-sacrificing woman. She was even willing to forgive her vicious attackers because, as she said, they had only acted upon the orders of their superiors. These poor soldiers who had raped and killed her fourteen-year-old daughter were not to blame because they themselves would have died, had they not done the job "right."

Then was it her naivete that had gotten her into trouble? Didn't she and her family know that their activities could be interpreted as political involvement? María certainly understands the political ramifications of her actions now. But hindsight is a great teacher, and she has had many years to consider the issue. Now what she wonders about is how other people managed to escape the horror that she and her family experienced. She is even suspicious of such people.

María: Once in a while other Salvadorans come to Costa Rica, bringing money from back home, where they have their little houses, and all that. . . . And sometimes . . . once in a while . . . families come, families that nothing has happened to. And I begin to say to myself, "What were those families doing that nothing happened to them?" But it happened to me.

2

Rita

"They invaded all the resettlement groups."

I bring a chair to the backyard of the Center where Rita is on duty watching the children. Without thinking, I ask, "How are you?"

Rita's answer is long and involved, mostly about the various aches and pains in her back and how she cannot sleep. I find her Spanish difficult to understand. Rita's rural dialect has stuck with her in Costa Rica, and one or two of her crucial teeth are missing. Like María, she seems to have some trouble focusing her thoughts.

We are soon joined by other members of Rita's extended family. Her niece, Rina, and her twenty-year-old daughter, Lupe, both come out of the kitchen to sit near us on the bench against the wall of the house. Although Lupe says little, Rina obviously wants to talk.

Rina announces for my benefit, "I went to the Canadian Embassy yesterday. They told me that my children and I will be granted visas next month."

"Are you going to Canada?" I ask, surprised.

"Well, my mother is already there," Rina answers. "And she says she won't be satisfied until all her children are up there with her. We will probably go."

"You realize that Canada is full of snow," I tease her.

"Worse yet, they speak English," Rina counters.

Laughing, I turn to Rita to ask if she plans to join her niece in Canada. Rina's mother, Teresa, seems to have no trouble negotiating for visas. Moreover, the Canadian government still appears willing to help the refugees.

Rita answers me in a tired voice, "I cannot work that hard, Robin."

"What do you mean? English isn't that hard to learn. And you could get a well-paying job," I say. "So could your husband."

By now, a number of other women have gathered around, listening to our conversation.

Carmen speaks up, "Rita's right, Robin. My cousin says that he works so hard in California, he hardly has any time to enjoy himself. He works for a packing company, and he has to account for every minute of his time. If he stops to talk with a friend, his boss gets very upset. You *gringos* work much too hard."

"Are you saying that people in the United States work harder than people in Costa Rica?" I ask. I am thinking of the long hours these women work and the low paychecks they receive.

Carmen answers, "Look at Rita, Robin. She has a bad back, and she is very tired. But here at the Center she can sit and watch the children, having a conversation in the backyard. Could she find a job in Canada where this is possible?"

She probably could not, of course. Rita has no special skills (except for cooking and sewing), and she doesn't speak English. A job for someone like her would undoubtedly involve heavy labor or long hours without much rest.

I return my attention to Rita's niece and ask, "Rina, what are you planning to do in Canada?"

"I can cut people's hair," Rina says. "I got my beauty certificate last year."

"You can? Maybe you'll cut my hair sometime before you leave," I say.

Rina smiles at me. Carmen laughs and teases, "Yes, Robin, you definitely need a haircut."

Rita's *testimonio* did not receive as much attention at the Center as did some of the others. For instance, while everyone pointed to María as an example of the horrifying aspects of the Salvadoran conflict, no one ever mentioned Rita in that light. Yet Rita's experiences were equally devastating. She lost three of her teen-aged sons all in the space of one year, and soon after that her favorite sister was arrested by the army, only to become one of the "disappeared." Rita's story depicts the daily atmosphere of suspicion and fear experienced in certain rural communities of El Salvador during the late 1970s. She demonstrates the kind of resignation one might feel in having no control over one's own destiny, a feeling that I heard expressed time and time again among the refugees.

Rita: Yes, I grew up in the state of Cuscatlán, in a province we moved to with my father. There were twelve of us in the family, five females and seven males. Yes, we were very poor, but even in our poverty we had peace. Because during that time when I grew up, there was peace. We lived in poverty, but if you are poor, if you are born poor, you do not need money. If you have food and there is peace within your family, you feel happy.

I grew up. I tell my daughter that I grew up very happy. I remember we worked very hard. My father worked in the fields, and my mother was something like a domestic helper. But we went on living that way, while God separated us, one after the other, you see?

Later, we had this problem. The *gringos* came to El Salvador to build a dam, to dam up the Cerrón Grande. Maybe you have heard something about this. At this time they took—well, I guess this is how I should put it—they took away the houses. Because it wasn't as if we had sold the houses, since we didn't get to decide on the price. It was not as if they came and said to us, "Look, we will buy your houses for whatever price you want." No, they decided how much they would pay for the houses. We had to sell them without wanting to, since we were being flooded out.

After they had built the dam, all that area became flooded. My father-in-law had had good land. Eighteen *manzanas* [measure of land, about the size of a city block] of his were flooded. The house where we had lived was also flooded. The house that my father-in-law lived in remained at the edge of the lake. But the best land was gone. Only the hills were left, where you can't grow anything, not even corn.

Then they told us that they were giving us the opportunity . . . ah, well, no . . . what they said was that they would buy the land. So we, the people of the entire district, got organized, and we all came up with the idea that we should ask for resettlement. So we began to request resettlement.

But what happened was not resettlement in which, say, they gave us a house similar to what we had had. No. Not even land like what we'd had. They didn't replace that either. Because they built the houses the way they felt like building them. And the land, they only gave two *manzanas* per family. Land . . . to the tramps they gave the good land, to others they gave bad land, that is how it worked.

Anyway, we agreed that they would build us a little house and that we would pay for it. Because they left us to make the payments. I don't remember now for how long, I don't remember if we had to pay within ten years or twenty years. That I don't remember. So this is how we left our home to go to the state of Chalatenango, to a place they called "Resettlement." But I liked the place where we came from better. It was much nicer.

When we moved over to the resettlement place, I felt very bad. Some of the houses were standing without any trees around them. They were standing there bare, just the houses. It was terribly hot. I remember my husband saying to me, "Look, if you want, we won't move over there. We can build a house up higher back home, so that we will be above the lake."

But my children were against this idea, those that were the biggest, the three boys who were already studying. They said to us, "No, we want to move." They wanted to continue studying. And over there in the new settlement they had built schools. So the boys insisted that we move.

My husband said to me, "My children are right. They want to study. Here at home, we will remain isolated. They won't be able to go to school. Because here I see nothing but hills and a lake." That is what you could see, nothing more, where we would stay. So we decided to go.

Rita's experience involving the confiscation of her family's land is a modern example of a land displacement process in El Salvador that has been going on for centuries. Nevertheless, the incident she describes is much more equitable than earlier practices, since her family received compensation for their land, however minimal. History suggests that this has not always been the case.

The pre-Spanish settlement in the region now known as El Salvador was "extensive and relatively dense" (Browning 1971:24), consisting of numerous well-populated indigenous communities from such diverse cultural backgrounds as Pipil with Aztec origins, Pokomam with Mayan origins, and Lenca. Although Spanish descriptions of the area allow for population estimates of 116,000–130,000 at the time of the Conquest (Browning 1971:21), more recent archeological data indicate the population of El Salvador to have been approximately 400,000 in 1524, though reduced to a mere 55,000 by 1551 (Sheets 1992:125).

Based on information about cultural groups throughout Central America (Browning 1971:5–20), the indigenous people of El Salvador were agriculturalists with a deeply spiritual relationship to the land and to the plants that grew on the land, particularly maize and cacao. Private and individual ownership of land was unknown to the native peoples, "as meaningless as private ownership of the sky, the weather, or the sea" (16). Instead, families were granted usage rights to plots of land that were part of the larger area of communal land that a village deemed its own.

In contrast, the Spanish conquerors that arrived to take over the region in the 1500s were not agriculturalists. They soon realized, however, that any wealth to be gained in El Salvador would come only through the appropriation of the interdependency between the people and their land, since the area was not rich in gold or silver. Initially, the conquerors exploited the indigenous inhabitants by taking control of their labor and the fruits of that labor, while still allowing the peasants to maintain control over the land. Despite colonial legislation designed to keep the Spanish and the Indian peoples living in separate towns (Browning 1971:36), native villages such as Izalco, Apastepeque, and Cojutepeque were gradually taken over by the Spanish overlords (38). As the Spanish administrators became more dependent on the local agriculture for their desired social status, they increasingly moved out into the indigenous communities in order to control the agricultural production, and the land displacement process began in earnest.

By the early 1970s El Salvador had become a densely populated country where 56 percent of the arable land was owned by a mere 3.3 percent of the people (Montgomery 1982:23). The inequity of land distribution, compounded by serious problems in agricultural labor practices, has created a serious gap between the haves and the have-nots.

Even though the rural poor vastly outnumber the rural rich, they remain powerless to control their own lives.

While it is generally believed that the Spanish Crown paid little attention to the colony of El Salvador following the Conquest, the influence of the Spanish can still be strongly felt. Even though there were official documents that attempted to prevent the enslavement of the Indians, including the New Laws of 1542 and the papal bull of 1537 (Todorov 1987:161), as elsewhere in the Spanish Empire, Indian labor was used to provide the Spaniards with access not only to the profits of agriculture, but also access to personal services of all kinds, including domestic help and sexual favors—anything that would make life in the colonies more genteel.

Early on, the Spanish colonists discovered that cacao was an excellent source of income. Prior to the Conquest, the Indians cultivated cacao because of the religious significance of the plant and the use of the beans as money; after the Conquest, the use of cacao as a beverage became popular throughout Central America and even in Spain (Browning 1971:53). Cacao orchards already maintained by the Indians soon were engulfed in a tribute system called the *encomienda* [royal land grant, including Indian inhabitants] (White 1973:29–31). Under this system the native growers were forced to give up a certain proportion of their crop as tribute to the Spanish *encomenderos* [commissioners in charge of the land grant]. Over the years the required tribute grew, forcing many of the Indian villages to make stricter demands on their Indian cultivators, or face punishment from their Spanish overlords.

After the decline of cacao as an export crop and the decimation of the Indian population due to disease, slavery, and deprivation, a number of Spaniards moved out of their colonial towns and set up huge *haciendas* [plantations] in the rural areas (Russell 1984:7–11; White 1973:32–33, 41). High demand in Europe for blue dye from the indigo plant led to the development of indigo as the next big export crop. During this period black slaves were often imported to manage these plantations, while native peoples were used mainly to help in the harvest. In spite of the laws against the enforced labor of Indians in the production of indigo, a labor system called *repartimiento* [distribution, in this case, of Indians] evolved, which provided the Spanish landowner with unpaid Indian laborers for a certain period each year (Bethell 1987:383–84). Indians who had run away from the stiff tribute and labor requirements of their villages became available as wage laborers during this period as well. Wage laborers were easily exploitable through "debt peonage" on the plantations (Bethell 1987:266). Under this system, the landowners would advance the Indians credit for goods at highly inflated prices, creating debts that the Indians could never hope to repay on the low wages they received. Such debts bound individuals to the plantation.

During the 1600s when indigo production was at its peak, Spanish plantation owners gradually confiscated more and more of the communally-owned land used by native villagers. Because there were no fences around these fields and no recognized title to these lands, colonists allowed their cattle to roam everywhere, thus destroying native crops. The indigenous tradition of shifting agriculture meant that a certain number of community fields had to lie fallow for long periods of time. Such unused fields became easy targets for confiscation by Spanish landowners (Bethell 1987:387–88; Russell 1984:8; White 1973:33).

Independence from Spain in the 1820s did not prove advantageous for the indigenous peasants (Montgomery 1982:28–29). The owners of the *haciendas* remained intent on maximizing their profits in the indigo trade. Even though the legal grounds for the collection of tribute no longer existed, the practice continued (White 1973:72). There was also continued confiscation of peasant land (Bethell 1987:389–90).

But by the middle of the nineteenth century, the world market for indigo had declined sharply (Russell 1984:22–25). Many Salvadorans began to invest in coffee as the new export crop. The *hacienda* owners who had made great fortunes in indigo now had little trouble shifting over to the new crop. They had the capital to live through the three to five years required for the coffee plants to mature. However, smaller landowners and owners of communal land were not in a position to wait this long to receive the income from their coffee harvest. Even worse, the Salvadoran government decreed that the state would now take possession of any communal lands that were not planted in coffee. Although the indigenous communities tried to comply with the decree through the planting of coffee trees, by 1882 the government had undertaken the total abolishment of communal property (North 1989:17). The philosophy was that private ownership of land was necessary for the development of a healthy coffee-exporting economy. Not only did this action place the most fertile regions of the country into the hands of the wealthy and experienced plantation owners, it also created a large group of desperate agricultural laborers who were willing to work for very low wages.

Rita and her family lived in a community back in El Salvador that was under constant surveillance. It was one of a number of "resettlement" communities, built especially to relocate some of the approximately 15,000 farmers (Armstrong and Shenk 1982:70) whose land had been flooded following the construction of the huge Cerrón Grande dam. The Cerrón Grande was a hydroelectric dam designed to provide energy for Salvadoran industry and for private homes. Since the dam was constructed under the supervision of foreign advisors (*Facts* 629; *Water* 321), the peasants were left with the impression that U.S.

imperialism was directly related to their personal grievances about having to move from their ancestral homes. The reluctance of the Salvadoran government to build the resettlement communities had not helped the situation either. Only after considerable pressure by the farmers and their families had the government agreed to meet some of their demands. When the new communities were finished and the people resettled, there continued to be grumblings of discontent.

Not only were the displaced farmers unhappy at losing their family houses and land, they were also dissatisfied with the resettlement communities that were built in compensation for their losses. In the *testimonios* Rita and others talked about being moved onto soil that did not produce crops without considerable investment in fertilizers (which few farmers could afford). They spoke of the lack of trees to shade them from the heat of the sun and of the newly constructed houses that were small and uncomfortable. Perhaps most important, they experienced a shattering in the stability of their traditional communities. Strangers were now living together in restless poverty. Neighbors mistrusted one another. Family members were all adjusting to new social relationships and unaccustomed forms of behavior. Such communities became fonts of social activism, and the army obviously sensed the danger. People were paid to spy on one another, and threats and sudden midnight searches became commonplace.

Rita: There came a time when the authorities entered the settlement every day to search the houses. You should have seen it. They would toss everything outside that they found in the dressers, down to the last piece of clothing. If they uncovered any money, they took it. If they uncovered any food, they ate it. And if they found men in the houses, they carried them away and made them "disappear." It was sad.

We would be eating sometimes when we saw them coming. They were masked and had these big hoods that made it look like their hair was falling down on their backs. But they were just people, maybe even our neighbors. They were part of the Death Squad. When you saw them coming, you couldn't eat because of the fear.

Once I remember that they entered the other settlement. And someone warned, "They are coming, they are coming, get inside quickly."

My husband arrived from work at midday and said, "I am hungry." So I set about to feed him lunch. I was just about to serve the food when we heard a bomb explode.

Someone said, "Ay, the army is over there in Settlement Number Two." I was carrying my apron in my hand, as if I were paralyzed. I had such a terrible fear.

My husband said to me then, "Give me the food, woman. Anyway, we already know it is the army that is over there." That man . . . seeing that I was standing there so scared! Ah, well.

We were only at the table for a short time, and then there was another bomb. Those bombs, you didn't just see them. You smelled the stink of decay. They put bombs into the houses so they would catch fire. Then when the houses were burning and finally came down, you just heard a deafening noise.

Well, by now we were no longer hungry. We couldn't eat. We went out to see what had happened, whose houses had been set on fire. As evening approached, we came home and locked ourselves in. Every day after six o'clock, the "animals" would walk around. The soldiers would come and circle the houses, looking to see who they could capture.

Another time we were asleep. Around midnight, we heard a lot of shooting. The bullets passed whistling over the rooftops. We all woke up and threw ourselves on the floor. The following morning, when the shooting was over, we got up to see who was dead. Because it was obvious the shooting was not just a game.

A neighbor said, "Ay, they killed the family that runs the little store, the Gómez family."

These were very nice people. They were good to everyone. We said, "But who was it that died?"

"They all died, the entire family. Everyone. Even the littlest ones."

In a tiny living room, they had killed seven people. They had killed the wife and the husband, his brother, and four children. One little girl was about two years old. The other little boy, who was about four, was lying next to his papá. He had protected himself by hiding underneath the bed. But when he saw that his father had been killed, he came out from under the bed and wanted to embrace his father. When the little boy got there to hug him, they killed him, too. His arms were still around his father. The mother sat hunched over on the edge of the bed with her two-year-old girl between her legs. They machine-gunned her down. She fell backwards onto the bed, and the little girl fell onto the floor. They also machine-gunned the little girl. So, there were seven that they killed. If you had seen it!

The old grandmother was there too. She told us how it had happened. Fourteen people had actually lived in this house. The others managed to save themselves. The shooting was in the dark. The others got under the beds and were not discovered. They didn't get killed. Only the owners of the house, their four children, and the man's brother died.

I went to see it. Everybody went. In a tiny living-room, there were seven bodies. The walls were full of blood, full of bones and pieces of things that had been splattered. When you went through the door, you got smeared with blood. I didn't really want to go inside. A lot of people went in. Not me.

The little old woman, the grandmother, told me about it. She said, "Ay! I would like to . . . !" But you should have seen that woman. She did not shed a single tear . . . the little old woman . . . the one with two sons, four grandchildren, and a daughter-in-law, all dead.

She was walking with a small pot in her hands, and I said to her, "What are you doing with this pot?"

"I am going to put water in it for a bath."

I advised her, "They say it is bad to bathe if you have had a shock."

"But feel my hair," she said. "See how stiff it is. The back feels like a piece of wood."

I asked her, "What from?"

"From the blood," she answered. "I hugged my son while he was dying. I feel full of blood. That is why I have to take a bath. But I would like you to sing me the 'Song of Salvation' for my sons."

But none of the people dared to pray, nor sing the "Song of Salvation." Men and women were standing there crying, some just acting foolishly.

During those times, I trembled a lot from nerves. I had gone to see a doctor. I took medicine. I didn't cry. I only felt a tremor in my chest. But I didn't feel like crying.

Since all the other people were crying, I said to a young man, "If you like, I will help you. We will sing the 'Song of Salvation'."

"Ay, I have a terrible trembling in my body," the young man said to me. "But if you help me, even if it is just with the words, we will manage it. Even if we shorten it a bit, we can sing it anyway, to please the old woman."

We sang the "Song of Salvation."

Then the old woman said, "Ay, I would like you to make me a burial gown for my daughter." From the way she acted, you wouldn't have known that she was the mother of those dead people.

I asked her, "And do you have something to make the burial gown from?"

"My daughter-in-law has a long dress," the old woman said to me, "and I also have some cloth here. Measure her so that it fits long, with white stockings."

So I said, "I will take it. I will do it."

When I returned to her house with the dress, the officials had already come to do the inspection. They needed to write up a report. But not just two soldiers came, not just ten soldiers, there was a whole troop of soldiers. It looked as if the whole army would arrive.

I said, "I am not brave enough to go and leave the gown. I am afraid." A young woman came and picked up the gown. I wasn't able to go leave it myself.

Control over the peasant population in El Salvador has usually been achieved without resorting to the kind of violence described by Rita, although a number of exceptional periods like this have been recorded historically. The passivity exhibited by Rita and her neighbors appears to come from the conviction that they are merely peasants with no rights, which is certainly how the government seems to view them. Fear alone does not explain why so many of the people do not fight back under such circumstances. They seem to believe that there is nothing they can do; this is their fate.

Not much is known about how the native leaders in pre-Conquest El Salvador exerted control over their subjects, even though the Pipil center of Cuscatlán certainly had a religious hierarchy with considerable influence (White 1973:21). The Spaniards arrived, however, armed with a worldview that placed themselves in a privileged position and their conquered peoples in a position of servitude. Not only did the Spaniards have the technological superiority to effect this kind of hierarchical order in the New World, they had the managerial skills, the political system, and the religion to reinforce it.

Conquest of the Central American region was accomplished in fits and starts, but the final outcome was inevitable. Native resistance was not equal to the firearms and cavalry of the Spaniards. Moreover, much of the Spanish advantage was due to a breakdown of native communities through the spread of epidemic diseases, like smallpox, pneumonia, and typhus, to which the natives had little immunity. By the 1540s the Spanish had the upper hand in the area (Russell 1984:2, 4).

Management of the greatly reduced indigenous population was accomplished throughout Central America by the establishment of native villages. While traditional Indian communities were often used as a base, in places like El Salvador the communities were often comprised of Indians from various groups, eventually leading to a homogenization of native culture and to a Spanish-speaking peasantry. Although indigenous organizations had broken down, village councils were formed using Indian leadership to distribute communal lands and to manage the local affairs of the native communities (Bethell 1987:70–72; White 1973:34).

Spanish administrators living in these Indian communities as well as in separate colonial towns held ultimate authority over the natives (Bethell 1987:180–81). These administrators collected the required tribute from the villagers and took advantage of the natives as a source of labor. Theoretically, the administrators were answerable to the Viceroyalty of New Spain, headquartered in Guatemala, and also to the Spanish Crown. Their isolation from these centers of power, however, gave them considerable autonomy. They were thus encouraged to ignore any decrees that were not to their liking, such as regulations designed to protect the local villagers.

The Church was another aspect of Spanish control over the indigenous population (White 1973:36–39). Much of the official justification for the subjugation of native peoples was for the purpose of converting them to Christianity. The souls of thousands of natives would be saved, and incidentally also the souls of the Spanish clergy for their missionary efforts. While the Church tended to view itself as the protectorate of the Indian peoples and often fought against the inhumane practices of the landowners, they nevertheless brought an ideology that only served to support the political and moral superiority of the Spanish elite, including themselves. The Church upheld the notion that Spanish authority and power was evidence of God's will. The Indians were taught to accept their inferior role in the world and to obey the will of God. Their reward for such obedience and acceptance would come to them in the afterlife.

The Church imported its hierarchical institutions along with its belief system. The pyramid structure of archbishops, bishops, parish priests, and lay clergy was established firmly throughout the Spanish

Empire. In the native villages a religious hierarchy called the *cofradía* [cargo system] was instituted to perform the yearly rituals to the saints of the Catholic Church. Although the upper hierarchy of Spanish bishops and priests retained their original European belief system, the religious ideology of the local *cofradía* was given considerable flexibility, allowing the Indians to create a synthesis between the Christian beliefs of their Spanish overlords and the indigenous beliefs of their own heritage (Perez-Brignoli 1989:51).

Besides giving the Indians a viable spiritual base, the *cofradía* enabled local peoples to maintain their identity as Indians and as members of specific communities. The yearly rituals of the *cofradías* were performed for the spiritual benefit of the community. But the expense of maintaining the religious hierarchy was high, only adding to the overall cost of survival for the Indians in the community (Bethell 1987:328–29; Perez-Brignoli 1989:50–51). The *cofradía* thus served to keep the Indian communities in a state of poverty. Local *cofradías* existed throughout El Salvador until the middle of the twentieth century, when all peasant organizations were banned as subversive (Montgomery 1982:15).

The political and religious hierarchies imposed by the Spaniards have had a profound influence on the mind set of the Salvadoran people. The elite believe in their own superiority and in their right to control the lives of others. And the peasants have, until recently, been resigned to their pitiful existence, convinced that their own role in the world order was determined by a higher will. But years of economic crisis, especially in this century, have led great numbers of people to question the system. Some people like Rita remain inactive in the general upheaval, hoping simply to survive the crisis, while others are actively protesting the conditions imposed on them.

Rita's family was lucky to have a plot of land. Even in the process of resettlement, they had acquired enough land to survive. Moreover, they were a large family with a lot of sons, traditionally considered a blessing, since sons were needed to help the father in the fields. Sons were also potential wage earners. The modern peasant family sent its sons to school in the hope that one or two of them could bring in money from a middle-class job.

But in the restless atmosphere of the resettlement community Rita's three sons and her numerous nephews drew unwanted attention to themselves and to the rest of the family. They were students in the local secondary schools and, along with other young men in the community, their activities were always under surveillance, as they participated together in student activities. They may not have been involved in any more serious political actions than these, though Rita's *testimonio* makes it clear that she did not always know what they were doing. In any case, the sheer numbers of her young male relatives and their friends, plus the fact that they met in groups to study and socialize, would have made them suspect in the kind of atmosphere that prevailed in El Salvador in the late 1970s.

Rita: Even though it was sad that we had to move from our old home, we were happy to be together all in one place. The boys found it hard to study in the resettlement community because they also had to help their father with his work in the fields. Sometimes they went to school in the morning. Then when they returned in the afternoon, they would go to the fields with their father. On Fridays they were supposed to study in the afternoon, so they worked in the fields until midday, returned to the house just for lunch, and then went off to school. Things went on like this for about five or six years.

After this the war began. It got worse and worse as time went by. There were already a lot of students attending school in the resettlement community. My three boys were among them. We were now sending them to secondary school, where things are very different than at primary school, with students pressuring each other into action. And persecution had already begun.

Then they decided to organize themselves, because the teachers and everybody were already striking. They were going on strike for all sorts of reasons, but one thing they all agreed on was that there should be change. Unfortunately, however, back in my country . . . well . . . how should I say it . . . just being a student is a crime. Even being young is a crime.

One of my sons was seventeen years old. He was at school with a friend. They left together to do some work, rather . . . some homework. They were always allowed to do their homework like that, together. It was the third of May. They left home with each other . . . and did not return. He disappeared on a Thursday, May 3, 1980.

He had said to me that morning, "Mamá, if I don't come back . . . well, I will certainly come by seven in the evening."

But at seven o'clock his student friends came by and asked me, "Hasn't David come home yet?"

"No," I told them, "he hasn't come." He didn't arrive that night either. At dawn the following day his friends returned and asked after him again.

"Nothing, nothing," I said to them.

Then one of my nephews said to me, "Don't worry, Aunt. He and his friend will appear."

"I hope so," I said to him, "I hope they will be ones who do appear again."

But he did not appear that day, and another passed, and another . . . and never, not later . . . not even to this day! I have not had any news of him for eight years now. It was in the same year that we came to Costa Rica, in 1980. It was eight years ago that he disappeared.

I searched for him. Well, I couldn't really search for him. I just went to the Human Rights Commission to announce his disappearance, but he has not appeared. The people from the Commission came to the settlement to investigate.

They told me, "Don't go searching for him, don't go to the army quarters. Because if you do, they will brand you as a subversive. You are already considered a subversive. And for that reason it won't do you any good. You will never be able to do anything about it. And they could turn around and persecute you. So you mustn't do anything."

Then on the sixth of June that same year, the army invaded the settlement where we lived. They invaded all the settlement groups, including ours. It was summer—boiling hot. All the young men who lived in the community left. My eldest son Emilio went with them. I didn't even know where he had gone, really. At about two o'clock in the afternoon a friend arrived and said that the army was putting a watch on the houses.

I said to my friend, "He is somewhere else. He did not come home to sleep."

And my friend replied, "He left to sleep in the mountains."

I couldn't sleep that night because Emilio didn't come. Then at about six the next morning, he came back. There had been a big storm all that day and all night. Antonio, another boy, was with him.

I asked him, "Where did you go to sleep?"

He replied, "I went to the mountains to sleep. But I am leaving. I am going now to my grandmother's." She had stayed back in that place where we had lived before.

"I am leaving," he said to me, "because they say that now the soldiers are coming to seize people. The guards will be coming. It is going to get worse. They are going to make arrests. I'm not going to stay here."

"Are you really going to leave?" I asked.

"Yes," he told me, "I must go. I will tell my father." My husband had already gone to work. "I'll tell him I won't be working, that I will be going to my grandmother's."

So then I said, "If you don't have the money to pay for it, to get you started, I'll give it to you." I gave him 25 *colones* [$10]—the Salvadoran *colón* is worth more than here in Costa Rica [both countries use the term *colón* for their currency]. I gave him 25 *colones* so that he could go. And he left.

I was at peace, believing that Emilio was with his grandparents. But the next day, around nine o'clock in the morning, my brother-in-law came and told me that they had killed him. "They killed him yesterday while he was going to his grandmother's."

I was shocked. "How horrible! Where did he die?"

"Over there in the surroundings of M——," he said. "They also killed Felipe and Jeremías." These were my nephews. And this brother-in-law was their uncle. My nephews were both gone, along with my son.

"They killed them also," my brother-in-law said to me, "they killed . . . they killed seven people over there."

"But why?" I asked him.

"They were executed," he said. "It was the army that did it. They watched the bodies all day long. They killed them in the early morning, and they watched them all day long so that nobody could go and bury them."

He told me that when he got there, night was already settling in. "A great storm arose, one like I have never seen in my life," said my brother-in-law. "The sky became all purple. And a great wall of water came. You should have seen it! And someone stayed to guard the place, where you could see the great storm. An airplane passed overhead, very low, making signals that the soldiers should leave. And they left."

Then someone who lived close by said that the soldiers had told him, "Look, those are guerrillas. Just let them stay there. Let those damned guys just stay there. Listen, stupid, either bury them on the road, or let them stay there. Let them just rot. Well, maybe you should bury them so that the stench doesn't get to you."

After saying this, the soldiers left. The people all got together and dug three graves, to bury all seven. Three graves, no more.

Then my brother said to me—because one of my brothers was also there—that he would never have had the courage to tell me about Emilio's death. "Such sadness," he said. "I . . . rather, we . . . we buried them. We threw them all on top of one another because their heads had been cut off. They were left without their heads, only their bodies. I wanted to put Emilio in the grave. But when I went to bury him, I didn't have the courage to throw the dirt, like that, directly on top of him."

He continued, "I went to look for an old cloth sack to toss over his front, so that I could throw the dirt on top of him in peace. But you see how sad it was. . . . You did not see it, but I did. I did. I buried my nephew. But you. . . ."

Well, several days later—just imagine—my daughter and I started to hold the wake, to say the prayers that we are accustomed to saying. We did not have the courage to pray loudly, since people might hear us. Nobody came to visit, the way they do when there is no war, when everyone in the world searches you out and accompanies you to the service. At that time, no. At that time you were alone in the house, locked in, to pray in secret, with the fear that the army would come and hear you praying, and would denounce you for praying, or that one of these prayers would . . .

After nine months, at the end of January, they killed my third son. I was told about it. I never saw it. I was just told that the soldiers had invaded another place where my son and some other young men were staying. They bombed the place where he lived. And after the bombing was over, they set the brush on fire. After they had killed him, they burned him. They set him on fire.

They told me that afterwards an old man who lived near there went to look. After they had done the bombing and lit the fire, after the army had left, he went to see who the dead men were. And one of them was my son. They killed him. They lit him on fire. They threw him onto the flames. Just like that, in one year they had killed all three of my sons.

When we went to mass, people said—neighbors and strangers, because some of them were from other settlements—they said to me, "I don't understand. How can you walk around with your three sons dead?"

I replied, "And what should I do?"

"You don't look like someone who has three dead sons!" they said.

So I said to them, "What am I supposed to do? I don't go around calling attention to myself by crying. I have already cried enough. I cry at home. When I go out on the street, I don't. . . ." Because you couldn't leave the house crying so that everyone would see you. You had to hold it all in. You didn't talk with just anyone either, since this was also dangerous for you to be out crying in front of people, maybe at some store . . . they would say, "You, why are you crying?" As if that would make my sons whole again. Crying will not bring them back to me again.

The Salvadoran army has not always been involved in the control of its own citizens. In the late 1850s, when the national army was first built into a substantial force, its primary focus was to protect the country against the threat of invasion by other Latin American countries. It was not until after the installation of a military government in El Salvador in 1931 that the army began to turn on its own people.

Earlier, wealthy *hacienda* owners had been expected to cope with the control of the peasants themselves. They hired private armies to do the job. If a peasant refused to pay his required tribute through the *encomienda* or tried to escape from providing the required months of labor through the *repartimiento*, private soldiers were called in to catch and punish the recalcitrant worker (Russell 1984:8, 25).

In the 1880s as the coffee barons were confiscating the communal landholdings of the native communities, these private armies began to nationalize, ultimately forming the National Police. Two additional national police forces were established in succeeding years, the National Guard in 1912 and the Treasury Police [*Policía de Hacienda*] in 1936 (Montgomery 1982:30–31). The responsibilites of these two groups often overlapped with those of the National Police, since any of them could be used to provide police services to the wealthy landholders. The primary task of each of these forces was to control the citizens of El Salvador.

By the late nineteenth century a small group of coffee barons had amassed an enormous fortune, becoming the strongest economic and political force in El Salvador. Not only did these so-called Fourteen Families own most of the best land in the country, they had also gained control of the government (Baloyra 1982:6–7; Russell 1984:67). The coffee barons provided most of the political leaders for the country up until 1931, when it became clear to the military leaders that the oligarchy did not have the necessary resolve to control the increasingly restive peasantry. At this point the military took over the reins of government with the installation of Gen. Hernández Martínez as president (Russell 1984:35).

One of the first actions of the military regime was to put down a peasant rebellion through a violent series of executions and attacks, now referred to as the *Matanza* [massacre] (Anderson 1971). Although peasant civilians had often been tortured and killed for alleged transgressions of questionable legality prior to this time, the *Matanza* of 1932 set a whole new precedent for horror. People were killed for having Indian facial features, for wearing peasant clothing, or for owning the most common of farming tools, a machete (Russell 1984:37). The goal of the new government was to eliminate any present and future potential for mass rebellion in El Salvador.

From the 1930s up to the 1980s, the military regime used the army as well as the national police forces to quell any opposition elements in the country (Russell 1984:35–50). The oligarchy retained the economic power in El Salvador—building up the banking system, constructing roads, and creating export services, activities all designed to strengthen the coffee industry. The military, on the other hand, held the political power. In spite of the sometimes uneasy association between the oligarchy and the military, each relied heavily on the support of the other. The oligarchy depended on the military to maintain order in the country and to keep the peasant workers in line. They also needed the government's help in limiting the path of modernization mainly towards the benefit of the coffee export industry. For its part, the military relied on the continuing public support of the oligarchy, as well as economic payoffs in money and land.

The harsh methods used by the armed forces of the country often went beyond what might be considered necessary to put down resistance. Killing or imprisoning the leaders of a rebellion is a common technique for holding onto power, but the military appeared to search for potential opposition, which made almost anyone fair game. Being "young" was a crime, as Rita says, because such a person had the possibility of turning into a guerrilla. By killing potential opponents in diabolical ways or causing them to "disappear" mysteriously, the military achieved another objective: fear. The army apparently hoped to make people afraid to do anything that might be construed as political. They could not hold trials for their so-called criminals and subversives because of the lack of evidence of a crime, yet they wanted the people to be aware that almost any activity could be considered "criminal."

Such was the case for Rita's sister, Clara.

Rita: I was the last of the girls. There was a boy who came after me, who indeed was the youngest child, but my brother and I were the last to be born. So I spent time, lots of it, alone with my mother and my father, because we were the youngest.

I got married right after my father died. My mother said to me, when I wanted to get married, "Don't do it. You will only be left alone."

But I replied, "I am going to marry. I have already decided about it. I am getting married."

My sister Clara said to my boyfriend, "If your first child is a boy, then give him to me."

"Yes, I'll give her to you," he answered. He was telling Clara that he would give the baby to her if it were a girl, but not if it were a boy.

Clara ended up loving my children a lot. She even spoiled them, especially my little boys. They loved her perhaps more than they loved me. Clara and I were very close. For me, she was my second mother. But unfortunately, she became one of the "disappeared."

After I got married, Clara also began to think about getting married. She was just about to have the wedding, when my mother said to her, "Clara, don't get married, not with this man. He likes to drink too much."

"But Mamá, the way things are now, I can only do things with you. I can't just live alone with you."

"Go and think about it, my daughter," she said. "And then, if you still want to, get married. God knows, you don't have to stay with me. I'll go on alone."

Clara got married in the end. You should have seen her husband, how he took the life out of her! Ay! He beat her. He hurt her. He was such a drunk! But she stayed married, and she looked after me. She always came to help me when there was illness, or when there was extra work to be done. She was always there. We were very close—as I tell everyone here. I have never been as close to anyone, except maybe my mother, as I was with Clara. I grew up with her taking care of me, since I was the youngest girl. That is why I was close enough to confide in her. And she did the same with me. When she got married and we were both leading the same kind of life, she helped me a lot in everything.

About a year after my sons were killed, the army returned to the settlement. They came in, bringing several truckloads of soldiers. At five o'clock in the morning they rounded us up with loudspeakers. We were all advised to get up and go to the soccer field. Everyone went. Children, pregnant women, women who had just given birth, everyone went to stand there, to get in line.

Well, we stood there. And a group from the Death Squad arrived to point out the so-called subversives. These people were set aside.

On this day my sister Clara was taken away. She was about fifty-five years old. No one really knew what she was accused of. We suppose that she might have been accused of giving food to subversives. She had so many nephews, and she was like a mother to them all. They lived right near her. Her nephews would go to visit her, because she lived alone with her fourteen-year-old son. All of them would go to eat at her house. She often went without food herself, so that she could give them something to eat. She had something like nine or ten nephews, including my three boys. So probably they accused her of giving food to subversives. But it wasn't true. Those were just her nephews that came to her house.

Anyway, the soldiers took her out of the line in which we were both standing. They separated her from the rest and put her in line to get up onto the back of a truck. That was at five or six o'clock in the morning.

It came to be eleven o'clock in the morning, and there she still was, suffering out in the sun—hungry, thirsty, and exhausted. Finally they grabbed her and threw her on the truck, along with two young men who were also there. This time they took three people.

We do not know what happened to my sister. Thank God my mother was already dead at this time, because I tell you, it would have been worse for her now. At least she did not have to see all of this. I almost died myself. They carried off her daughter, and they killed about ten of her grandsons.

After this we stayed in the settlement community about two years longer, but the life we were living was so . . . sad . . . because somehow we weren't alive, you know what I mean?

Well, after this there was only slaughter on all sides. Almost every day death threatened. They would take this person or that away to some place to kill him.

One day, as usual, we were not able to sleep in the middle of the night. We were still awake at about midnight when we heard dogs barking. My husband said to me, "The army is walking around out there."

"Yes," I whispered. You didn't dare talk out loud. You didn't want them to hear you. There was a commotion all around the house. I sat praying furiously, begging God to save us from a terrible death at the hands of these people.

They stayed quite a long time there, going around the house with the light from their flashlights coming in under the doorway. They shined their lights under the beds through a crack in the door. And we were inside, just waiting for them to enter the house and kill us. But no. Thank God who is our Lord. They finally went away. . . .

By now we couldn't sleep. We just lay there thinking, whispering about the kinds of things that could have happened. When we got up to look outside, we no longer had our grinding stone, nor the tools that the men use for their work, like machetes and shovels. All of this had been carried away. Our grinding stone was gone.

They had stuck a piece of paper on the wall which said, "You are relatives of communists . . ."

I said to my husband, "Look, you can't stay here any longer. You have got to leave."

"Where am I going to go?" he asked. Because sometimes he is very timid, really. "Where am I going to go?"

"Go to San Salvador."

"If I stay here," he said, "even if I don't sell anything, I can defend us both. But if I go off to another place, they will surely kill you."

I insisted, "No, you go. I will save myself. I need to sell our corn."

He said to me, "How are you going to sell the corn? You?"

"I can sell it," I said. I had seen the announcement in the settlement telling when the buyers would come.

"I will sell the corn," I said. "And then I will gather together my clothes and leave."

That Saturday the nuns arrived at the settlement. I told him, "I will go to see the nuns and tell them what is happening, so that they can get me out of here."

My husband said to me, "I am going to take Ricardo. Because if they come, it will be just the males that they are searching for. They will want to take him from you." Ricardo was our twelve-year-old son.

"Take him," I said, "and leave the girls with me." I had four daughters in the house. They were still little, under twelve years old.

Ah well, he went away with all of them, including the girls. That night I didn't sleep there, out of fear. I went to sleep at one of my sisters. And on Saturday, I went to visit the nuns. They said that, yes, they would get me out, that I should sell everything and that then they would take me to a refugee center.

That is the way it was. I sold everything and came to the refugee center. It was not a bad place, but since it was run by the nuns, there was no mixing allowed. They did not let men in, only women and children. My husband had to stay outside with my son.

After three months went by, my sister who was already in Costa Rica said that we should join her. I felt sad when we left. They told me that our trip was now possible, but it was not a happy time for me. All that night I cried. You cannot imagine the crazy thoughts that came into my head. I was thinking that my sons were dead. I was crying as if I were chasing after them, as if I had left them, as if I had left them all alone. And for that reason they had died, because I had left to go to Costa Rica. All that night I cried. . . .

After hearing Rita's story I puzzled over the way she was being overlooked at the Center. Why was she not considered a prime example in the political struggles of the group? A large part of the answer to this question lies in Rita's personality. Even though she was one of the initial group of women who founded the daycare center, she was never a leader. She personally had hoped that the group would receive funding as a sewing cooperative rather than as a daycare center. Although she went along with the daycare project, she worked in the shadow of her elder sister Teresa, whose energy and enthusiasm was crucial in pushing through the daycare project. Now that Teresa had emigrated to Canada and was arranging for her many children to join her, Rita remained at the Center with no thought of leaving Costa Rica. She performed her duties at work with less of the enjoyment experienced by some of the other women.

Her daughters had grown up and married, so Rita was left alone with her husband. She rarely spoke of him, but when she did, she often referred to him obliquely as "he." Once a hard working farmer who had spent his days in the fields, he became a recluse with little opportunity for work. Although Rita's $170/month salary from the daycare center provided them with a minimal existence, Rita was unhappy with the situation. She felt that she was shouldering all of the responsibility for the family, and she found her health was failing.

3

Carmen

"It is my turn to weep."

Carmen is Doña Ligia's assistant and best friend. Together the two constitute the hub of activities at the Center. Even though decisions are formally reached by consensus in general meetings, the informal procedure involves lengthy discussions between Carmen and Ligia prior to these meetings. Carmen then goes to talk over the ideas with her allies in the classrooms and in the kitchen. Thus, while Ligia remains somewhat aloof from the other staff members, Carmen's more open personality serves to bridge the gap between the director and the others.

Carmen works hard to make me feel comfortable at the Center. She is the one who makes sure that I get invited to all the special events, like the Mother's Day celebration and the anniversary of Archbishop Romero's assassination. It is her affable and teasing manner that sets the tone for my reception among the women.

One day I make an attempt to exchange the enormous pieces of fruit they have hospitably given me for a snack in return for more moderate-sized pieces. Carmen pokes me in the ribs and says, "Latin men like having something substantial to grab." I then deny that I am currently looking for a Latin man, whereupon she rolls her eyes toward the ceiling in mock exasperation, making everyone laugh, including me.

On the day of our interview, I find Carmen sitting in Doña Ligia's office, chatting with the director and another teacher, Carolina. They tell me they have some arrangements to make for an upcoming holiday and ask me to wait for a few minutes. I take the opportunity to watch the babies being fed in the hallway.

Four little toddlers are sitting in wooden highchairs lined up against the wall, two younger babies are propped up in plastic infant seats on the low table in the corner, and an older pair of children are seated at the same table in preschool chairs. Rita and her niece Rina are busy feeding everyone. They each have a bowl of mashed fruit in one hand and a spoon in the other. The babies are fed as they open their mouths, like baby birds in a nest. While I am pondering the health consequences of shared spoons, one of the women thrusts a communal washcloth into my hand and requests that I wipe all the little hands and faces. I am just getting into this task when one of the toddlers takes a good hard look at me and bursts into howling tears.

Carmen emerges from Doña Ligia's office. She motions to me through the child's noisy tears that we can begin our interview session now. She opens the door dramatically to the classroom, and turning back to the others, Carmen says with an impish grin, "Now, *señoras*, it is my turn to weep."

Since the nineteenth century the coffee export industry has been the economic mainstay of El Salvador. In order to remain competitive on the world market, the coffee barons have felt it necessary to control the most productive coffee growing lands and keep the agricultural wages low. Unfortunately, from the point of view of the peasant, these goals are not always in keeping with the more immediate goal of putting sufficient food on the table for his family. Because of the scarcity of available land, many rural peasants have had to move onto the large plantations to work for wages to secure their family's survival. Others have become sharecroppers or renters. Each of these sets of circumstances leaves the peasant families almost totally at the whim of their more wealthy landowners. Even farmers with small tracts of land often find it necessary to work for wages on a larger estate in order to make ends meet for the family.

As land has become concentrated in fewer hands, great numbers of rural peasants have moved to the cities to look for work. While many of these people have remained poor, living as street vendors or domestic servants, some of them have been luckier. They have been able to find work as part of the support industry for the coffee export economy. Jobs are available in government, transportation, finance, and education. Some of these people have even raised enough capital to set themselves up as shopkeepers.

Carmen's family is an example of this emerging middle class. As the owners of a small shop in a suburb of San Salvador, they always had enough to eat. Their main economic struggle as a family was centered on raising their standard of living beyond this minimal level. Unlike María and Rita, whose rural families had never encouraged their girls to go beyond the first few years of school, Carmen was expected to get the kind of education that would eventually lead to a middle-class job in the city.

Carmen: I come from a rather large family. We were raised completely by my mother. My father died early, when I was only four years old. So it was my mother who dedicated herself exclusively to struggling so that we would be able to get ahead.

It was the eldest son who was first able to graduate with a degree in secondary education. Then he had the obligation to assume the role of father and to help me continue my career in secondary education since I was the next child. I had to get good grades and receive a scholarship so that I would not have to pay for my secondary school. He helped me and together we helped support the rest of the family.

I studied every day, but on the weekends I went home. Everyone arrived home on Sunday to help my mother to sell things in her little store, so that she could rest a little. Since Sunday was the best day for business, it was good to have several of us there selling. This helped her to earn a little bit more money so that she could get ahead, so that she could afford to pay for all the expenses that having a house implies. We didn't have luxuries or anything. We barely had the necessities. But it cost us a lot of sacrifice. We helped her in her little store, and we cooperated economically as a family.

Carmen's decision to become a teacher undoubtedly arose out of her natural spontaneity with children. Looking in on her class of two- and three-year-olds at the Center was always a pleasure. She and her partner Carolina would sing and dance in circle games, landing on the floor in plump cheerfulness whenever the game called for it. On other occasions, the two teachers would drape blankets over all the furniture in the room to create a sprawling playhouse for the children.

But true to Latin style, the teachers were strict when it came to learning academic skills or discipline. A child needed to hold a pencil correctly. She needed to be able to draw a straight line and not scribble all over the paper. And when the National Anthem of El Salvador was being sung, the child had to stand at attention in line and not allow his eyes to wander. Inability to conform to such standards usually led to ridicule. "Watch how badly Lina cuts with her scissors," the children were directed. "Marta does it much better."

Carmen probably learned most of her teaching methods by going through school herself. The minimum qualification for becoming a schoolteacher in El Salvador is the completion of secondary school. Newly certified young teachers are usually sent into a rural school setting, allowing them to gain valuable skills in the field. Much of their learning is therefore practical. Of course, the social significance of this for the rural families is that their children are most often taught by unproven and unskilled educators, and the turnover of teaching personnel is high. On the other hand, the energy level and idealism of a young teacher, as Carmen indicates, can have an important impact on the rural community, and the subsequent political consequences of the teacher's experience can be far-reaching.

Carmen was eighteen years old when she graduated and got her first job in a rural school. This experience was a genuine eye opener for her.

Carmen: When I first went to work at the school out in the country, I felt that I was finally going to have an opportunity to practice all that I had learned. But I began to be aware of something. Even though I had come with the desire to teach and put my knowledge to work, I saw that I was learning more from these people than I was teaching them.

The relationship was very nice. I got to know the actual conditions under which the people lived, especially the people who were suffering the most, the rural farmers. I worked for four years in the rural zone, sharing day and night with these people. And this, whether you like it or not, gives you a different view on life. From the girl who arrived from the city with a desire to teach the people, to educate the children to read and write, I became aware that this is not possible in practice if there is no solution to the true needs of the rural farmer. There cannot be any education, to my mind, or any teaching to read and write, without a person's becoming identified with the problems of the people who suffer most.

And this is how my manner of thinking has changed. Now I ask myself how it is that these people live under such conditions. The children arrive at school under incredible circumstances—full of worms, without shoes, and having to cross rivers and everything. And sometimes they come without eating. You are made aware of this problem. You would like to be rich so that you could find a solution. But you see that as just one person, as Carmen, you cannot really help.

You finally say to yourself, "Well, the problem here is that these people do not and can not have access to that to which a small minority have access, like adequate education."

You discover something else. Anywhere there is a school with at least first through third grade, where the people can learn to read and write, to count, to add, and to subtract, you discover that there are people with excellent qualities. Some of the children have perhaps more life and more intelligence than a child from the city. So reality begins to change you. And you begin to wonder about who is responsible for this problem.

As a teacher I said my role was to identify myself with these people. And they felt it. They came closer to me, as if I were a person they could turn to, and whom they could ask for help. I tried to do everything I could, but the problem was not simply one of education. It was housing. It was health. It was all the basic necessities.

And so, in cooperation with the community, we held activities for the improvement of the *cantón* [district]—because back there the little place or the village where you have activities, fiestas, or whatever, is called a *cantón*. We raised funds and worked together for the good of the community. But this was only while I was in the village, during the week from Monday to Friday. On Saturday and Sunday I returned to the city where I came from. Traveling back and forth, going from one situation to the other, I could see many contrasts.

The place I grew up offered no great opportunities, but I was able to gain certain skills and techniques, even though these came at considerable sacrifice. I come from a humble family, but all the children have had a chance to study, even though we have only been able to afford a moderate level of education, such as getting our *bachillerato* [equivalent to high school degree].

So at this point I decided to better my education. My contact with the rural area had made me acquainted with many new things. I had been able to investigate the conditions that existed in my country through my work. So now I decided to enroll at the university, the Catholic University of El Salvador, the UCA. At first, I went back and forth from the *cantón* where I worked to San Salvador, in order to study at the university. I wanted to continue getting a little practical experience at the same time that I was working on establishing the theoretical basis for understanding the people I was working with.

Even though the job was near my town, traveling back and forth made it very difficult to study, and so I asked for a transfer to a more convenient location. They sent me to another little school. It was still not very close to San Salvador, but the availability of buses allowed me greater access to the university.

This new school was much more involved in the Salvadoran political movement. As a teacher who is aware of the conditions under which the people live, you try to orient them as a group. You want to help them get out of their present situation. You know that as an individual, a person cannot do anything. He cannot resolve the problem, even though he would like to, even though he feels it, and it hurts.

So, I began working as part of the general effort to organize the teachers. And in the teachers' union, ANDES [*Asociación Nacional de Educadores Salvadoreños*, National Association of Salvadoran Educators], we demanded rights for teachers and for other people, including the peasants and the people living in the slums, who exist in under subhuman conditions, in houses made of cardboard, and everything. That is how we struggled to orient the people. We tried to help them learn to fight for themselves . . . so that if they didn't have seeds, they could get them more cheaply . . . so that if the land didn't produce, they could get it fertilized at a cost more accessible to their pockets . . . so that they wouldn't come out losing.

During this time there arose a strong movement of the masses. The majority of people were incorporated into the movement. As teachers, we fought for teachers' rights, such as increased salaries that would be on a par with the high cost of living. We fought for better medical services. Since we were paying a percentage of our salary towards the welfare of the teachers, it was the obligation of the government to answer to our health needs. We also fought for lower rents on housing, as well as for solutions to many problems experienced by the people at this time. All of us who were on salaries felt the same economic burden.

Carmen soon became aware of the dangers of getting politically involved. Unlike María and Rita, who were going about their lives much as they always had, somewhere along the line Carmen had made the conscious decision to participate in protest demonstrations. One of the things she had learned in the rural school was that if she hoped to contribute towards improving conditions for her students, she had to enlist the cooperation and support of the families in the community. She could not do anything alone.

This was the kind of lesson Salvadorans were learning all over the country. Rural priests were advocating community efforts toward social and economic change—both through rural cooperatives and through protest demonstrations. Union activity was another feature of the growing movement. Teachers, students, factory workers, and peasants were all organizing themselves into unions to create greater leverage for their demands. They were advocating land reform, higher wages and improved working conditions, and better education and health care for all Salvadorans. They viewed their demands as involving a more equitable distribution of the wealth of the country. Groups of people making such demands were labeled "communists," whether or not they were influenced by Marxist doctrine. Union activity was considered "subversive" because it undermined the power and wealth of the coffee barons and the military government.

After the *Matanza* in 1932, any union or political activity in the rural areas that questioned the domination of the coffee baron oligarchy was prohibited by the government. The coffee barons were strongly adverse to any type of modernization in the agricultural sector, because such development would necessarily give rise to questions about the inequity of existing land-tenure practices. On the other hand, the urban population experienced an increase in political democratization, because the elite were interested in the modernization of urban industry, especially that which supported the export economy. As the middle and working classes expanded in the cities, the urban population became increasingly concerned with having a voice in the governing of their lives and with raising their standard of living. Unions of all kinds started to form.

Through the 1960s, while the workers' unions remained fragmented and comparatively weak, the military government had little trouble controlling them. Most business enterprises were small, enabling employers to maintain a paternalistic attitude towards their workers. Certain concessions were sometimes made in answer to the demands of the workers, since the workers were necessary to the success of the enterprise. Nevertheless, union leaders were usually dealt with harshly (North 1985:56–57).

By the 1970s, however, the government had become alarmed by the increasing influence of the unions. Strikes and demonstrations were being organized by all kinds of groups. The separate unions were not only demanding salary increases and better working conditions for their own workers, but they were also looking nationally to agrarian reform and defending the rights of the peasants to organize themselves. Neither the coffee barons nor the military government that supported them felt that such radical ideas should be tolerated.

From what Carmen says, it would appear that by the late 1970s the repression experienced by teachers in the city was not substantially different from the repression felt by peasants like Rita or María in the rural areas. Teachers were now seen as subversive because of their potential for inciting revolutionary action. Thus, urban families could have the same fear that they would be singled out for attack by the police or the army. Teachers had no easier access to a system of appeal against their accusers than the peasants had.

Carmen: During this period I was working in the little school close to San Salvador. The situation was intense. Teachers were being killed in front of their students. You were sent papers, notes, with the signature of the "White Hand" on them. These were from an organization that exists in El Salvador on the extreme right. The sign of the "White Hand" was an indication that your life was in danger. If as a teacher you participated in a demonstration, your name was already on a list, or if a percentage of your pay was given to the cooperative ANDES, you were also on the list. ANDES was a union, but it also served as a savings and loan cooperative. Since all of the teachers gave a percentage to the cooperative, we were automatically vulnerable to whatever they could do to us.

The repression was against all teachers. If you traveled on a bus and there was a roadblock, they made everyone get out. And if you said in answer to "And you, where do you work?" that you worked at such and such a place, "I am a teacher, and I work at a school," they detained you. For example, lots of times there were roadblocks, and they grabbed me and asked me this question. I never told them I was a teacher. I never told them anything. I said, "No, I come from San Salvador to visit a family." "Where do you work?" "I don't work." And they believed me because at that time I was only about twenty years old.

So you constantly felt threatened. If someone came to visit you at your house, you had to leave the door locked and peer through the window to see who it was. Lots of teachers were killed at home. Sometimes a person would be sitting there watching television with his family, when there came a knock on the door. Without thinking, he opened the door. Masked men, members of the Death Squad, had arrived in special cars. The cars had window blinds, with polarized glass all the way around. They had come to ask him, "Are you so-and-so?" They never let him speak or anything. They just killed everyone there.

So this created a kind of psychosis and a nervousness in you. You began using different methods to avoid detection. For example, in order to get to my house I no longer waited at the same bus stop. I took the trouble to wait at one of the stops ahead or two stops behind. Sometimes I changed the route altogether. I did a number of things differently.

You were persecuted for being a teacher, whether or not you were involved. The teachers' union ANDES is an organization that has the power to demonstrate publicly. Supposedly, it has the legal endorsement of the government to operate freely. But in practice things are different. In reality, the paramilitary groups—like that of the "White Hand," ORDEN [*Organización Democrática Nacionalista*, Democratic Nationalist Organization; ORDEN means "order" in Spanish], or the Death Squad, as well as civilian security forces—were always searching out the teachers. Teachers were traitors and subversives who were destined to be killed.

But it wasn't only the teachers. Everyone was under attack. The cruelest kind of repression developed from 1978 to 1980. On your way to work, you would encounter sacks full of dead bodies tossed by the side of the road. Someone would say, "Come on, let's go see the bodies!" Ay, it was horrible indeed . . . the fingers . . . ay, it was terrible . . . ! Why does a person remember such things?

Or you were traveling on a bus and you saw the human heads, chopped off at the neck, heads with the teeth broken and with something like a piece of tobacco in the gritted teeth. Once I saw three heads, each perched on a stake. The bodies were nowhere to be seen. And you understood the message: "For being a guerrilla," or "For being I-don't-know-what," since their identification papers had been taken away.

The notion of education raises numerous contradictions in El Salvador. From the point of view of the elite, it is necessary to have educated people in many of the urban jobs required to support the coffee export business. Education is also needed if the country wishes to industrialize and modernize. On the other hand, the coffee business relies on labor-intensive agriculture, meaning that the wages of the agricultural workers must be kept low if the profits are to remain high. In order to keep farm laborers from demanding better working conditions, education for the peasantry must be kept minimal.

Teachers and students are faced with another set of contradictions. The higher a person goes in her educational training, the more likely she is to become exposed to some of the problems facing El Salvador. Practical training, such as Carmen received while teaching in the rural school, is only one of many ways of gaining knowledge. Another is the general atmosphere of inquiry amid which teachers and students tend to thrive. During the 1970s, strikes and demonstrations were among the more extreme expressions of this tendency to question, but even people who were not active in the teachers' union or the student associations were influenced by the prevailing unrest. The contradiction arises because the schools and universities are supported financially by the government. Teachers' salaries come out of the public coffers, and students are supposedly preparing themselves to participate in a society that supports the status quo.

Carmen: It was a situation of repression, of persecution, of torture, of death. You could no longer feel secure at home. We couldn't sleep. There were four of us, well, four women—my younger sister, my mother, my grandmother, and myself. My brother was there too, studying. My younger sister had finished school and was working as a secretary. And I had a job as a teacher.

All the districts were under surveillance. The guards already knew a lot about us. My brother was studying at the institute. When there were student strikes at the institute, the houses of students came under surveillance. So did the houses of teachers. And at night the guards would come to watch the streets. You could hear all the soldiers marching out there. They would scatter out. We watched from the house through little cracks, as the soldiers scattered and spread out on the ground. Who knows what they were out there looking for, really! You could feel the person outside on the ground, with his lights out and looking, watching. It made you psychotic. It was awful. Who could he be watching for? And you had the fear that this time they would be coming to knock at the door and take you away.

They would arrive and take people off in the middle of the night. Sometimes when I was so afraid that I couldn't sleep, I would go someplace else to spend the night. When you are young, you get afraid. Still, you make up your mind that since they are going to kill everybody, they are also going to kill you. It is your mother who really suffers in such a situation, however. It isn't until you have your own children that you finally realize what your mother has suffered on your behalf.

I remember that one time we went to a demonstration during the regime of Romero [General Carlos Humberto Romero]. This was one of the most repressive periods for the masses. The masks of the government were removed. Romero denounced the demonstrations directly, to create order. We had gone, my sister and I, to a demonstration that was in San Salvador. And the government denounced this demonstration on the radio.

We were not destined to die that day. We were able to escape, even though tanks and soldiers were shooting at everything. We fled into a slum to hide. A woman gave us a spot to squeeze into, and we were able to escape with our lives. They searched for those who were hiding. A lot of people were killed.

My poor mother was at her place in the province, watching the news and knowing that we were involved in the demonstration. We didn't get to her house until about five o'clock in the afternoon. She already thought we were dead. And when she saw we were still alive, she was incredibly happy.

"Ay, child," she said, "if you could only imagine how worried I was. When they denounced the demonstration, they said that people had been killed. Ay, I was sure that my children had been killed. I was so anxious. Now my child, you must go. You must leave the country. Even though I will be without you, I would prefer to have you leave rather than stay here. I'm afraid I'll get the bad news at any moment. And I would suffer so much. How much it would cost me if they were to come and say to me, 'Look over there at that body to see if you can recognize who it is.' No, I could not stand it. You must begin immediately to gather together your papers and do whatever else you have to do to leave. You must go to another country, I don't care where." And she continued to say, "You must go, you must go."

And still we didn't do anything. I thought to myself, "How am I going to go off to another country when I have never been away from here? I would have to quit my job. I couldn't work. Who knows what I would do, but I wouldn't be able to work. I cannot go through such anguish."

We have half-sisters in the United States, sisters on our father's side. They are my father's daughters; they are older, but not my mother's daughters. And they love us as if we were real sisters, sisters of the same father and mother. They said, "What a problem, come and stay with us." But I had never really thought about going to the United States. (Well, actually the idea had occurred to me; I knew that although they have had to work hard, they have been able to survive.)

Anyway, my mother insisted that I should go to the United States, to Costa Rica, or anywhere, so that she could feel more at ease. She thought I would be better off outside the country than in El Salvador. But really, when you think about actually leaving, about abandoning your life. . . . Nevertheless, I began to work on getting my papers. I applied for a passport and all the other necessary documents in preparation to leave.

The decision to go to another country was a traumatic one for Carmen. A young Salvadoran woman expects to move away from her family, either to get a job or to marry into a new household. However, rarely does such a move involve large distances. Carmen's teaching position in a rural area still allowed her to visit home on the weekends. In fact, she and her siblings were expected to return home every week to help their mother in her small store. Such obligations to the family are given high priority because helping a family member is the best and often the only way of securing one's own future. Grown children in El Salvador can expect their parents to take them into the household during troubled times, and grandparents almost always live out their final years with one or more of their children. But moving to another country changes all these reciprocal relationships. Carmen was well aware that she would be forced to rely on the help of strangers if she moved to Costa Rica. And she knew enough to realize that her half-sisters in the United States might not be as willing to support her as her Salvadoran family would.

Carmen: But at this time many things were happening. Once while I was working at the school, two men came to the house in civilian clothes. I was not at home, thank God. Only my mother was there. Two men arrived—tall, well-mannered, large, full-grown men. Lots of my friends came to visit me at the house, but these men were people my mother didn't recognize.

"Is your daughter here?" they asked.

"No, she isn't here right now."

"And what time will she be coming?"

"I don't know," my mother answered. "She never tells me what time she is coming. She could arrive soon, or she could arrive late. And why do you wish to know?"

"It is just that we want to speak with her in person."

About twenty minutes after they left, I arrived. And I found my poor mother all upset. "Ay," she said, "Two men came looking for you, who were not your friends. They were not your acquaintances. I asked them questions about where they had gotten to know you, and they said that . . . that . . ."

She didn't think these people really knew me. "I don't trust these men, Carmen. Who knows who they were? It makes me very worried."

She began to insist again that I leave. Indeed, I had to move to San Salvador, to live with some relatives there, because soon after this incident, they came to search the house. Searches were common. People weren't even surprised by them anymore. What they did was search throughout a whole area, including several blocks. People already knew that the guards might be coming to look for things. The guards would find nothing, because the people with guns and things had them well hidden. Usually what they found was just a newspaper or something.

Thank God again, I was not there when they came to the house to search. I owned a typewriter. My sister was a secretary and practiced on the machine. And I had a paper that I worked on every Saturday. It was a preschool paper for the kindergarten. The school district had given me departmental cardboard, bond paper, stencils, and other things. I kept them all in the dresser. The guards took all these things, claiming that I was using them for subversive propaganda.

My mother tried to tell them, "No, it is because my daughter is . . . this is her work, she types on the machine." I don't know what my mother explained to them, really.

Robin: Were these the same two men who had come to the house earlier?

Carmen: No, this was later, after the two men had come. These were guards who came to search the house. "Search" means that the guards arrive and choose a *manzana* of houses, or let's say two or three houses, and they lift up everything, they look into the closets, they look at everything that a person has, in order to see what they find. They found absolutely nothing in the house because there wasn't anything there. But they came and seized the typewriter, the bond paper, the stencils, and the other things that were there. And they told my mother that they were taking these things because it was possible that they could be used for subversive propaganda.

This was the last straw for my mother. She said to me, "No. Right now. You see what you have to do. You are going to San Salvador, to another place, but you are not coming back here anymore. Those men already came to look for you. Now the local guards have come, too. They are after you. You must not wait for any more clues."

So I finally left for San Salvador in order to arrange for all the necessary papers to leave the country. And on the fourth of June, I came with my sister to Costa Rica.

Standing outside on the quiet street in front of the daycare center, I am surrounded by energetic two- and three-year-olds. The sun is finally out after several long days of steady rain, which has kept the children cooped up in their small playroom. The little ones express their joy at the warmth on their faces by running up and down the sidewalk in vigorous games of chase. At last, the excess energy is spent, and the teachers ask all the children to sit down on the curb. I sit in their midst.

In her arms the teacher Carmen cradles a doll, which only a moment before was carelessly tossed from hand to hand in a relay race. She stands on the street with her colleague, Carolina. An impromptu drama begins. The playful Carmen is transformed into an unhappy young refugee widow whose baby girl is about to starve to death because her mother no longer has enough money to feed and clothe her. The more serious Carolina turns into a sympathetic neighbor who first listens to the mother's sad story and then begins to offer suggestions of help. A discussion between the two refugee women ensues, illuminating a variety of possible solutions to the problem. The drama is resolved when the neighbor takes the baby to raise as her own. At this, the two women fall out of character and become preschool teachers again.

Carmen hands the doll to one of the little girls. She says, "Now you be the mother."

The child takes the doll and stands shyly out in the street, sucking her tiny fist. Another little girl is chosen to play the sympathetic neighbor. She too seems a bit reluctant to act out her part in front of everyone. With encouragement and even some ridicule by the teachers, an inaudible version of the same drama takes place, considerably shortened. Both girls look relieved to rejoin their classmates when it is over.

The messages in this little drama were varied. One was that problems can be solved through discussion. Another was that Salvadorans take care of each other's children, a philosophy I saw expressed in a host of other ways at the Center. A third message was undoubtedly addressed to me as ethnographer: take note of what our lives are really like, Robin, and put that in your book. However, there was an additional more subtle message; this was the idea that impromptu theater was a culturally encouraged expression of social values among the refugees.

Role-playing and imaginative drama are perhaps the most important educational tools at the Center. The refugees do not have much money to spend on crayons and toys and books. Such expensive items are carefully stored in the closets and only brought out during special times. So the children are encouraged to play house and other imagination games, using the furniture and blankets as props. In a more formal setting—yet still on a daily basis—individual children are asked to become the center of attention in front of an audience of teachers and children. One child may recite a serious poem about love, using stylized hand gestures. Another child will sing a song about animals that requires him to act out the ducks and the rabbits. While some of the children are ridiculed onto center stage, others are obviously happy to be there, but everybody takes a turn.

Theater plays a large part in the more public social events of the

Center as well. At most holidays a church mass is held in the largest room which is normally used for eating and napping. All parents and friends of the Center are invited to bring their children and sit on the tiny chairs. The mass for the refugees is a dramatic affair, with stirring songs about patriotism, revolution, tragic losses of husbands and sons, and the pain of homesickness. The participants are not asked to bear their ills quietly, but rather to express their feelings. The service takes on the form of an impromptu drama. The priest reads a passage from the Bible, usually something that is directly relevant to the refugees' situation in exile. The participants are then asked to comment on the passage. The discussion that takes place is not an intellectual analysis of the topic, but an emotional appeal for peace and human compassion. The speeches that are heard often leave one in tears.

The church services at the Center follow the general format of those described elsewhere for "liberation theology," which first developed in Latin America in the 1960s and eventually took hold in El Salvador during the 1970s (Armstrong and Shenk 1982:80; Thomson 1986:48). The "Popular Church," as liberation theology is called in El Salvador, started a tradition of religious services that was in opposition to the former Catholic position of "obedience and acceptance of God's will" (Armstrong and Shenk 1982:78). Study groups were formed, where passages of scripture were read and the parishioners were encouraged to find the meanings of these passages in terms of the problems of their daily lives. The purpose of such an approach was to raise the political consciousness of people who had never had a chance at formal education. The idea was to make people aware that the difficulties they experienced on a personal level were part of the more widespread social problems that existed in El Salvador. It was a form of "social activism" that the government of El Salvador wanted to discourage, since it was only a few steps away from revolution against the regime. Among the refugees in Costa Rica, the problems emphasized during church services are those of exile and homesickness, but the method used is the same.

Political awareness is also expressed dramatically in more secular settings outside the Center. During a celebration of the patron saint of El Salvador on August 6, the festivities included impromptu plays on political issues. In one performance that I witnessed, a soldier gave a payoff to a poor elderly Salvadoran peasant woman in exchange for snitching on her neighbors; the soldier was looking for "subversives" and was finally able to drag someone off to prison. The political message was serious, but it was presented as a farce. The silly costumes and exaggerated gestures allowed the audience to ridicule and jeer at their enemies. Such theater may help to alleviate the pain of the more genuine tragedy, based on real life, which is, of course, that the soldier won the day.

The sense of drama expressed throughout refugee life was extended to my contacts with the staff at the Center. Doña Ligia was clearly directing the action by controlling my interviews with the women. Moreover, there was a concerted effort among all the refugees to impress me with their experiences. The women relived their tragedies in that little room with me. Then afterwards they would compare notes with each other about who had cried most during the interviews and who had managed to make me cry. There was also some friendly competition as to how many sides of my tapes had been used up. They talked about how nervous they had been; they knew they were on show.

4

Mirabela

"We, as women, . . . cannot remain with our arms crossed."

Mirabela is the only one of the refugees that I would call a political activist. I heard that she was thought of as a "communist," but this term seemed to refer more to the intensity of her opinions than to her political perspective. She herself said that the other women looked on her as a political "fanatic," which she seemed to feel was a fairly accurate representation of her views. She was angry about a great number of things and most of her bitterness assumed a political slant.

Mirabela arrives late and a little breathless, all dressed up for the interview with her party make-up on and probably her nicest dress. We set up the tape recorder in Ligia's office and sit down at a table to talk. Before starting the tape recorder, I give Mirabela some general instructions and tell her that I will probably not interrupt the interview with specific questions now. She agrees and begins her *testimonio*.

Although we are in a private room, the place is not quiet. Children are running back and forth in the hallway, because playtime has just begun. Mirabela does not seem to notice the noise. She is so intensely engrossed in the telling of her story that I feel it would be unwise of me to interrupt. About twenty minutes into our interview, the door of the office suddenly bursts open, and a small boy runs into the room. He is crying and demands the whereabouts of his mother. As he rushes across the room, he trips over the electric cord to the tape recorder, and the machine lands with a bang on the floor. The boy's entry causes a flurry of nervous activity, during which my tape recorder is tested and found no longer to be working. At my suggestion, a more isolated room with less noise is located. Ligia's fancy new tape recorder is brought out and loaded with a new tape. Our session begins anew.

The second version of Mirabela's *testimonio* is very similar to the first, both in tone and in content. It is my first strong clue as to the number of times Mirabela has probably repeated this same story. Moreover, after she realizes that her initial recording has been garbled by the running and laughing noises of children, she is anxious to repeat her *testimonio*. I am amazed that she can begin again following our interruption, but it is clear that she wants to be heard.

Mirabela: In 1972 we were married. I am from a little town called Ereguayquín, in the province of Usulután in the eastern part of El Salvador, the part most under conflict. I went to San Salvador then because Hernando lived in Ilopango. He worked there during the day and studied at night. He was employed in a crayon factory, one of Zafier's factories. Well, it was here, working in this factory, that he began to see for himself the kind of exploitation to which the factory workers were being subjected. And they decided, he and two other workers, to form a union in the crayon factory.

And it happened at a certain point that the union began to grow. They started having confrontations even with the owner of the factory. Because my husband was secretary of the union, he was the one who had to come face-to-face with the factory owner Zafier. Well, the union gained what it was after: fair wages, overtime pay, and everything that a worker should get, as worker.

It was from this time on that the persecution of my husband really began. They would come to the house in search of him, when they knew we were there—the SIT [the secret police of the Interior Department] and the detectives of the National Guard. They didn't say who they were, in truth, but a person can always recognize them from the way they act. They try to make people afraid of them.

After they had come looking for him at the house, we moved from there and went to live in San Miguel, an area in the east. My husband went right on doing the same kind of work. He was active in the utilities unions more than anything else—the unions dealing with electricity and water—all of which were under persecution.

At this time the period of Colonel [Arturo] Armando Molina as president was coming to an end [Mirabela has her facts mixed up; Molina *started* his presidency in 1972]. During these years, 1972 through the beginning of 1974, there was terrible persecution. Our friends began to disappear: my brother-in-law [Hernando's eldest brother], a friend of mine named Sonia Estela, and a number of other people that I knew. And then the struggle continued, to gain freedom for our friends who had been captured.

But there was no response to our requests. . . .

Later, when General Carlos Humberto Romero took over the government, the repression of the people became more open. He issued a decree, called the *Ley de Orden* [Law of Public Order], which allowed him to seize all those people who were going around handing out propaganda and painting slogans on walls. And he managed to capture all the rest of our friends.

All of these people were tortured. I know because I succeeded . . . I was able to see, when my own husband was taken prisoner in 1978, that he was being held personally by the head of ANSESAL [*Agencia Nacional de Seguridad*

Salvadoreña, Salvadoran National Security Agency, part of the security structure that the United States played a major role in creating, yet which was suspected of coordinating the repression under presidents Molina and Romero (Byrne 1996:47)]. This man was the retired major who was the leader of the Death Squad, Roberto d'Aubuissón. He was the person who murdered Monseñor Romero [Archbishop Óscar Arnulfo Romero, who was assassinated in 1980; no relation to Gen. Romero], as well as thousands of rural farmers, workers, students, market women, teachers, and people living in the slums. Hernando was held almost a month with the National Guard, where they tortured him by giving him electric shocks. When they moved him on to the jail at Santa Tecla, he arrived in such a state . . . well, totally . . . so . . . well . . . psychologically destroyed.

From the 1930s the Salvadoran military gradually gained an increasing role in the governing of their country (North 1985:58–59). The military started out by protecting the economic interests of the coffee baron oligarchy, but after World War II, military leaders had begun to take an even more active role in the system, including becoming managers of numerous state agencies. During the 1950s through 1970s the government became more and more engulfed by the military, such that military leaders took over other high political offices in addition to the presidency.

Corruption became typical of the era. Military men were given economic and political rewards for protecting the oligarchy. Electoral fraud in 1972 gave a military officer, Colonel Arturo Armando Molina, the presidency, even though objective sources stated that the civilian leader José Napoleón Duarte had won the election (Armstrong and Shenk 1982:60–62; North 1985:71). Under Molina's regime, which had a facade of agrarian reform, or "transformation" as Molina called it, repression by the government escalated (Armstrong and Shenk 1982:83). There were attacks against priests and Jesuits for "communist subversion" based on the Church's support of peasant organization and agrarian reform. Unions, teachers' associations, and dissident politicians also came under attack (North 1985:75). Resistance to this repression led to the formation and consolidation of numerous organizations—such as the Popular Forces of Liberation-Farabundo Martí (FPL-FM founded in 1970), the Popular Revolutionary Army (ERP founded 1971), the United Popular Action Front (FAPU founded 1974), the Popular Revolutionary Bloc (BPR founded in 1975), and the Armed Forces óf National Resistance (FARN founded in 1975) (North 1985:79). The Farabundo Martí National Liberation Front, or the FMLN, was formed in 1980 as a broader united effort at resistance (Byrne 1996:40). Part of the government response to this resistance was the utilization of the semi-secret paramilitary group ORDEN, which had "the ostensible mission of combatting communism and defending 'democratic' values in the republic's rural areas" (qtd. from Webre 1979:162 in North 1985:71).

Most Salvadorans found it impossible to remain neutral under such disruptive conditions. Both the army and the FMLN needed manpower, and both sides of the conflict used forcible means to gain recruits. The Salvadoran army employed a number of techniques, including parking buses outside of movie theaters in order to cart off the young men as they left the movies, or raiding public fiestas or dances for induction (Payson Sheets, personal communication, 1997). Only those men whose parents had enough money could buy their way out of army service; all others were taken off to basic training. The guerrillas used similar forcible tactics, grabbing men on foot, though, rather than hauling them off in buses. Sheets, who was working in El Salvador as an archeologist on the Cerén Site in the late 1970s and early 1980s and who spoke with a number of these ex-recruits, reports, "Some poor guys had to serve on both sides and survived both to tell the tale."

In 1977 the military again controlled the elections, turning power over to General Carlos Humberto Romero, who had served as defense minister during Molina's regime. Romero took immediate action in November 1977 against the ongoing civil unrest in the country by establishing the *Ley de Orden*, allowed for political assassination and persecution under the widest possible definition of "subversive," including anyone having the potential for opposition to the government (Armstrong and Shenk 1982:97). Violence in El Salvador only grew during the enactment of this law, both on the part of the government and on the part of the increasingly mobilized opposition, such that El Salvador became the focus of international scrutiny (Armstrong and Shenk 1982:98). Inquiries from a number of international groups, including the Inter-American Committee on Human Rights and the Catholic Church, led to a uniform condemnation of the human rights abuses of the Romero administration. Romero was finally forced to repeal the *Ley de Orden* in February of 1979, and his presidency ended a few months later in October (Baloyra 1982:83–84).

The junta that was formed to take over the government, ultimately led by Duarte, was unable to solve the enormous economic and political problems of the country, and after a brief hiatus, human rights abuses continued, as the stories of the refugee women attest. The attack on María and her family came in 1980, and as we shall see, Mirabela finally emigrated in 1980 when her husband had become one of the "disappeared."

Mirabela: Well, my mother-in-law was, and is, illiterate. She can neither write nor read, and she isn't very well acquainted with the capital city. I had to go around with her. We went to the Human Rights Commission of El Salvador [*Comisión de Derechos Humanos de El Salvador*, or CDHES, founded in 1978] to ask for help, straight to the president of the Commission.

The president and founding member of CDHES was a friend, Marianella

García-Villas. She was later assassinated on the La Bermuda estate together with thirty other companions [the exact nature of Marianella García-Villas' assassination on March 14, 1983, has never been clearly established], due to her extraordinary struggle in defense of human rights. The army tried to give the impression, over the military channel COPREFA [Army Press Office], that these people had all died in combat, when in actual fact they had been massacred on the estate. And it was there that our friend Marianella García-Villas died. But as I said before, this woman worked hard to gain freedom for the many associates who had been made prisoners, including those who had been working in the unions, as well as those catechists of the Popular Church, who were also being pursued by the government.

And it was Marianella who finally was able to see my husband at the jail. Even though I was with her, they didn't let me go in. Marianella spoke to the director of the Santa Tecla jail and explained to him that I was Hernando's wife and that it was I who wanted to see him. Well, they were vehement in their refusal, saying that they had orders from their superiors and that they couldn't let me through. But they did allow her to get in.

Well, my friend Marianella was able to see my husband and she noted how they had left him, with handcuffs on and with marks all over his body . . . that more than anything else . . . wounds on all parts of his body where they had marked him. That is what I saw above all, the two times later I tried to see him and they finally let me inside. So that is how I know. When I saw him, all pale and totally messed up, well, really. . . .

Hernando told me everything that d'Aubuissón had personally done to him. D'Aubuissón had accused him of being a subversive. "Maybe I am a subversive," he said to d'Aubuissón. "Well then, I'm willing to die for it. If you could only see the injustices that you are committing against the people. If that is what makes me a subversive, then I am. But what you are doing to the people is indeed unjust."

They kept Hernando prisoner for a year-and-a-half. Then from that jail, they transferred him to the jail at Otera. This jail was built by Maximiliano Hernández Martínez, who was responsible for the 1932 massacre in which 30,000 peasants were killed inside the jail [she is referring to the *Mantaza* of 1932; however, the peasants were killed all over the country, not just in jail]. Now the jail was full of political prisoners. But through the efforts of the Human Rights Commission, many gained their freedom and were allowed to leave. My husband was also able to leave prison during the false amnesty that existed in El Salvador in 1980. Many of our friends were set free, but I don't believe that any one of them is left alive at this point. Some of them, after two months of being out, were murdered. Others disappeared again. And this is how things were going on in El Salvador, a whole lot of bloody happenings.

I ask Mirabela about her political involvement as wife of a union leader. She answers that as Hernando's wife, she served food to the union members when meetings were held at the house. She also stood guard outside the house during these union meetings to assure the men inside that nobody was watching them from the street. After the disappearance of her husband's brother in 1974, she took an even more active role, accompanying her mother-in-law in the search for him. Although they never succeeded in finding Hernando's eldest brother, Mirabela found herself getting more and more involved politically.

In 1977, even before her own husband was imprisoned, Mirabela joined a group of ten women in El Salvador to form the Committee of Mothers, or COMADRES [*Comité de Madres de los Presos Políticos, los Desaparecidos y los Asesinados "Monseñor Óscar Romero,"* Committee of Mothers of Political Prisoners, Disappeared, and Assassinated "Monseñor Óscar Romero," founded in El Salvador in December 1977]. These women initially worked together to obtain information about their own missing relatives, ultimately pressuring the Salvadoran government to answer for the killings and disappearances of thousands of ordinary citizens.   Such activities were extremely dangerous in El Salvador because of the political nature of the group's demands. The Committee also provided other kinds of support for women, such as helping them with health care, thus paving the way for similar kinds of services to women refugees abroad. Mirabela was part of the initial Committee, first searching with her mother-in-law for her husband's elder brother and then trying to obtain the release of her husband following his imprisonment in 1978.   She continues to work with a refugee branch of this group in Costa Rica.

Mirabela: Indeed, there was a group of women—mothers and sisters— who were going around in E1 Salvador looking for their sons, their husbands, and their brothers.   But the women had not received a single response to their requests. We became part of the Committee of Mothers, of the "disappeared" and murdered political prisoners in El Salvador. We wanted to show our response to the government and to the groups of repression in El Salvador. We wanted to demonstrate that we women were capable of demanding freedom for our loved ones in prison. We wanted a complete clarification of the situation involving the "disappeared." These groups should tell us what had been done to our people, and they should ask for trials and punishment for the criminals.

Among these criminals was Chato Castillo who was the director of the National Guard and who was in charge of public justice.   And there was Santibáñez, Eugenio Vides Casanova [Salvadoran Minister of Defense], and Colonel Sigifredo Ochoa [Commander of the Fourth Brigade]—all of whom are still in power in the government, reprimanding the people because they want their rights. They reprimand the people for demanding their freedom and for demanding that, instead of exploitation or misery, there be peace and social justice for everyone—not just for the Fourteen Families. The majority of people are peasant farmers, and we have the right to live as human beings in a new land where there is peace, but a peace that is real for everyone.

Hernando was taken prisoner in 1978. While he was in jail, Mirabela no longer had any secure income. In order to survive she began selling off her furniture and other household items. However, she was pregnant again and had her two other children to support as well, so she was finally forced to return home to her parents' house. There her third child was born.

When Mirabela's husband was finally released from jail in 1980, the Human Rights Commission gave him enough money to survive on while he renewed his fight for the rights of the union members. He remained in hiding, however. Mirabela saw him only a few times during brief, secret meetings in her father's village before Hernando finally "disappeared" permanently. In August of 1980, Mirabela left El Salvador for Costa Rica with her eldest son. She now presumes that her husband is dead.

Historically, U.S. involvement in Latin America has focused on preventing European intervention in the region. As early as 1823, the Monroe Doctrine showed U.S. support for the independence of the Latin American countries from European colonialism (Molineu 1986:15–19), and much later in 1948 the United States joined the Organization of American States (OAS) to create a military alliance for deterring external threats and keeping peace in the Western Hemisphere (Molineu 1986:25–28). The approach characteristic of the United States towards Latin America from the 1950s was a continuation of this policy; the "containment of communism" was based on the view that the Soviet Union, with Cuba as its ally, hoped to inspire communist revolution in the area (Molineu 1986:7–9).

As a corollary to the policy of preventing European intervention, the pattern of "dollar diplomacy" arose, involving the use of troops to defend U.S. investments and business interests in Latin America (Molineu 1986:45–48). Thus, governments run by the wealthy, as in the case of the coffee baron oligarchy of El Salvador, or military dictatorships, as existed in countries throughout Latin America, found themselves aligned with the U.S. government, which was dedicated to supporting economic and political stability in the region. Even during the era of President Franklin D. Roosevelt, when the policy of "good neighbor" meant the withdrawal of troops and the signing of agreements pledging noninterference, the United States did little to prevent military dictatorships in these countries (Molineu 1986:22–25).

U.S. policy was thus contradictory from the beginning. Latin American countries were dependent on the United States for their very independence and economic stability. While the U.S. belief in democracy was ostensibly "containing communism," U.S. support of military dictatorships actually prevented democracy from taking hold in these countries and even led to many of the human rights abuses that occurred.

Slavery and its offshoots like *repartimiento* and "debt peonage" have existed in Latin America for centuries, though such exploitation has not been viewed internationally as "human rights" abuses. It wasn't until the Alliance for Progress under the Kennedy administration in the 1960s and the human rights campaign of the Carter administration in the 1970s that U.S. aid to Latin America became tied to economic and political reform in an effort to reduce these abuses and promote democracy in the area (Molineu 1986:28–30). Thus, the contradiction became official U.S. policy in Latin America. On the one hand, U.S. strategic interests in the area meant military aid to prevent the intervention of communism, and on the other hand, U.S. interests in human rights meant attempts, largely ineffective, to pressure these governments into more equitable domestic policies.

Expression of this contradictory policy in El Salvador over the years varied between benign neglect and gentle arm twisting. Clearly, the U.S. government believed that its own national security interests in the country required a strong military force, as well as a weakened peasant class. Between the years 1962–1982 El Salvador received more military aid than all but five of the largest countries in the Western Hemisphere (Molineu 1986:94–96), and this aid went indirectly toward these national security ends. Although the United States occasionally put overt pressure to bear on changes in the Salvadoran government prior to the 1970s (especially during the overthrow of Martínez in 1944, the consolidation of military rule in 1948, and the reestablishment of military rule in 1961 [Baloyra 1982:75]), the same goals were accomplished when the United States remained aloof during the electoral frauds of 1972 and 1977 that brought the military leaders Molina and Romero to power. During the *Matanza* of 1932, the United States turned the other way when innocent civilians were being slaughtered, and over the years U.S. officials did little to try to pressure the coffee baron oligarchy to work toward land reform and more egalitarian treatment of agricultural workers. Thus, the U.S. government attitude was that we should let El Salvador solve its own problems, our own national interests often being best served by this neglect.

External involvement in El Salvador changed radically during the 1970s with the intensification of human rights abuses, especially during the enactment of the *Ley de Orden* under the Romero government. Death threats against Catholic activists caused the Carter administration to search for ways to exert U.S. pressure on Salvadoran domestic policy. One of the strongest measures taken was a linkage of U.S. military aid to the observance of human rights in El Salvador. Like some other Latin American countries, El Salvador refused to take the aid rather than comply with international pressures to reduce the violence against its citizens. The Carter administration was then forced to isolate the Romero government in order to keep its pledge towards human rights (Petras and

Morley 1990:128–31).

After Romero was ousted by a coup in 1980 and the new junta failed to solve El Salvador's urgent problems, the United States strongarmed Duarte into becoming a member of the junta, in the hope of restoring some kind of legitimacy to the Salvadoran government. The Carter administration also insisted on a land reform program combined with a system of repression designed to curtail popular support in the countryside (North 1985:90). This program of concession-repression was backed by renewed U.S. military aid.

The Reagan administration brought sharp increases in military aid to El Salvador, plus the commitment of fifty-six non-combat military advisors, with the expressed purpose of helping to combat leftist guerrilla activity (North 1985:90). The U.S. government was even considering the possibility of sending troops to fight against the increasingly well-organized and determined revolutionary forces. Much U.S. military aid became funneled into terrorist activity, however, through paramilitary death squads and unchecked government security forces.

Mirabela: So we, as women, as mothers and wives, cannot remain with our arms crossed in the face of all this. In spite of everything that might have happened in El Salvador, my strength to go forward in my work has not weakened. Although I have been here in Costa Rica since 1980, I am able to maintain that same strength and even have greater strength than before. When I see and hear the news that my people are disappearing on a daily basis in El Salvador, or that they are being killed, it makes me go on with my work to bring down the dictatorship that has been imposed on El Salvador for the past fifty years.

Even though here we only occupy a little space, we must take advantage of this small space to push ahead with our work of consolidating the people of El Salvador—and not just in El Salvador, but also in all of Central America, and North and South America. Because along with El Salvador we must mention Nicaragua, where North American imperialist aggression works daily to prevent the Nicaraguan people from deciding for themselves how they should conduct their own revolution.

We can also look at the case of Panama, which now at this very moment has about 20,000 North American advisors. In Honduras the advisors are there to commit acts of aggression against the Nicaraguans, against the Salvadorans. Or let's say, the Reagan government is attempting direct intervention. But the countries of Central America are not alone. The Panamanians, for example, are defending their own sovereignty. The Panama Canal belongs to the Panamanian people. The Torrijos-Carter treaty should be respected, and the imperialists should not try to snatch the canal away from Panama.

And it is in this sense that we, as women who have suffered, who have been exploited, should not remain with our arms crossed. On the contrary, we should unite our forces and from here where we are, we can set up a front against imperialism and say to the Reagan government that they cannot pass. Because Central America is not alone, it is a united people that is ready to defend itself at the cost of blood or whatever it might be, but we will not be colonies of North America.

I came to Costa Rica on the twenty-ninth of August, 1980. I came here alone with my oldest boy, because he was the one in the greatest danger. I left the other children at home, against my family's wishes. [Her other two children were sent on to Costa Rica later.]

But I feel good about myself, how I am and how I think. If my parents were to die while I was here in exile, I believe that they would die wrong, well, because I really think that in life one should do all the good that one can. Seeing such injustice, one cannot simply remain silent nor with arms crossed. Instead, one has to move forward.

Mirabela's political position is something of an anomaly. She grew up in a rural family, as one of eight children, but her father had more than enough money to give them all a comfortable life. All her brothers and sisters were able to go to school and prepare themselves for middle-class jobs, as secretaries and teachers. Though Mirabela was offered the same opportunities as the others, her life has become a struggle on behalf of her poorer neighbors. In her fight for justice and equality for the poor, she has become one of them, alienating her family and forfeiting her own chances for a comfortable existence. Her sacrifice has not been without bitterness.

One thing that originally set Mirabela apart was her contraction of trichinosis as a child. This illness resulted in unbearable headaches due to the accumulation of fluid on the brain.

Mirabela: My brothers and sisters, they all became secretaries or teachers. They are all educated. The problem with me was that I only got through the second grade, no further, because I suffered a lot in my head. I was very sick, so I didn't keep going to school. But I was the only one in my family who didn't finish school.

In her *testimonio* Mirabela mentions an operation to insert a valve in her brain to drain off excess liquid. However, this operation was not performed until she was an adult, when she was in the hospital in 1977 giving birth to her third and final child. The operation helped alleviate the pain, but she still gets numerous headaches. (I notice that she often talks with her fingers tightly pressed against her temples.) Her family claimed that her increased political involvement after the operation was due to problems in the process of recuperating her health, but Mirabela says that she had legitimate political reasons to act strangely during the year following her operation.

Mirabela: The operation took place in 1977, while I was in the hospital having my last child. My husband became prisoner in 1978. So I really had recuperated. When he left, I was running around in circles, going crazy. This was when my family told me that I wasn't even taking pity on myself, that I was just getting involved in trivialities [political activities] that were of no importance to me. I never paid any attention to them.

What I always did was to bring my children to my family's house and then leave. I would come back after a week or two. But one time my mother, perhaps just to make me stay, said, "Watch where you are leaving your children, because you are not going to see them anymore."

I got angry and said to her, "If you are going to be that way, I had better take them with me."

When she saw that I was serious and that I was really going to take them, she got upset and said, "Oh, go ahead and leave them here. You go on, and I hope you fall on your ass."

"O.K., I am going," I said. But she did that just to try to make me quit being involved in what I was doing.

Nobody could ever stop me from doing things, but it was her way of trying to make me quit. My sisters also came and told me that they would not see me anymore. However, they were not able to stop me either. I kept on doing what I had been doing before, working with the Committee of Mothers. I also went on searching with my mother-in-law for her eldest son who had disappeared. She now has two sons that have disappeared and two sons killed. Yes, there are four. A peasant woman who can neither read nor write, who doesn't even know the city. I had to walk around with her . . . in this direction, in that direction . . . and such a fighter she was.

Mirabela's disagreements with her own family actually started much earlier than this, although the conflict apparently did not come out into the open until she became an adult.

Mirabela: My family never gave me any support in anything. Instead, they rejected me for my way of thinking about the people as a whole. They told me that I was being influenced by Cuba, that my husband had brainwashed me. I began to have problems with my parents and the rest of my family. I began to lose respect for them, because I never really had agreed with their way of thinking.

For example, my mother said, "Those who are prisoners, let them stay in jail, as prisoners."

And I said, "No, I cannot simply allow that to happen."

Then she said, "Just think, you were so intelligent, and you just used your intelligence to learn foolishness."

My husband was in his second year of studying law, so I was able to say to her, "Oh, Mamá, you are interested in the kinds of things I have learned. You want the people to be free. And you don't want the workers and the peasants to be exploited. Even we, as children, were exploited by our own father."

And this was when I really began to fight with my father. He said, "Your husband has ruined you, that man with his Cuban ideas!"

"Don't screw around with me," I told him. "Don't you see that even you, instead of giving your farmhands something to eat, you feed only your dogs?" But his answer to this was that he was in charge of taking care of the dogs, but not in charge of the farmhands.

So I said to him, "Everything that you have, you got at the expense of the peons, of those you have exploited. . . ."

My father got furious and told me, and my mother too, that it would have been better if I had died as a small child. I was the only one who ever gave him any trouble.

Thus, they pushed me aside, they abandoned me. . . .

Even as a child Mirabela probably was not at ease with her family. Mirabela says that her father was the "boss" of the town, not in the sense of being an elected head—although in later years he was chosen to be mayor—but in the sense that he was extraordinarily feared and envied for his wealth. His house was the first in the town of Ereguayquín to acquire a television set, and it became the custom for the neighbors to come by and watch. The children of the house were expected to collect five *centavos* [cents] from each villager who came to watch television. Mirabela's brothers and sisters always managed to make everyone pay, but she felt uncomfortable with the practice and often allowed viewers to slip in free.

Mirabela's father was the undisputed head of his household. When he arrived home, he demanded absolute silence from each of his eight children; and he got it. He treated his wife harshly, beating her and taking up with other women. He spent a lot of time away from home drinking. He would walk up and down the streets of the town with his mistresses on his arm, and even parade with them in front of his own house, where his wife and children could watch. One of these other women had five children by him, another had two, and a third had a child who died at birth. When Mirabela asked her mother why she did not try to escape this intolerable situation, her mother's reply was, "Where would I go? And what would I do with eight children?"

However, Mirabela's illness and her bitterness towards her family were only part of the gradual growth of Mirabela's political conscious-ness. The most crucial factor was undoubtedly her childhood friendship and slowly developing love for Hernando, the man who was eventually to become her husband. Even though Hernando was much older than Mirabela, they became friends at school very early. Hernando's family was poor. His father was a landless peasant who worked as a caretaker on someone else's farm. Although Hernando wanted to continue with his education, his family's poverty forced him to leave school to go to work at age fifteen. He got a job with the National Campaign Against Malaria and was soon sent to the town of Majagual to distribute anti-malaria medicine to the people. After two years there, Hernando managed to return to his native village of Ereguayquín to complete his schooling and receive his *bachillerato*.

According to Mirabela, Hernando was a serious and retiring

young man. He was obviously persistent and bright as well. In spite of several interruptions in his studies, he was able to get to law school. He was working on this degree when he was finally arrested in 1978. With Mirabela, he was patient and kind, explaining things to her and including her in his life. Mirabela did special things for him, too. When he was a boy, too poor to participate in the Independence Day parade on December 15 because he lacked the money for the required uniform, she somehow got the money from her family so that he could take part.

When she was about sixteen years old, Mirabela realized that she and her friend Hernando had fallen in love. But they were very restrained about sex because they were both painfully aware of her father's disapproval of the union. According to Mirabela, she knew little about sex and its consequences. She said her parents had never talked with her about sex, this being the custom in rural areas of El Salvador. When I asked if she had ever talked about such things with her friends, she replied that she and her brothers and sisters were kept virtually isolated from the neighborhood children.

So, ten years later, when Mirabela was twenty-six years old, she was surprised to find herself pregnant. Her periods stopped, and her father angrily rushed her off to see one of his physician friends. At the doctor's she learned for the first time that the suspension of menstruation was one of the signs of pregnancy. Mirabela claimed to me that she and Hernando had never actually had sex. I am not sure what she meant by that. At any rate, when it was established that she was pregnant, Mirabela and Hernando got married. Mirabela's bitterness about her father's objections to her marriage is still evident in her *testimonio*.

> Mirabela: My father was a wealthy rural farmer, someone we call a "donkey loaded with dough" [*burro cargado de este pisto*]. When I got married, my husband didn't have any place to live, since his family were only caretakers on someone else's land. But my father was from a certain social class. And he wanted his daughters to marry men whose families were of the same class. A person isn't supposed to marry someone because she likes him. She is supposed to marry him because he has money. So we had a problem when I got married. My father didn't want to give me away in the church. He said that since I had married a man who was poor, I had dirtied his soul. . . .

Mirabela's political stance has left her with a strong sense of martyrdom. The heroes and heroines of her *testimonio* range from well-known political figures such as Marianella García-Villas, through the lesser-known figures of her husband and his friends, and on down to innocent civilians like her mother-in-law who understand almost nothing of the conflict. She expresses a parallelism in the suffering of all of these people. And who does she blame for the political injustice that she sees? The villains include people like Roberto d'Aubuissón, known for his association with the Death Squad, and even her own father who mistreats his agricultural workers and creates misery for Mirabela's family. Beyond this, she condemns "North American imperialist aggression" in Central America, implying a complicity between the U.S. government and the people in power in El Salvador. She obviously associates national security forces and paramilitary groups with the imprisonment, torture and disappearance of her husband and of many other Salvadorans; and she blames them, as well as her family, for her own personal exile and loss.

Such political martyrdom does not exist without a firm ideology worth fighting for, and even worth dying for. But what is this ideology? The U.S. government committed its military aid to fighting leftist guerrillas, more commonly labelled "communists" or "subversives" in El Salvador. But while Mirabela's parents have accused her of being "influenced by Cuba," she does not have the rhetoric one might expect of a communist. She speaks mostly of justice, equality, and freedom—ideas most often associated with democracy. She never talks in her *testimonio* about communal ownership of property or governmental control of factories or farms. The closest she comes to these ideas are her comments about workers having certain rights regarding wages and benefits. She does not say that her father should turn his farm over to his laborers, but rather that he should feed them at least as well as he feeds his dogs. In condemning "North American imperialists," Mirabela does not seem to be referring to capitalism as an ideology, but instead to political and economic tactics that turn Central American countries into colonies. For Mirabela, the struggle is between the rich and the poor, the powerful and the powerless, and not between capitalism and communism.

This association of martyrdom with political action is a relatively recent phenomenon in Latin America, arising from liberation theology and the Popular Church. The upper echelon of the socioeconomic hierarchy has traditionally manipulated the religious concept of martyrdom to its own ends. The teachings of the Church—that the poor should accept their suffering with grace, waiting patiently for their rewards in the afterlife—have served to keep the peasants in their place. Any guilt experienced by the wealthy has been alleviated by the notion that people are born into their particular station in life according to some divine plan. Just as the poor were destined to be poor, the rich were destined to be rich.

However, the Popular Church in El Salvador has encouraged the people to question the social order as the source of their suffering. In this new atmosphere, martyrdom is still seen as saintly, but there has been a shift in its meaning. Whereas people were previously supposed to accept their suffering, now people are being asked to act against the worldly source of this suffering, a process that leads to even greater suffering and often death.

Women play a special role in this atmosphere. Their sacrifices, which have always included the acceptance of poverty, hard work, and the inconstancy of men, now encompass the personal loss of sons, husbands, and fathers. Their suffering now means a general breakdown of the extended family support system and all that this has traditionally entailed—someone to take care of their children, a family homestead to which they can return in times of stress, and their sense of community. While some Salvadoran women have entered the armed conflict as guerrillas, the vast majority have proven their martyrdom in ways that fit more closely with their traditional roles of suffering wife and mother. Even Mirabela, who believes in political activism more than any of the others, does not advocate that the women take up arms against their oppressors in a "revolutionary" stance; she asks only that they join her in condemnation of the system, as martyrs.

The martyrdom expressed openly by Mirabela is apparently felt by all the women. This becomes evident to me during a mass at the Center when the Salvadorans celebrate *Día de la Madre* (Mother's Day). On this occasion the children, all in colorful peasant costume, perform songs and dances for the mothers who are present. Speeches are made about how the daycare center is dedicated to the care of Salvadoran children. Mothers who must go to work for the survival of their families have a place to keep their children safe during the day. Even orphans can receive a semblance of mothering from the Center staff. The daycare center is a place where the children can learn the customs and values of their homeland.

Then comes the climax of the service. The priest reads a passage from the Bible, which I do not recognize, but which leads to a passionate discussion by the group of the suffering experienced by women during the conflict in El Salvador. They speak of rape, of violence, of imprisonment. They tell of the "disappeared" and the murdered, of sons and husbands and fathers and daughters and sisters, all lost in the struggle. They weep and pray together for the suffering of all the mothers of El Salvador, for those who have died and for themselves.

It is a moving moment. The refugees, in what looks like a spontaneous outburst, have associated their own lives with those of the saints. They too have suffered; they too are martyrs—even if only on a smaller scale. It gives them hope and a reason to live. It gives strength to their political message to the world.

5

Alicia

"My entire family fell apart."

Doña Ligia warns me about Alicia before my first interview with her. At the very beginning of my research I suggest to Ligia that I interview each of the women at my home so as not to disturb the running of the daycare center. After discovering that Ligia's office is too noisy to obtain a clear tape recording of Mirabela's session, we move to one of the classrooms, but I feel that using a classroom may be an imposition during future interviews. Doña Ligia insists, however. First of all, she says that the Center's collaboration with me means certain sacrifices on their part. This is one of the things they can easily offer me.

"Besides," she says, "I feel more comfortable when my staff remains close by. We might need them." Then she continues, "I must speak frankly with you, Doña Robin. There are certain people who might take advantage of you if they go to your house." I assume Doña Ligia is referring to the possibility of theft, but I want her to be more specific about it, since she has brought it up. So I ask, "What do you mean?"

"There is one person who might start to ask you for this and for that. Well, of course, María wouldn't do that, even though she is very poor. And Carmen would never do that. But someone might." Doña Ligia pauses.

"Who do you mean?" I ask. I have set up three additional interviews, and the only name Ligia has not mentioned is Alicia's.

"Well, Alicia might. She is always making friends with *gringos* and getting things from them, like . . . taking advantage of them. Frankly, Robin, I wanted you to know that you must be very careful."

It took me several months to figure out what Doña Ligia was trying to tell me about Alicia. Although many thoughts passed through my mind, I settled for a long time on the notion that Doña Ligia and some of the other women were simply jealous of Alicia. I saw right away that Alicia was a gifted storyteller. She kept me on the edge of my chair during her entire *testimonio*. Not only was her story energetically told, but it was full of intimate detail and suspense. Alicia was also young and pretty. Her two latest children had been fathered by two different men here in Costa Rica, and she was still searching for a husband to replace the one she had lost back in El Salvador. And as Ligia had told me, Alicia had managed easily to befriend a number of foreigners—among them a reporter and two relief aid workers. These friends even sent dollars occasionally from abroad. Indeed, Alicia had given the other women plenty of reasons to be jealous.

But Doña Ligia had said that Alicia might try to take advantage of me, and I suppose Alicia did try to manipulate me a bit. I was immediately charmed by her story and by her active overtures toward friendship. Alicia's manipulation of me, however, seemed no more serious than the manipulation I felt from all the other women. Everyone wanted to influence me. But as time went on, I noticed that Alicia's attempts to guide my behavior were often in direct competition with similar such attempts made by the others. While the other women aligned themselves more closely with the political goals of the group with regard to my research, Alicia's goals were intensely personal. She was not working for the solidarity of the group at the Center. She was a woman alone, intent upon the survival of herself and her five children.

Alicia: I am originally from Chalatenango, which is north of San Salvador. I was born in Santa Teresa, a little town that is part of Potonico, which is under the jurisdiction of Chalatenango.

My father is a peasant farmer, and my mother is, too. The greater part of my childhood, you could say, was spent together with them, working in the country. Out in the country a child is given work to do when she is still very little. From the time she is five years old she starts to work, helping her parents, harvesting the corn, taking lunch to them in the fields, or taking them afternoon snack. She also helps to fetch water, because out in the country there isn't any running water in the houses, and does other kinds of chores, like feeding the animals.

Then when I was twelve years old, I had to leave home, where I belonged, and go to work in San Salvador in order to help my mother to take care of my sisters and brothers. I also worked to save money so that I could continue going to school. When I was five years old, I went to first grade, and by the time I was ten, I had finished sixth grade. I was an excellent student, and I wanted to go on studying. But my parents couldn't pay for my studies. When a person finishes sixth grade, which is primary school there in my country, he begins secondary school, which is seventh, eighth, and ninth grade and the first year of high school. But they couldn't pay for this, because you have to buy books and notebooks for school, all of which cost 14 *colones* [$5.60] in Salvadoran money. And they weren't able to buy them.

So I had to go to San Salvador to work and earn money to help my mother with my sisters and brothers and to save money so that I could continue in school. I spent two years there. I worked for two years, starting at 25 *colones* [$10] a month. Of that, I gave 10 to my mother, and 15 were left for me, which I put in the bank for my studies later.

After two years they gave me a raise, but only to 30 *colones* [$12] a month. So I decided . . . after two years of working, I decided I wouldn't continue there, and I went instead to the place where my parents were. However, this was no longer in Santa Teresa, but rather in a place called El Asentamiento [settlement], or better yet Reubicación [resettlement]. They built a dam named Cerro Grande [big hill], but everyone called it Cerrón Grande, I really don't know why. Even the person who was president at that time, Molina, said: "the dam of the Cerrón Grande." Well, it really is El Cerro Grande. Anyway, they built this dam in order to get energy for export. So when the dam was built, all of us who lived in those *cantones*, we had to leave because the area was going to be flooded. And my parents were among those who left . . . who had to leave. They were taken to this resettlement place. They call it "resettlement," but to me it was not resettlement because "resettling" means taking people from one place to another without it costing them anything. But in this case they kicked us out of our houses and off the small parcels of land that we had. They paid us very badly, and the houses they had made for us, where they took us, cost more than what we had been paid for our houses and land. So for me it was not resettlement. It was a maneuver which they used to make it known on an international level that the people who had been hurt by the dam had been resettled in another place more . . . more feasible and closer to the city. Of course it was true that we were closer to the city, but it wasn't the same because the land was different. Our land back there was very fertile, and here where they brought us, the land was not very good. What I mean is that in order to get a harvest, you had to invest a lot of money in the maintenance of the land. This was one thing. And the other thing was that our lives were different. The community spirit was gone, because all the people in this new place were from different areas. They were all brought from different *cantones*. The only good thing about this new place was the fish. The people could fish, and many married couples and many households were able to survive on this.

We always used our land. We planted corn, watermelons, garden vegetables like cabbage, melons, cucumbers, and of course there was always fish. So that's how we lived. And I studied on my own, got through seventh grade, and then I got married.

Robin: How old were you then?

Alicia: Seventeen years old. That's right. . . . I got married and immediately I began a whole new life. I was already responsible for myself. I had gone through seventh grade all by myself. It was there that I met my husband. Well, first we were friends. Soon he became my boyfriend, and very quickly we got married.

Not long afterwards I had to move to San Salvador, because my husband was being pursued for belonging to the union in the place that he worked.

Robin: Where did he work?

Alicia: He worked in the Tropical Bottling Company, which is really . . .
quite certainly . . . well, the owners of the bottling company are apparently from the
United States.

So he was one of the members, or rather he was one of the ones who
helped form the union, mostly in order to ask for better pay. Because what they
were paying was 150 *colones* [$60] a month and you can't live on 150. The union
began with a strike and had very good results. They got 200 *colones* [$80] a
month in pay and an improvement in the food. The company had been giving
them unclean food, food that wasn't any good. Spoiled food is what they had been
giving them. So this is what they had asked for in the first strike they had. And
the union succeeded, but afterwards the repression began.

The union was successful, but the repression came soon after. The
authorities began to take workers that had supported the strike and throw them out
of their own houses. Others they threatened. And still others were taken from
where they were standing and waiting for a bus, or from where they were eating
lunch or whatever. They were carried away and finished off. Or they disappeared.

So then I had to . . . I traveled with my husband to stay in Chalatenango
for awhile . . . sometimes we lived in San Salvador, and other times we stayed in
Chalatenango. We had three years of marriage before he was murdered. He had
. . .

Robin: In the city?

Alicia: In the city of San Salvador, yes. He was captured at the bus stop
of the UCA [*Universidad Centroamericana*, Central American University]. The UCA
is a Catholic university of San Salvador. He was at the bus stop and was captured
there . . . it was a Monday, the seventh of April, 1981. My boy had been born just
three months before, the littlest one. My husband left me three children, and the
third was three months old.

When he didn't come . . . at this time there was a curfew from six o'clock
on, and it didn't end until five in the morning. So when the hour arrived, the hour
of the curfew, and he still had not come, I got a bad feeling in my spine that
something had happened to him. Because always after work he came home, and
there wasn't any problem. He didn't . . . we didn't ever have problems, at least not
in our marriage. When he would leave and go to another place, like that, he
always told me. But on this day he hadn't said anything to me, and he didn't
arrive. The next day I went to search for him. I came close to the bottling
company, and they told me that . . . that there had been a meeting of the union
members at the UCA.

One of the members that hadn't gone to the meeting said that they had
all been captured. Seven of them were captured. This person told me that he had
been saved because he had not arrived on time. He got there late, after they had
already been taken. The people were talking about it when he arrived, and he
pieced together the news himself. This person then was forced to move out of his
house immediately with his wife and his son. He had only one son. And since I
was out looking for my husband, I met this man, and he told me. . . .

I began to go around to the various organizations. I went to the International Red Cross, I went to the Salvadoran Red Cross, I went to the morgue at the hospital, at Rosales Hospital, indeed I went everywhere and didn't find out anything. There wasn't a trace of him. My uncle was helping me, too. And after three days had gone by, my uncle found him murdered in the cemetery of Soyapango. All seven were there, the seven companions.

Robin: They had just been put there, or had they . . . ?

Alicia: Yes, but it seems as if, or rather, they had not been killed there. They had been killed on the train line from San Carmelo in Soyapango—Monte Carmelo, that is. That is where they were murdered. But I never would have imagined that my husband was over in that area. I thought he would be somewhere else perhaps, or taken prisoner, or beaten up . . . in a hospital, I don't know, but I never once thought he would be in that place.

My uncle, nevertheless, kept saying to me, "Child, let's go over there and search."

I didn't even have the courage to follow him there. I was only twenty years old and had three children. I felt so bad. More than anything else I wanted to die, if my husband didn't reappear. So my uncle took off. He always rode on his motorcycle. He had a motorcycle that he used to ride around on to collect money from the different agencies, because he used to work in a warehouse.

Robin: This uncle?

Alicia: My uncle, yes. So when he went to collect some money, he said he saw that a great many people were entering the cemetery at Soyapango. The people said that the International Red Cross had brought some bodies there to the cemetery in hopes that their families would come and identify them. It had already been three days, and the bodies were decomposing.

So my uncle became curious and went inside to look. And the surprise was that first in the row—they had placed all seven in a row—was my husband. My uncle came straight home to tell me.

It was very sad, because my children were calling for him, mostly the biggest girl. He used to put her to sleep and feed her. She wouldn't eat for me unless he was around. So when my uncle came, I became very hopeful. I felt such happiness when he told me he had found my husband. I never imagined that he would be dead. I was expecting to find him alive . . . alive, no matter how—beaten up, without any hands, or whatever, but alive.

When my uncle saw how happy I was that he had found my husband—I had gone to change, to get dressed to go with him to wherever my husband was—he said to me, "Alicia, but you have to be prepared for . . . for this, because you don't realize what state he is in."

I said, "It doesn't matter how bad it is! I'll go and see him and bring him back. And I will take care of him."

Then he saw that I was not ready to receive the news that he was dead. He called my father and told him that my husband was dead and how should he go about telling me. And my father said, "Just tell her."

So when I said, "Uncle, are we going to go?" he answered me, "Look. He is dead."

I felt like . . . like . . . like I didn't even exist. . . . I lost consciousness, I forgot my own name, I didn't know if these children were mine, I didn't know anything. I completely lost my head, as if someone had turned me round and round in circles.

Then my uncle saw that I wasn't ready and that the news had made me act that way. He couldn't figure out what to do. I ran out into the street, desperate, with my littlest girl in my arms, and with my other bigger girl and my father after me. And behind us my uncle called out, "You go with her!"

I stopped a taxi, though I didn't even have five *centavos* [$.02] with me. My uncle gave my father some money for the taxi fare and told him not to leave me alone.

I went directly to where he had said, to Soyapango. He hadn't really said, he hadn't given me an address, he hadn't given me anything. I just grabbed my little girl, and I don't know. . . . When I came to my senses, I was in the cemetery. Actually, it was when I saw him [her husband's body] that I came to my senses again. I had my little girl in my arms, and I looked at him. Then, giving the little girl to my father, I went straight toward him.

And another thing. Somewhere in my consciousness . . . I didn't get out of the taxi at the cemetery, I got out before and began to run from there. I got out at the market of Soyapango, and from there it was something like eight blocks to get to the cemetery. I really ran.

When I arrived, I gave the little girl to my father, and I went directly over to the body. I walked around it. He didn't have any impact from bullets. I stood there looking at all of the bodies, but mostly at him. He didn't have any impact from bullets. He just had his ribs broken, and there was a whole lot of blood . . . like . . . dry . . . and on his head he had some black pelts, as if they had banged him against the floor. And his ears were full of blood. They had burst his eardrums.

He had a piece of shirt tied around his throat, from one of the same shirts that had been taken off their backs. I went to untie it. As I was loosening the piece of shirt, all the people who were looking at the bodies came over near me. I wasn't trying to hide anything. I didn't feel anything at all. They came up to me and said, "Poor young man, look, he's been decapitated." Because he had two holes in his throat.

I stopped. And I turned him over, because he was . . . was . . . I turned him over. And after I got him turned, the people were upon me again. He was bound. He was tied here, by his fingers. And his fingers were all swollen and purple. He didn't have any impact from bullets. His pants were ripped, he wore no shirt, his socks were torn . . . I don't know how they did it, but they surely killed him by means of torture.

My uncle had come after us, and he didn't enter the cemetery. He stayed by the gate while I was looking at the body and doing all these things. I reached into my husband's pocket, the only pocket of his pants that was still any good, in order to see if his identification card was there, or his papers, because he carried around photos of me and of my children. There was nothing.

A man, or rather a very fat boy wearing a cap and dark glasses, came over to me and asked, "Is that your husband?"

I said to him, "Me? No, that is not my husband."

My husband had told me before, "Alicia, if I don't come home some day, don't look for me, please. Because what I really want is for you to stay alive . . . and to go on with my children." He presented it to me like that.

So I said to this man, "No, it isn't my husband."

And I didn't shed a single tear. Even my father admired me. He said, "How this woman behaved!" I didn't shed a single tear. I denied everything . . . everything . . . everything, I denied. And only I knew how I felt inside. It was going against everything I felt, but I didn't reveal anything.

When he asked me, I said, "No." Then he went away. He walked over to something—I think it was a radio, I wasn't able to tell—but my uncle knew. He told me later that this man was from the National Guard. My uncle had stayed outside. But the people had noticed that I was interested in one of the bodies. After the man had asked me this, he went back to where he had been standing.

Right afterwards an old woman, a little old woman, came up to me and asked, "Is this the little girl's father?" But my little girl didn't call out to him—this was another miracle—she didn't call out to him the way she usually did, "*Papito! Papito!*" She just stood there. But she didn't say, "*Papito.*" She didn't say anything. She acted just the way I did.

The old woman came up to me and asked, "Is that the father of the little girl?" There they don't say "*chiquita*," but "*niña.*" I answered, "No, no, that isn't her father."

"And why," she asked, "are you interested in the body?"

"Ah," I said, "it's that he looks like somebody I know, but I am not sure. And I want to be sure before I inform the family."

"Oh, then it isn't the child's father?"

"No," I told her, "it isn't the child's father." And I denied it all. I wanted to be left alone.

After the old woman withdrew, I turned around and looked at my uncle, who was standing at the very entrance to the cemetery. My uncle just returned my look and gave me a signal, like this [Alicia makes a gesture], and I . . . I don't know how it was that I understood I should go, that I should get out of that place, that it was dangerous there. I backed away from his body and went to look at the other cadavers, so that the people wouldn't think any more about me.

So I walked around looking at the other bodies. Each one had met a different kind of death. One of them had all . . . everything that was part of his face removed. He still had a little bit of his hair and some of the back of his head, but he didn't have any face left. Nothing. The rest of his body was all right, but he didn't have anything of . . . just the little piece here in back.

Another one had two bullet holes here. Otherwise he was whole. Just the bullet holes. Another had his hand amputated and his foot cut. He lay there dead even though the rest of him was all right.

There was a woman . . . they had removed her breasts and one arm. And they had left her like that. Only one woman among the seven. . . .

Well, all of them had died differently. But no one had been tortured the way my husband had been. No one was tied up the way he was. Or at least, none of the other bodies was tied up. Only him.

After my uncle and I had looked at each other, and he had signaled to me, I understood that he wanted me to leave. So I said to my father, "Let's go, Papá."

I felt pains in my stomach, back there in the cemetery, but I didn't feel them that strong yet. I was perhaps forcing myself, I don't really know. When I left the cemetery, my uncle stopped a taxi. I got in the taxi, and my uncle said to me, "Well, you know what you have to do."

So I went in the taxi. But as we were driving along, I just wanted to yell . . . yell . . . then my little girl started to cry, and she said to me, "*Mami*, they killed my *Papito!*" She could already talk. She was two-and-a-half years old. "*Mami*, they killed my *Papito!*"

I said, "No, my love." You see, I was afraid of the taxi driver, because he turned to look at us in the mirror. I was riding in back with my father and my little girl.

"No, my love, that wasn't your *Papito*," I said, "Your *Papito* is at work."

But she said, "I saw him, *Mami*, I saw him! It was *Papito*, it was *Papito!*"

And I answered, "No, my love." But I felt as if I were going to explode, right that very instant.

Finally I said, "Let's get out here, Papá." We got out of the taxi right there . . . almost . . . something like two kilometers from our house. I began to feel terrible pains in my stomach, as if I were going to have another baby. I wanted so badly to scream. I didn't want to be walking out on the street. I didn't want anyone to see me. I had such a desire to cry . . . and my little girl was weeping at my feet. . . .

During all this time, we didn't know what had happened to my uncle. When I left, in the very moment that I left, a truck from the National Guard had arrived, full of guards which that boy had . . . perhaps my uncle had seen that that other boy had been talking over his radio. So the truck arrived full of guards. And my uncle wasn't able to start his motorcycle, maybe out of pure nervousness, he couldn't start it. The guards grabbed him and asked him who I was . . . who was the girl or the woman looking at the body. And he said that she was a niece of his, but that . . . they asked him who the dead man was. He said that he didn't know, because I had left . . . since it wasn't the person that we were looking for.

My uncle said, "It's that her husband is a drunk and hasn't come home, so she thought he might be here. But no, she left because it wasn't . . . it wasn't him."

And they replied, "You tell us. I know that you know who that dead man is. You tell us. You tell your niece that she had better say who he is, if she knows him. She knows him. She'd better tell us who he is. We will bury him. It's not going to cost you a *centavo*."

But my uncle was so afraid, and he said to them, "Well, I don't believe that he was anyone she knew, since she left. She left. . . ."

The boy who had watched me and had come to ask me about the body turned out to be one of my husband's relatives, and he knew that I was the man's wife. He wasn't able to pressure me . . . I don't know . . . there was . . . maybe his conscience bit him . . . or he was waiting for . . . or who knows! Anyhow, nothing happened to me.

And my uncle, when they caught him, he didn't say anything. He said that it wasn't my husband and for that reason I had left. That I was not interested in the body, and whatever else. And well . . . they hit him in the head.

Robin: Your uncle?

Alicia: My uncle. He says they wanted to make him tell the truth. He told them, "But if she left, what can I tell you? I can't tell you anything. If I didn't . . . I didn't even know this man!"

That is what he said. He really did know him, but he denied it. And the man did not have the courage to *echar al agua* [arrest] my uncle. He was the one who had sent the message over the radio. He didn't have the courage. Because if he had talked, if he had told anybody that this was the uncle of that man's wife, my uncle would no longer exist. He wouldn't be alive. But he didn't talk. The man just said over the telephone, over the radio, that there was someone interested in the body. But he didn't say who it was. That is why they didn't ask him questions.

And behind the truck of the National Guard came the coroner of the military. They said my uncle should tell them who the body was, because they were about to bury the body. And I should give them the information and they wouldn't collect any money. They only needed to know where the house was, my house. That is what they wanted to know, where I lived with my children. But since I had gone, they couldn't find out.

Then they left my uncle alone. As there were many people looking at the bodies, they left him. He grabbed his motorcycle and went. But since I had told my uncle that a person should never go straight home, when he is being followed by a taxi or a car in order to find out where he lives, my uncle didn't go home. He made a few turns towards Mejicano and other places on his motorcycle until finally at night, he arrived at the house. In order not to be followed. That is what happened.

I was on the way home. I hadn't arrived yet, and I began to feel the most horrible pain. I gave the little girl to my father. I couldn't stand it. I kept holding onto the trees by the houses—in Salvador they have trees for shade—I couldn't stand it anymore. I felt so cold all through my body, until I finally arrived.

When I got there, I had just walked into the house when I began to hemorrhage . . . a vaginal one . . . or rather my whole body was hemorrhaging. I spent three months without the strength to move, because I was hemorrhaging, until one of my husband's friends went and brought a doctor to help me at the house. They gave me a blood transfusion. This same friend also gave me the blood. Thank heavens, he was my blood-type. I have RH positive.

Well, all this . . . and as this man was such a good friend of my husband's, and they were the same kind of workers—he didn't go to the factory anymore, because he had been threatened, and he had been involved in the same type of things—he gave me a lot. And there was another man that I gave food to at my house. He took care of my little boy. And my father was there . . . he did almost nothing . . . or rather, he couldn't figure out what to do.

After three months of this, I had to leave the house. I was risking my life, staying in the same house. My husband could have talked . . . about where we lived and all that. But thank heavens, he didn't talk, because they didn't come to search for the house. After three months I left there, so that they wouldn't notice that my husband wasn't there. The neighbors didn't realize that my husband had been killed. They knew that he worked and all that. But as he never was the type to go around and visit the neighbors, they didn't notice.

The people helped me. The friends of my husband helped me look for another house. And I moved to another place, still in San Salvador. During all this my father was living with us, and my mother was somewhere else. My mother was living with my uncle somewhere else. The whole family disintegrated at once. My entire family fell apart. My brother also had to leave the house. He is the one that was born after me . . . I was responsible for my mother and my younger brother and my sister, who are now here in Costa Rica, in addition to my three children. It was terrible until . . . well, it's over.

What I did in order to live was make tortillas at home. I made stewed *yuca* [manioc] with *pepeisca* [little fish, salted and dried], as we say back there, and little *chimbolitos* [bigger fish, fresh or fried] . . . I made *vigorón* [manioc with deep fried pork fat and tomato] to sell, and pastries—here they call them *empanadas* [turnovers]. I had a refrigerator where I could make *chocobananas* [frozen chocolate-covered bananas], *charamusca* [homemade popsicles], and ice cream to sell. I sold frozen ice fruit in order to survive, to pay the rent and to buy food for the children.

That is how we lived until there came the opportunity for my father . . . well, he had to become a refugee. And I stayed with my mother and my three sisters and brothers. The one that was born after me was already there. He had arrived home and was already there. My father had to go into hiding, and we sold a pair of bulls that my father had, so that my mother could come to Costa Rica, because our lives were threatened. My mother was not one of these strong women, or . . . or one of these women, let's say . . . that is able to stand too much pressure without talking.

I had already had a lot of problems, partly because I was going around without identification papers in El Salvador. About six months after they had killed him—no, I'm not telling the truth—about four months after he had been killed, I went to Apopa to bring corn. And when I returned, there was a roadblock. I was just bringing corn to make the tortillas. They stopped the bus to check papers and when they did this, they detained me. They made me get out of the bus. They took me over to one side and asked for my identification card. I gave it to them, since I had it. Then they asked me whether I was married. On the card . . . they asked about my husband. Of course, I wasn't going to tell them that he was dead. It didn't even say on the identification card that I was a widow. So I told them that he was working. They asked me where he worked, and I told them that he worked in the Tropical Bottling Company. Then they wanted to know what my name was. I told them Alicia Flores, and well, I thought that was all. But no. I heard them say to me, "Look, go to that truck over there."

I felt that my children were now orphans, and that my mother, well, wouldn't know anything, because they would do something to me . . . well, a person has to pray because God is the only one that can do anything in such cases. God was the only one who could help me at that moment. What I did was start to pray.

And I tell you . . . they took down my sack of corn from the bus, and they stuck their big knives into it. They said that I was carrying arms in the sack. They kept on until most of the corn had fallen out of the sack into piles all around it. They took away my identification card and carried it over to a fat old man with a vest and with a mask here, so that no one could recognize him and all that. And he said . . . they talked secretly over there . . . and he said . . . they brought my card back over to me again and asked me what my name was, what my husband's name was, where he worked, and all that. And I repeated the same things over and over about four times.

Then, when the bus started up to leave, I said to him, "*Señor*, I want to go. I have to go and cook the corn for my tortillas."

He said to me, "You are not going to go. You are going to stay here with us."

And I said, "No, I left my children alone."

Then they went back to asking me about my name, as I was saying before. And when they already were talking to me and when I saw that the bus was moving fast, what I did was begin to pray "Our Father." That was all that I did. Then suddenly the old man came over to me, with his mask on, and said, "You can go."

I said, "I can go?!" I felt like . . . who knows?

"Yes," he said, "Go on, go on already. Before I change my mind."

So I said, "And my identification card?"

"Go on," he said, "if you want to go."

They didn't want to give me my identification card. They sent me away without my papers, so that I was running the risk that somewhere up ahead there would be another roadblock . . . that's possibly what they thought, that there was another roadblock up ahead.

And I went running so fast. You should have seen how fast I ran from there. I reached the bus, since it kept stopping for people. I reached the bus—the bus driver knew me—and I got in. And I began to pray from the time I sat down in the bus. I prayed, "Let there not be another roadblock, let there not be another roadblock . . ." again and again, like that. Until I finally got to the house, I didn't believe I would ever arrive.

I told the story to my mother. I said that I was now without papers and could never again walk out on the street. Then later my uncle came to visit me. I told him what had happened. He said, "I'll take you to get your identification papers."

So then I went to the town hall of San Salvador to get an identification card. I wasn't really supposed to get it there, but I got it by lying. I was supposed to get it in Chalatenango, but I couldn't go to Chalatenango. I could no longer go to Chalatenango.

I arrived at the town hall, and the person said, "What did you come for?"

"To get my identification card," I said.

"Aha, go over there," he said.

I went over to a room, and the person there said, "And why are you . . .? How old are you?"

"Uh," I said, "Twenty years old."

"And why did you wait so long to come get your identification card? You know that you have until you are eighteen years old to get it, and then you must get it immediately."

"Look," I said, "I am originally from Potonico. My parents are farmers. You know how farmers are. They don't think a legal document like an identification card is important."

"Anyway, I am a woman," I said, "and back there only the boys have them, the sons. But the women almost never . . ."

And it's true. In the country almost nobody gets an identification card, only when they are about to get married.

Then I told him, "And now, since I am working here, I see the importance of having an identification card." If you could have seen how I was trying to convince him . . . "And now I . . . I can't walk around on the street. It's even worse in this situation, as you can imagine. I can't even leave from work," I said. "I am working here."

The person said, "Let me see. Go over to window three."

So I went over to the window. And they began to ask me the same questions: why hadn't I got my identification card, and why . . . ?

And I said, "Look. I didn't get it." I said that it was for this reason and for that, the same thing that I had told the other person. I couldn't change even a single word, because if there is a single word different, you go. So I said exactly the same thing.

Then he said, "Go over there," pointing to a room full of other people. One of them said, "Aha, you came to get your identification card. Yes? Stand over there. Look." And he stood me there and measured me and said, "You've never gotten your identification card?"

"No. This is the first time." If I had said that I had gotten it, they would have tossed me aside. So I said, "No, this is the first time."

"Are you married?" he asked.

"No. I'm single." I still have my identification card here [in Costa Rica], saying that I am a single woman.

I left the town hall with my card in my hand. I already felt that I had something special like . . . it wasn't as if, let's say, the identification card would save my life. Never. But at least I was better prepared for a roadblock. I left with papers that were good for six years. The card didn't expire until last year.

I went home and showed my mother, "Ay, look what I have done!"

"Ay, daughter, look at you. You are very clever."

"Ay, you think that I am not in distress," I said, "You are worse."

And she said, "You watch. I'm going to die there. I'm going to die."

Well, that's what really happened to me. . . .

Two days later our house was searched. There came a "tun-tun" at the door. They said they were going to seize everything, and asked us where were we keeping the arms, and all that.

And I said, "What arms? I have the eyes of my children here. If you want, look closely at everything. Turn everything upside down, if you want."

My mother cried and cried. We always used to have *guaro* [cured corn liquor] for pains in the stomach, for twisting bellyaches or for diarrhea. It is very good. My mother kept the bottle behind a door, so that she could get at it to drink. There she was with the bottle in her hand, drinking and trembling, full of tears. And I followed behind the guards who walked around inspecting the house.

When they had left, I told my mother, "Mamá, you cannot do it. You can't stay with us. It pains my soul, because you are my mother, but you can't stay with us."

Well, the search was over. And I said to myself, "She is my mother, and she was crying because she said that I didn't love her and . . . but our lives are really in danger here, forever!"

They had said to me, "And your husband?"

"He is working." Look, they had not even had the intelligence to call the . . . ! See, even after I had said, "He is working." Then I had analyzed the situation. "He is working." "Where?" "In the Tropical Bottling Company." If they had called, we would have been in a mess. But see, God did me a favor, because they didn't call. I just told them that he was working, and the man didn't say anything. And since my identification card was all right, there weren't any problems.

Robin: But it said "single" on your card.

Alicia: Yes, single, so I told them it was a common law marriage. When a person doesn't get married, then it's common law marriage.

So in answer to their question, "And your husband, where is he?," my reply was, "He is working," since I had the children. That is what I kept saying.

About fifteen days later there was another search. But this one was massive. They took my brothers and sisters all out into the open, asking them questions and hitting them and everything, all in front of me. They didn't grab me. I kept going after them. I followed them. When they asked my brother questions, I answered them. Then they said to me, "We are not asking you. We are asking them. He is the one who has to answer."

And my brother gave exactly the same answer that I had given. I kept on following them. But they didn't ask me any questions. My children were crying. Back then the children were very small. My little boy was just beginning to walk. Such crying from the children and from my brothers and sisters! And my mother sitting over there alone in the corner. They didn't ask my mother any questions. But my mother said, "Ah, yes, they killed him . . . they killed him." The guards didn't pay any attention to her, because they thought she was crazy. All she did was keep saying, "They killed him . . . they killed him. . . ." Of course, who would think that it wasn't just nerves, her drinking and saying, "They killed him . . . "?

You know, I couldn't figure out what to do. My brother, the one that was born right after me, said, "Look. The only thing we can do is, we have to tell our father that we must sell the calves and the bulls. We've got to send our mother to Costa Rica, now while there is a chance. She can go on a microbus. Because our mother is going to get us all killed here."

So I talked with my father about it, and he said that, yes, we should sell the bulls that we had left back in Chalatenango. My uncle sold them and brought us the money. We paid to bring the microbus, and we sent her off, weeping . . .!

She said, "I'm already an obstacle to my children. I don't know why it is when, ay, look. . . ."

I felt terrible . . . and she came here to Costa Rica. She arrived here at five in the morning. Well . . . she arrived here the second day. It took her two days.

Once she was here, she saw that there were opportunities to send for the rest of the family through the United Nations. So she went to the U.N. to say that I was left in El Salvador with my brothers and sisters. In addition to me, there were my three brothers and sisters and my three children. She told them she wanted us to come to Costa Rica.

I was given an appointment in El Salvador and asked to come to the U.N. offices there. When I arrived, they told me to bring all the interested parties, because they were going to give me a group passport to travel to Costa Rica. So that is what I did. But my brother, the one that was born right after me, didn't want to come. He stayed there.

That is how I left. After my mother had come . . . in October . . . no . . . my mother came in August.

Robin: What year was that?

Alicia: 1981. I came the twenty-seventh of November, 1981, through the United Nations, the U.N.

I found Alicia's story most intriguing. Like Mirabela, Alicia was the wife of a union leader, and it was this association that eventually led to her becoming politicized. Although Alicia does not mention it here, she also joined the Committee of Mothers back in El Salvador in order to search for her husband.

On another level, however, the two women differ enormously. Alicia's *testimonio* is personal and dramatic. She is clearly aware of the political implications of the events she describes, but in contrast to Mirabela, she does not choose to tell her story from a political point of view. It is the inside story of a woman in constant confrontation with danger. She tells how she feels, how she sees people acting toward her, and what she does in response to them. Unlike Mirabela, who depicts people as either good or bad depending on which side of the political fence they sit, Alicia's description implies that people are both bad and good at the same time. Their motivations and actions are not clear-cut.

Unlike Mirabela, Alicia's struggles with Salvadoran officials have little to do with political ideology. In her case the struggles involve a battle of wits, where the authorities are the hunters and Alicia is the hunted. Her cleverness is greater than theirs in the end, because even though the officials come close to catching her several times, she and the rest of her family are finally able to escape.

Alicia's mistrust of authority continues to haunt her in Costa Rica. She is not alone in this. All the women are reevaluating their home country's firmly established sociopolitical hierarchy, but Alicia's negative reaction to authority, and to the type of conformity it implies, creates significant problems for her at the Center. She is an individualist to the core.

A few days after the first interview with Alicia, she comes up to me in the kitchen of the daycare center where I am watching the women make tortillas for lunch. Right there in front of everyone, she asks me, "And when are you coming to my house to visit?" I can feel all the eyes in the kitchen on me as I answer, "Anytime you like." I would prefer that such an arrangement be made privately, but Alicia does not leave me any choice. I cannot decide whether this is her way of making sure I will accept her invitation or whether she wants everyone to be under the impression that she and I have established some kind of special relationship, thus making them still more jealous of her. Possibly both these interpretations are true.

At any rate we make our arrangement in the kitchen. I agree to come to Alicia's house the following Sunday, bringing my daughter with me to play with her three children. Together we draw a map to get to her house up in the hills behind the town, but as I am leaving the kitchen, Alicia calls out to me once more:

"I don't want you to give my *testimonio* to Ligia," she says in the presence of several women. "You can do whatever else you like with it, but I don't want you to give it to Ligia." What is this? A public insult to Ligia?

Whatever Alicia's intent, this public declaration has serious implications for my research. It is obvious to me that Alicia has every right to refuse to allow her *testimonio* to be put in the files of the daycare center. I recognize immediately that this individual right of Alicia's supersedes any rights of Ligia to use the *testimonios* of the women, even if Ligia's purpose is to raise money for the daycare center. So I say to Alicia, and incidentally to all the women there with us in the kitchen, "Of course. Before I hand any of the *testimonios* over to Ligia, I will check with each of you first, to make sure you are in agreement."

Alicia seems satisfied with this promise, and I leave the Center. But I have a strange feeling in the pit of my stomach. I am getting involved in some kind of emotional tangle between Ligia and Alicia, and I am not at all sure how I am going to handle it. I know that I cannot afford to take sides with either woman, since I want to continue talking with them both. On the other hand, how am I going to remain neutral, or at least appear to remain neutral?

6

Ligia

"Exile has been a kind of school."

One day when I go to the daycare center, Doña Ligia calls me into her office. I can see that she is upset. She says to me, "Alicia has accused me of things that are not true. She told you that I was planning to sell the *testimonios*, and that is not true. I only wanted to have a copy of each one on file."

I can see that Ligia has been given the wrong story about my conversation in the kitchen with Alicia. I try to protest, "But Alicia did not say that you were planning to sell the *testimonios*. She only asked me not to give hers to anyone without her permission." This is not quite true either, since Alicia specifically requested that I not give her *testimonio* to Ligia.

Ligia insists that her version of the story is true. Her argument—and I can not dispute it—is that I am not a native speaker of Spanish and therefore can not always understand exactly what is being said. I decide to back off and let Ligia have her say, even though I am quite sure that Alicia has been falsely accused. After all, Ligia has been publicly insulted by Alicia, no matter how I look at it.

Nevertheless, I tell Ligia that I am planning to respect anyone's request regarding the *testimonios*. If any refugee wishes that her *testimonio* not be quoted or not be put on file, I will honor that request. I do not know the legal rights of Costa Ricans—or refugees in Costa Rica—but I feel I have a moral obligation to the women to insist upon these terms. Doña Ligia is obviously angry with me, but she holds her anger in check.

Or rather, she shifts her anger back to Alicia. She says, "Alicia is the only one who will behave in this way. All of the others will let me have their *testimonios* for the file."

I say, "I am not so sure she is the only one. One or two of the others may have reasons for not putting their *testimonios* on file."

"Who else? I don't believe there is anyone else," Ligia insists.

"Well, Eduardo might not. He told me when we started our interview that he had never talked about any of this to anyone before, not even to his present girlfriend. I promised him that I would use his *testimonio* only in the most general way, to write about the typical experiences of teachers in El Salvador."

Ligia returns to the subject of Alicia, which is really what concerns her. She tries again to impress upon me the necessity of being careful with Alicia. Alicia is a person who takes advantage of others, invites them to her house, gives them *pupusas*, gets them all sympathetic, and then tries to extract money from them. Moreover, she is always causing friction among the women and creating problems for the Center. I want to ask for more specific information as to what Alicia has done, but I am not sure that this is the appropriate time, so I keep silent. Instead I ask, "How do you handle someone like Alicia, when she creates problems for you?"

Ligia says, "Maybe we would get rid of her, but she is a woman alone, about to have a baby. Without the daycare center, where would she go, how would she eat? And we have the little baby to think of." I feel that Ligia is softening up a bit.

I decide at this point to state my position as an anthropologist. Ligia has already stated her position with regard to Alicia. I try to point out to Ligia that my study of the Center is an attempt to understand the women who work there. I want to know what kinds of people they are, what kinds of problems they have, and how they are conducting their lives. I feel that Alicia is important to include in the study because she has typical kinds of refugee problems. She has lost her husband and is now living in Costa Rica alone with her children. In order to appease Ligia a bit, I go along with the assumption that Alicia may be a troublemaker. I say that perhaps her problems stem from tension as a single parent in a strange country with lots of children and very little money. Maybe even her pregnancy is affecting her. Ligia agrees.

I then tell Ligia that I have made plans for a visit to Alicia's house that Sunday. Ligia undoubtedly already knows about the invitation anyway. Her reaction is quite reasonable, considering the anger she has expressed only a few minutes earlier. She says that, of course, I am free to contact any of the women after daycare hours. However, she adds, I should beware.

From the beginning of my research it was clear to me that Ligia was hoping to use the *testimonios* of the women to raise money for the daycare center. She spoke of putting copies of the stories on file for some future occasion when the Center might have to apply for more financial support from international agencies. Ligia's choreographing of the *testimonios* and her inclusion of Alicia's story among them (in spite of her obvious distrust of Alicia) only underscored her intentions.

At the same time, however, Alicia's fears that Ligia might have other motivations for keeping the stories on file were not totally unfounded. Ligia and Alicia come from separate socioeconomic classes that have traditionally mistrusted one another. Maybe Alicia thought that Ligia might try to sell the *testimonios* to make money for herself. Or worse, perhaps she even believed that Ligia might someday use the stories as political evidence against her.

Doña Ligia does not want to give me her own *testimonio* and, in fact, claims not to have one. What she means, of course, is that her reasons for leaving El Salvador were far less urgent than for the other women. Her life and the lives of her children were never in danger. Even her profession as a teacher did not cause her to experience any form of repression; the private city school where she taught was never targeted by the army. Her family's expensive house with its cadre of servants shielded her comfortably from the outside world.

It took Ligia a long time to make up her mind to leave El Salvador. It was only with the greatest difficulty that she tore herself away from her father's house to join her husband in exile. Her eventual decision to leave was not so much political as it was personal. I get the impression that she feels her reasons for coming to Costa Rica as a refugee are somehow "illegitimate," even though she can easily claim that she came because her husband was under persecution. Maybe she is ashamed for having preferred to stay at home in luxury.

Because Ligia claims not to have a *testimonio*, she does not set up an interview with me for herself. It takes me several weeks to persuade her that I am interested in hearing what she has to say, and at first, she only allows me to take written notes. Finally, long after the others have granted me their interviews, I am able to get a recorded statement from her. Ligia's story of her life back in El Salvador is brief, but it reveals the complexity of her decision to leave.

Ligia: Well, my husband worked on human rights. In El Salvador the situation is such that if a person shows a certain degree of humanity, that person is then seen as a communist. My husband had to leave the country because of such things. In the case of a person who serves others—especially in the case of a medical doctor—he cannot discriminate by saying "this one I shall heal, that one I won't." So another group of colleagues accused his group of being communists. He had to . . . let's say, emigrate obligatorily, leaving his family behind.

I was left with a two-month-old baby boy (Marco, who now goes to school). So I stayed with my family, at my job. In the beginning you believe such things are important, but later you see that your work is not enough. The disintegration of the group affects a person. Even though I had my children with me, my mother, my brothers and sisters, my nieces and nephews, and my friends, you miss the support of your husband, for yourself and for your children.

I stayed there a long time because I had the responsibility of my nieces and nephews who were my sister's children. She had emigrated to the United States. I had always watched out for her children, and she left them in my care. I felt then as if they were my own children, and I still feel that way. I was not easily able to disturb my family by tearing it apart—my three children plus three nieces and nephews, six in all, and my mother, who makes seven. I didn't want to disturb them all by moving to a country where I had only been a visitor on vacation. I had merely come to Costa Rica to see my husband.

Even so, I felt the necessity of making a new home alongside my husband. Two and a half years passed, more or less, with me coming here and then returning to El Salvador, struggling with my desire to be in both places. I wanted to stay here, and I wanted to return there, to be with my nieces and nephews, whom I had left back in El Salvador. But when my sister saw what was happening, she decided to take her children with her, so that I could start a new home. Everything was disintegrating anyway, due to all kinds of unexpected things, not because anyone wanted it to happen, but because it was our fate, as we say.

My sister's decision to take her children back was really hard for me. It was as if something precious were taken away. I had been raising these children. And besides, they didn't really want to go. They wanted to stay with me. They even called me "*Mami*." This was a problem. I couldn't fight for them. They weren't legally mine, even though they were mine emotionally. My sister wanted to have them, and they didn't want to be with her. But in the end "it is the captain that gives the orders, and not the sailors." So they had to go. My mother traveled with them to the United States at the end of 1983.

With the children gone, I began to look seriously into the possibility of coming to Costa Rica. I did not come here under the same illusion that many of the Salvadorans did. They believed they were coming for only three months and thus brought only three changes of clothes. They said to themselves, "We will be returning right away. This will be enough." No. I came here fully conscious of the situation.

And that is what was so terrible. I had left one place and come to another where I knew there were no jobs for me. And coming here was not like they tell you, really. They always say Costa Rica is the Switzerland of the Americas, a democracy, and a wonderful place to live. But there is the problem of work. Back in my country I had a job, and I knew I wouldn't have one in Costa Rica. . . .

Most of the refugees at the Center came to Costa Rica during the height of the Salvadoran conflict in 1980 without much thought as to how they were going to survive. Most of them had a little money, which they hoped would last them throughout their stay, figuring they could get temporary jobs in Costa Rica to cover the difference. Having come much later, in 1984, Ligia was a special case. She had visited Costa Rica to see her husband and had observed the conditions of life for the refugees who had arrived earlier and were already settled.   In addition, her husband had experienced many of the problems that she would now have to face. Thus, Ligia's decision to migrate was more realistic, and possibly more agonizing, because she was aware of the kinds of sacrifices she would have to make.

Settling into Costa Rica for the long term meant giving up her job and perhaps even her career, quite a blow for Ligia, because she had never been taught to stay at home and mind the children. Her family had servants for that kind of work.   She was raised in a family of professionals and had married a professional. Her expectations for her own life centered on the premise that she would have a fulfilling career of her own. However, from what she understood of the situation in Costa Rica, such a career would not be possible. She had seen her husband struggle for permission to work as a physician; he had finally been allowed to treat refugees and local farmers in a rural area.   The limitations on his work had ultimately led him to concentrate more heavily on his activities as a human rights advocate for El Salvador, since this work was paid for by international organizations and did not require Costa Rican permission. Her husband's problems had made Ligia acutely aware of what she was giving up to join him as a refugee.

Ligia: People take refuge in Costa Rica because they hear so many good things about the country. Discrimination always exists against refugees, against people in exile. This is true anywhere, not just here. But you are attracted to Costa Rica because you feel that this country is different. When I was back home and came here only to visit, people would say to me, "How wonderful that you were in Costa Rica! I hear that Costa Rica is really beautiful." And what they said was true. As long as I had just come on a visit and had brought plenty of money with me, it was really nice. Any country could be nice under those circumstances.

But it is different when you come to settle down. In my case, the Costa Rican Ministry of Education refuses to recognize my degree. They believe that if they were to recognize it, I would only take a job away from a Costa Rican. But I cannot even get them to recognize it so that I can continue my studies. I already knew that they were never going to give me a job.

Costa Rica was theoretically the ideal country to which Salvadorans should migrate for refuge. It is a democracy and has no army, the so-called "Switzerland of the Americas." The standard of living is relatively high, with the state providing many services—such as health care and public education—and controlling the prices on food staples and the rents on housing. Moreover, since Costa Ricans speak Spanish and their culture is Latin, the Salvadorans would presumably have few adjustments to make by relocating there.

There is a strong belief among Costa Ricans that they live in a "classless" society, a belief often shared by rich and poor alike (Biesanz

1982:47–70).   Even though the government and the economy are controlled by a handful of wealthy families, there are a number of egalitarian tendencies in the country which soften the disparities of power, wealth, and prestige that do exist. For one thing, land is widely distributed among small and medium landholders. When coffee became the important export crop there, the coffee barons concentrated their efforts on the control of coffee processing and on easy access to credit and world markets, rather than on the control of the coffee-producing lands. The landowners themselves remained in close contact with their laborers, often working alongside them in the fields and attending the same social gatherings.

Perhaps the most striking tendency towards egalitarianism in Costa Rica has been the development of a large and influential class of government workers. The government labor force, which is well-paid and highly unionized, comprises an astounding one-fifth of the entire work force, "one of the highest rates of government employment in the world" (Biesanz 1982:198). Even though these government workers have created an almost impenetrable bureaucracy in every area of public life, this group has also been responsible for social legislation that has benefitted even the poorest of domestic servants. By keeping so many people employed, the government acts as a kind of welfare system that puts a damper on serious social dissent.

A local man who sold me his old family car gave me a typical explanation. I was expressing my amazement at the intricate Costa Rican bureaucracy involved in the transfer of ownership of the car, when he launched into a tirade:

"Robin, this is just an example of how my [the Costa Rican] government hires ten people to do a job that would be better accomplished by a single official. Each of the ten persons performs a small step along the way. One official stamps the paper, another collects the paper, a third checks the stamp, a fourth takes your money, and so on . . . you see how it works. The point of all this is to give everyone a job. People need to work and feed their families. All these jobs provide benefits, but the work itself isn't meaningful. And the worst part is, when one person along the line of operations is sick, or even out to lunch, the whole system breaks down."

These tendencies towards egalitarianism among the general populace have kept the poorest of Costa Ricans from resorting much to collective action against their employers and the government. Nevertheless, recent economic problems facing the country have pushed agricultural workers towards strikes and demonstrations.   Seasonal agricultural laborers have failed to experience the social benefits of other Costa Ricans because the protective legislation does not always include their concerns, but the myth of a classless society is so strong that it prevents the average Costa Rican from recognizing the social and economic disparities that do exist.

> Ligia: Back in your own country, you believe that everything is going to be different here in Costa Rica. But it isn't. The Costa Ricans are experiencing an economic crisis. And the people are beginning to demonstrate here, just as they do back home, and there are strikes. But many Costa Ricans still live very isolated from the real world.
>
> Once when I went to the Legislative Assembly, there were a number of workers striking out there on the street. They had spent days there on the street, sleeping and eating. I said to my Costa Rican friend who was accompanying me, "Look. Your countrymen are on strike."
>
> She answered me, "Those are not Costa Ricans. Those are refugees."
>
> But the truth was, she did not want to accept the fact that some changes are going to have to take place in her country as well as mine. The Costa Rican lives *durmiendo en sus laureles* [resting on his laurels], as they say. He believes that everything in his country is "*pura vida*" [pure life, that is, "just great"], but this is merely a saying, because "*pura vida*" doesn't exist here.
>
> "*Que barbaridad!* [How rude!]" I said to my friend, "You are even ashamed of your own countrymen. Don't tell me . . ."
>
> "Those are not Costa Ricans," she insisted. "They are Nicaraguans or Salvadorans."
>
> "Don't kid yourself. Look at these people up close. Listen to them. They are your own people, demonstrating for better living conditions."
>
> People who have enough to live on forget that there are many others that are starving.

While Ligia understands clearly the contradictions in the Costa Rican view of themselves as a classless society, she seems less aware of the contradictions in her own behavior regarding class hierarchy. She thinks of herself as having come from the middle class in El Salvador, but there is obviously a wide disparity between her own family situation and that of her friend and associate, Carmen, who also claims membership in the Salvadoran middle class. Ligia's family was made up of well-paid professionals, with enough income to provide servants for performing the daily tasks of the household and a liberal choice of schooling for the children. Carmen's family, on the other hand, had to pinch pennies and pool their money carefully to gain the luxury of a secondary education; the hiring of servants was out of the question.

Ligia would probably not have socialized with Carmen back home, but in Costa Rica they live more on a par with each other. Ligia is still much better off economically than Carmen, mainly because her husband has a steady job while Carmen's does not; nevertheless, their similar experience as primary schoolteachers has created a strong bond between them. Family pressures to maintain certain social networks are no longer applicable. Both women recognize that their new lives in

Costa Rica require them to work and socialize across traditional class
boundaries.   One of the significant aspects of refugee life is the
obliteration of such boundaries, at least on the surface. Everyone has
been reduced to a similar economic level. In Costa Rica refugees are all
poor but surviving, and each family receives the benefits of free medical
care and public education.

For Ligia more than any of the other women, life as a refugee has
been a step down. Although she speaks highly of democratic procedures
at the Center, she finds it hard to accept some of the egalitarian aspects
that are implied by such procedures. Her upbringing has led her to
believe that she is better than most other people. Her education and
family background place her well above all her associates at the Center.
Both Ligia and the other women are aware of this. On the other hand,
no one is eager to maintain the social and economic hierarchy inherent
in such thinking. Even Ligia is hoping to break down the social barriers
that have existed in El Salvador for so long.

Ligia: We cannot feel sorry for ourselves forever. Eventually, you have
to realize that even though being in exile is hard, you can learn something from the
experience.
In my country I was part of the middle class. But here I have had to learn
to change diapers for the babies. It disgusted me at first. I felt bad about it,
because it belittled me to do such things. But slowly I became aware of the
consequences of this kind of thinking, and now I do it anytime. I do it gladly. I am
agreeable about changing diapers, because I say that the same thing was once
done for me. Exile has been a kind of school, where you learn things you will
never forget. Sometimes you learn things and forget them right away, but exile
has created such an impact on me that you never forget the things you learn.

Even though Ligia claims not to have a *testimonio*, she
nevertheless lays claim to martyrdom. Her choice to live in exile, rather
than in the comfort of her parents' home, has given her this right. She
too has suffered. She has made the "correct" political choice in leaving
her country, and at great sacrifice. Thus, she can associate herself with
all the mothers who have lost their husbands and sons to the war. Exile
has turned her into a political believer and a martyr. Ligia has not only
been influenced by her husband's political orientation, but her work at the
Center has changed her. Observing the needs of the refugee children has
made her sensitive to the ravages of malnutrition and civil war, and the
suffering of homesickness enables her to see herself as a martyr like
everyone else.

Ligia: When I came, it was February. I had been in Costa Rica about a
month when I received a call from the director of the school where I had worked
back home, "My dear Ligia, would you like to come home again? Your job is still

waiting for you." But I had already decided to stay, even though I felt like going home immediately. I had gotten used to living on my own salary at home, and here I had no money. I had no work. Well, at least my husband is a very responsible man, and he has always kept my spirits up. He told me that somehow we would overcome these bad times.

Then the month of May arrived, the time of Mother's Day. It was terrible. I was invited to a Mother's Day celebration given by the daycare center on the university campus. At that time I was pregnant with my little girl. Pregnancy is something, of course, that you can't just plan when and if you want it to happen. You say to yourself, "There is no work. The conditions are not good for having a baby." Well, my little baby girl arrived, and we said, "Welcome." But in addition to the indisposition of pregnancy, I had the indisposition of exile. It is really hard to be in exile. It is nice to come here on a visit, because you come and know that you can return whenever you like. But when you have to stay for who knows how long, it is different.

Anyway, the Mother's Day celebration took place, and I was helping. They played the Salvadoran National Anthem. It reminded me of the "*Poema de Amor*" ["Love Poem"], which tells about how the Salvadoran people feel. It talks about the suffering in the banana-growing regions, in the Panama Canal zone, and in the flight to the United States—the things that happen to you, the things you have to suffer on the border between Mexico and the United States. All of this is in the "*Poema de Amor.*" But there is also a part which talks about "those who cry during the National Anthem." I had always said to myself, "Heavens. Who would cry?" When I had come to Costa Rica just for a visit, I had never felt like crying during the anthem. But during the presentation on Mother's Day, when the cultural show began, they said, "We will begin with the stirring notes of our National Anthem." And it happened. I started to feel a knot in my throat, a horrible lump. I couldn't swallow it down. The people who had been here longer were perhaps already accustomed to their new lives. But I had just arrived and for me it was an incredible experience, just to become adapted. So when I began to feel the tears, with my eyes all wet, I realized that it was true. When you are in exile, you cry upon hearing your national anthem. And you don't just cry for the song itself, you cry for all the things you left behind.

And later when they were doing another presentation, there was a moment of silence for all the mothers who had died in the struggle, in the war, because really a lot of people have died. And another thing, you could see that all the people were crying. Many of them had left behind their brothers and sisters, their children, their husbands or wives, their friends, their parents . . . well, their family and close friends. Yes, these people all felt it.

In spite of Ligia's enthusiasm for my research, she remained at the periphery of my activities. She was invariably cordial and pleasant with me, asking about my daughter regularly and talking occasionally about her husband and children. But she never fully relaxed her guard, as all the other women seemed to do. I decided there was purpose in her attitude. Maintaining the respect of others (including me) required a certain distance on her part. Everyone called her Doña Ligia, "*doña*" being a respectful form of address for a woman. (I myself was often referred to as "*doña*"; such respect might have been required because I was a guest, an outsider, or even because I came from a superpower—and perhaps for all three reasons.) The women seemed to use "*doña*" in a friendly way, but the term nevertheless conveyed a sense of inequality, and of potential bitterness.

Because of Ligia's aloofness, much of my understanding of her arose from what others said about her and how they interacted with her. Ligia's presence may have been more invisible than the others, but her influence on my research was enormous. Probably I came to understand Ligia best through her often stormy relationship with Alicia.

Part II

The Women Together

7

Carmen

"This is the way we can collaborate for now."

In early 1980 the influx of Salvadoran refugees to Costa Rica began. The initial group to arrive were the 200 rural farmers who had taken over the Costa Rican Embassy in San Salvador. The Salvadoran farmers were first housed in the open on the *hacienda* El Murciélago (owned by the deposed Nicaraguan dictator Somoza), and were eventually transported to the agricultural project Los Ángeles, a refugee camp in the province of Guanacaste. Although other Salvadoran refugees were also sent to this camp, the great majority of arrivals chose to remain in the Central Valley of Costa Rica, near the urban areas. Some stayed in temporary camps such as the Fátima Refugee Center in Heredia, and others stayed in houses rented by the refugees themselves (Universidad para la Paz and Universidad Nacional 1987:137–38).

Getting into Costa Rica initially involved only simple paperwork. Refugees traveled by bus or by airplane and counted on being hurried through immigration when they arrived. Most came with the notion of returning to El Salvador quickly—in a few months or, at most, a year or two. The Costa Ricans must have thought their stay was temporary, too, because for a while officials were issuing refugee papers to the Salvadorans without bothering to check into their personal histories. Later, the bureaucracy for admitting refugees became well established, and it was more problematic for a Salvadoran to receive refugee status (CEDAL 1986:63–75).

At first the refugees in Costa Rica remained under the protection of ACNUR [*Alto Comisionado de las Naciones Unidas para los Refugiados*, United Nations High Commission for the Refugees]. This agency funded basic emergency help in the form of food, housing, and medical care, all of which were dispensed through various local

nongovernmental groups, such as the Costa Rican Red Cross, the Episcopal Church, and others.   Much of this emergency aid was sharply
reduced in 1983, when the Costa Rican government took over the
handling of refugee assistance from ACNUR (Universidad para la Paz
and Universidad Nacional 1987:143).

Carmen: When a person leaves his country and comes to another place
where, at least he doesn't hear . . . or see the guards, the army, dressed in green
and everything . . . he doesn't have to think about . . . a person enters into a state
of calm, of restfulness . . . even though in his mind he does not act that way
because . . . because unconsciously, at night, in the day, he cries out. Eight years
have passed, and right now I can tell you that I dream . . . I dream things at night.
And sometimes I am awakened by nightmares, even though they are not about the
guards, or anything like that. It is something that I have inside me, and it is very
difficult.   Sometimes I say, "Well, even though I am living a more peaceful
existence, I still have another kind of worry. I may not be experiencing the war,
the bullets, or anything like that. Nor do I have that same anxiety, that anguish.
But everything that I have bottled up inside me, in my unconsciousness, comes to
me at night, or when I watch a program on television, or at times like that. It
doesn't feel like a lie to me. I feel as if . . . as if I were really living in that situation.
        So a person doesn't forget. I think it would be difficult to forget, even after
many years. These things are going to lie in wait and haunt you. But the moment
arrives when it comes to you, I don't know, when you start to talk about these
things. You imagine that you are experiencing them. In my case, at least, I don't
really like to remember, because . . . because you cross over into that world, you
live through it again, and well, you feel the situation all over again . . .

Robin: Hmm . . . did you have any problems getting into Costa Rica?

Carmen: Problems? Getting into Costa Rica?

Robin: Or leaving your country, or . . . ?

Carmen: I just came. There were no problems. At that time there
weren't many problems here in Costa Rica. It was 1980. Because of the war in
El Salvador, everything was unraveled—at the political level, at the economic
level, at the military level, and at the international level. The world knew about
what was happening in El Salvador. People knew all about the repression. There
was such repression during this period that it could no longer be kept secret. The
Human Rights Commission condemned it. There were deaths and assassinations
in El Salvador, full of torture. The army was not content simply to kill the people.
Instead, before doing that, they had to torture a person. They pierced the body
with needles, with razors, or they took out the eyes. Well, it's just that it was . . .
I don't know . . . it was like there was a question of blood . . . the madness of war
and of death.
        All of this became known on an international level. And maybe we came
when most of the refugees were arriving in Costa Rica. Costa Rica began to

accept the refugees when the government realized what was happening in El Salvador and saw that there needed to be a country which would take in the refugees. And so Costa Rica opened its doors, permitting us Salvadorans to enter its territory. They made it officially possible to get entry visas and everything, without any major obstacles.

While the emergency aid handed out by relief agencies was helpful in keeping the refugees alive, it proved to be only a stopgap measure. Emergency aid was doled out during the early 1980s with the idea that the recipients would soon be able to survive on their own. After all, these people were not vagrants and ne'er-do-wells; they were hardworking peasants, factory workers, and teachers. All of them were accustomed to long work hours and low wages, and except for the teachers, they were also used to heavy labor, so it was only a matter of time until they got jobs.

The Costa Rican government was sympathetic to the plight of the refugees and was generous in a number of ways. The refugees were allowed to send their children to the public schools, and all family members were soon able to take full advantage of the extensive socialized medicine of the country. However, due to high unemployment among Costa Rican citizens, the government remained reluctant to let the refugees take jobs that otherwise might have gone to their own people. Gaining permission to work became a lengthy and often futile procedure for the refugees, one that required considerable money and effort.

The refugees were unable to work in schools, hospitals, factories, businesses, or government—even in menial positions. They were only allowed jobs that were offered to them by private individuals or jobs that were specifically created for refugees through international funding. Costa Rican citizens, for example, could hire Salvadoran refugees to work as domestic servants or gardeners in the privacy of their own homes. While such jobs are regulated by the Costa Rican government to protect Costa Rican workers from exploitation, it was not clear that the refugees were similarly protected. Another category of available work was that of the seasonal agricultural laborer; many Salvadorans worked temporarily as coffeepickers, but such work was not offered year round.

Carmen: Here in the Costa Rican environment, with the Costa Rican people, it is difficult to get the opportunity to work. It is very difficult because you have to have a resident visa, you have to have permission to work, and all that. And as a refugee, a person cannot become part of the life here. You can only work on Salvadoran projects, or with certain Costa Ricans.

A person who leaves his country doesn't plan to stay away. He thinks that he will go abroad just until the war is over. I thought I would be here for about three months. I left, without requesting permission at work. I didn't quit or anything. I said, "I'll just stay for three months, and then when I return, I'll find work." But the truth is, my three months have become eight years! 1980 to 1988—eight years have gone by without my being able to return to my country! And the war is still going on. A person, when he leaves, does not think in terms of a prolonged war. He thinks he will just stay out until the repression is over. And it is then that he sees the situation.

Indeed, when I entered Costa Rica, I had no major problem. And anyway, I had a little money, just a little, which made it possible to survive in this country. When I left El Salvador, I brought about a thousand dollars, for my sister and for me, in order to halfway survive while we were looking for work that would help us along. But the truth is that when a person comes here, he finds out that temporary jobs are difficult to find, because there are no opportunities and because there are so many thousands of us.

Well, when we first came to Costa Rica, we stayed at a hotel in the center of San José. And we had to pay for it. At this time we had to pay 200 *colones* [$23] per day, to sleep in a tiny little room and to pay for our food—breakfast, lunch, dinner, and all that. But soon you see that the money you brought isn't enough. A month passes and your money is getting low. At this time the exchange rate was 10 or 12 *colones* to the dollar [it was actually 8.6 *colones* to the dollar in 1980], something very little. And so pretty soon you say, "No. It is all going to be gone, and when I return there will be nothing left." But the truth is that the situation in El Salvador is not getting any better.

Several of the women had spent some time in the Fátima Refugee Center. The accommodations provided through the Fátima Church were not luxurious by any means, but they did offer a temporary haven for the Salvadorans who arrived during those early years. It was communal living, in which everyone helped out with the cooking and the childcare, even the men.

The Fátima Refugee Center was run by a colorful priest named Higinio Alas, who had himself escaped El Salvador into exile. Not only was he rector of the Fátima Church, but he was also active on the Human Rights Commission in Costa Rica, helping to publish the periodical *Derechos Humanos en Centroamérica* [*Human Rights in Central America*]. He also achieved recognition as the author of a book entitled *El Salvador* (1982), in which he explored the historical and current reasons for the conflict in his native country. In July 1988, at the fifth anniversary celebration of the daycare center, he received official recognition as one of the Center's founders.

In her *testimonio*, Carmen describes the communal life at the Fátima Refugee Center and speaks of Higinio Alas' contribution to their lives.

Carmen: We settled in Heredia, at Fátima. We came under the care of Higinio Alas, who was one of the priests, well, who were concerned about us. He had already left El Salvador because of the persecution and had come to live in exile in Costa Rica. He had been given a parish here at Fátima Church. So when

I heard that he was here, I looked for him. We began at Fátima, with his help.

He sent us to the United Nations' relief group, because we didn't know anything about being a refugee, not a thing. For me, such a thing didn't even exist. And I certainly didn't know I was going to be a refugee, or anything like that. I never imagined that. Never.

When I arrived, they said to me, "Look, this is the way things are. This is how you have to do it."

Well, I said to them, "You see, I brought this money, but it is running out on me. I've been here a month, and there isn't even enough to return to El Salvador, not enough for the tickets or anything."

So we went to ask for help from the United Nations. They gave us food and a roof, at least. We no longer had to spend our money on that. We went a long time without work. We had to depend instead on help from the United Nations.

Robin: How did they help you? When they gave you a roof, did you live with a family? Or how did it work? Did they give you the money for . . . ?

Carmen: In order to live? No. At that time what they gave us was food and other kinds of help. The church provided the roof, the Fátima Church, over there in the community of Fátima.

Robin: So you lived inside the church?

Carmen: No. It was like a house, a communal house. It's something that the church has.

Robin: It's a house that belongs to the . . . ?

Carmen: It was a house belonging to the church, a big passageway, more like it. The conditions were very difficult, really. The rain came in, and so did the cold, because it was only made of laminated roofing. But there we were.

Robin: And were there a lot of people?

Carmen: There were a lot. We were about ten families at that time. People who were concerned about El Salvador came and gave us clothes and things. We cooked our meals together. We cooked plenty of food. Sometimes we had meetings. We had to organize ourselves so that we could figure out how to leave that place. And we had a schedule as to who would fix the meals. On one day a certain person would help, on another day another person. We organized the cleaning, the cooking, and what kind of attention we would give the children. As for me, I liked working with the children the most. We took them for walks, we gave them recreation. Sometimes also, if some of them got sick, we would help by taking them to the health center. And at first they did not give us medicines at the health center. They sent you to the pharmacy over there near the refugee center.

Well, we spent six or seven months in Fátima. Then we moved into

houses. Three families would live in one house. They were big houses, paid for
by relief funds. The priest was working on proposing projects. He was requesting
funds to rent houses, so that groups of families could live there. We would cook
the meals collectively, and we were given mattresses and everything.

My mother, after everything happened back home that I told you about
. . . when she told me to come here . . . after we had already come ourselves, I
brought her here too, with the help of the United Nations . . .

Robin: Where is she?

Carmen: She was here. She was working on a project for young people,
helping them with a home-school that they had set up. She was working here, and
everything. But she came together with my grandmother. And my grandmother
couldn't stand it here in Costa Rica. She had to return to El Salvador. She went
back there to die . . . she died because of her heart. Well, a person can endure
these conditions only so long, before she gets to the point where she cannot stand
them physically. She was very old and . . . she died. On January first of 1987,
last year, she died.

It was painful for us, because my grandmother was like a parent, like the
father we never had. . . . She filled the empty space that my father's absence
made, by supporting my mother. And in exile a person really feels the death of a
loved one, because you cannot go and see her.

So my mother returned to El Salvador, and she is still there . . . working.
Back there the displaced people, the refugees, are also organized. Now she is
working on a project with children—like me—with orphans back in El Salvador,
with children who don't have mothers and fathers.

One morning as I am visiting Carmen and Carolina in their lively
classroom of two- and three-year-olds, we hear a knock at the window.
Framed in the glass is the handsome, smiling face of Carmen's husband.
Carmen bounces over to the window, remarking to us over her shoulder
in a wry voice, "Duty calls."

Carmen and her husband Federico talk quietly for several
minutes, while Carolina and I turn our attention to the preschoolers, who
have become abnormally active at the appearance of this visitor. Soon
I agree to take over Carmen's place for an hour while she and Federico
go for a walk. As young parents of three small children, they rarely have
a chance to be alone together.

After her return, Carmen comes to me with the request that my
daughter and I visit her family on Sunday with my tape recorder.
Federico wishes to give me his *testimonio*.

Carmen and Federico met each other during their early years as
refugees in Costa Rica. Federico was sharing a small house with a friend
at the time, and Carmen was living in a house that she and her family
shared with other refugees. They became acquainted through the growing
Salvadoran community, and soon afterwards Federico moved into

Carmen's group home in order to be close to her.

Federico had always been interested in the political situation as a student back in El Salvador, which was one of the reasons he had felt it necessary to leave.   As a refugee, he soon joined a group of people—both Salvadorans and Costa Ricans—who were concerned about the political events in El Salvador.

Federico: I went to this group in San José because I was interested in what they were doing. I had heard that they talked together about how to gain solidarity with the Salvadoran people. They had a house where they worked toward solidarity, and I went there to work with them. From this group I was able to learn things about what was going on at home. I was with my own people, so I wouldn't lose sight of my country. And I could always get help from them if I needed it.

I wasn't working at this time. There was no possibility of a job here in Costa Rica. So the only thing I had for amusement, to keep myself occupied, was to work a little with this solidarity group. I felt that their activities were good. Well, they didn't actually do anything active—nothing out of the ordinary, nothing illegal, nothing at all, really.

I was doing this, when a series of problems began with Immigration here in 1981.   They started to cart the Salvadorans away, to deport them.   The authorities from Immigration would stop you often, even on the street, and ask you for your papers. Of course, I had permission to be in Costa Rica, so I wasn't very worried.

The main problem had to do with . . . with . . . some embassy. I don't know what it was exactly. Someone put a bomb in the embassy. I don't know what happened. You might have heard about it.

Robin: Yes, I believe so. [In March of 1981 rockets were fired at a U.S. government van carrying marines to guard duty at the American Embassy; a guerrilla group calling itself the Carlos Aguero Echeverría Command claimed responsibility, saying the attack was in protest against U.S. actions in El Salvador. As a result of this attack, plus an additional explosion near the Nicaraguan Embassy, the Costa Rican government expelled thirty-six foreign political exiles from the country. *New York Times* 18 March 1981:13:5 and 12 April 1981:21:1].

Federico: I'm not sure if it was the U.S. Embassy, or some other one. Yes, I think it was the Embassy of the United States. Well, the result of all this was that it became even more of a problem to live here in Costa Rica.

One day I was surprised as Carmen and I went out walking. This was in March of 1981. We were just returning home when we found everything in a mess. The authorities had come to search the house and to register the people living there. Everyone's papers had been examined, and the documents were all found to be up to date. But they had left the message that Carmen and I should present ourselves at Immigration to be sure that our papers were in order, too.

I didn't go to Immigration right away. I had already heard of several cases in which fellow Salvadorans had been deported. Instead, I asked Father Higinio's advice. And I also talked to other people. I went to my doctor. She had helped me before. And I went to see another Salvadoran who had been acting as my lawyer here in Costa Rica.

I finally went to Immigration to present my papers, along with another Salvadoran who needed to do the same thing. The lawyer and the doctor accompanied us both. We all went together to show the officials at Immigration that our documents were in order. We had permission to be in Costa Rica. At Immigration the officials interviewed us for almost four hours. They took away the papers we had been given, and they kept us standing there.

Finally another official arrived, and we were told to go with him down below. We followed him down the stairs. And at the bottom he said we were to get into these large vans. I didn't like what was happening, so my lawyer went up to the official to protest.

The official answered my lawyer, "Look. You had better not ask anything. This doesn't concern you. Now, if you really want to find out what is happening to them, then we will take you too."

Next the official said to me, "And you, if you want things to go well for you, then you had better watch out."

This sounded to me like a serious problem. It was obviously some kind of detention. They didn't tell us anything. They just made us get into the car, while the doctor and the lawyer stayed behind. The officials took us to headquarters, keeping us prisoner the whole time. But I felt that we had committed no crime. I had tried to get close to the Salvadoran community, tried to participate somehow in their efforts at solidarity. But I had never considered these actions to be serious crimes. Yet they kept us prisoner, even writing up reports, as if they were keeping a file on us.

We were kept in jail for several days. The United Nations became aware of the problem, probably through my lawyer. The U.N. lawyer tried very hard to present our case in court, but little happened.

Finally the lawyer for the United Nations came to us and said, "Look, I've done everything for you that I can. But you will not be able to remain here in Costa Rica. The government has decided that you both must leave. The Costa Rican government, through the judicial power of the court . . . well . . . has decided that you qualify as undesirables."

He continued, "So now you must choose. You have two alternatives. The most we have been able to achieve for you is to avoid your being sent back to El Salvador. This was the most complicated issue, the most serious issue for you. But they are now making you choose between going to Nicaragua or going to Mexico."

I thought it would be better for me to go to Nicaragua. This was still in Central America, nearer to El Salvador. I have always been close to my parents who are in El Salvador. If I went off to Mexico, I would be farther away from them. Also, I was already serious about Carmen. We would be nearer each other if I went to Nicaragua. We could still see one another.

We arrived in Nicaragua, and the people took us in. The United Nations paid for us to stay in a hotel during the first few days. It was a nice hotel. Maybe they felt that this would help us pull ourselves together. From there we were sent to a Nicaraguan refugee center.

Robin: Was Carmen with you in Nicaragua?

Federico: Not yet. She came soon, though. When she came, we talked about formalizing our relationship. We decided to get married. Then she returned home to Costa Rica to talk with her family, with her mother really. And I stayed on in Nicaragua. I started right away to look for work, because now I would have a family and all that.

Luckily, I went to an office for work cooperatives, a state institution, associated with the government there. It was similar to the place where I had worked back in El Salvador. I presented my papers and showed them my work experience. I told them I had worked as an advisor to cooperatives in my own country. So they gave me a job. After only fifteen days in Nicaragua, I had already been offered a job. I didn't even have to spend a month at the refugee camp. I became a delegate for the cooperatives. My boss was responsible for establishing and maintaining the cooperatives. And I worked under him as his assistant, as his delegate.

That's how things were when Carmen returned to Nicaragua. We settled in Managua. I worked up in the northern zone, but we set up housekeeping in Managua. We stayed in the city on the weekends, and the rest of the time we spent wherever I was working up north.

The situation was clearly better for me in Nicaragua. I didn't know much about the Sandinistas, it's true, but I felt that the changes would be for the good. Things went very well at my job. The government established cooperatives in which the members themselves became the owners of the business. I consider this to be good, because the worker then has access to part of the profits.

During this time Carmen and I were exploring, to see whether or not we could establish a home as a couple. We were trying to see if it would work. We didn't get married right away. We just lived together. Well, we agreed on that at the time. It was not as if we planned to spend our whole lives like that, just living together. We spoke to each other as husband and wife, even though we were just getting to know each other a little better. That's how things were. We were still getting to know each other, when we finally decided we should get married. We had spent almost six months living like that. We even considered the possibility of having a family. We thought about having our first child. Our relationship was serious enough to make it legal. This was still in 1981.

Two years later twin boys were born to Carmen and Federico. By that time trade embargoes by the United States and internal government mismanagement had combined to create an economic crisis in Nicaragua. Many essential goods had become expensive and difficult to get, including things like milk and other products that were necessary for the health of the twins. Moreover, Federico and Carmen had begun to experience a negative reaction to their continued presence in Nicaragua. Neighbors and acquaintances began to talk of them as outsiders, in spite of Federico's job with the government. People viewed them as using up scarce resources that rightfully belonged to the local citizens.

The young couple decided to return to Costa Rica. Carmen had no trouble regaining her refugee status there, along with her newborn twins; Federico, on the other hand, was not given refugee papers. So he entered the country as a tourist and remained there illegally, instead of returning to Nicaragua as was required by his visa. After that time, through the efforts of his lawyer, he was granted a series of legal documents that each allowed him a temporary stay in Costa Rica. Because he was not offered a permanent refugee visa, his status was constantly in question.

Carmen's relationship with Federico was beset with problems due to the instability of his legal residency, but this was by no means their only source of conflict. Federico's advanced educational level and his work experience made him dissatisfied with the kinds of jobs that were available to him in Costa Rica. Although he was occasionally asked to teach a class for refugees at DIAKONÍA [the Swedish funding agency], he remained largely unemployed. He reacted to all this stress by becoming suicidal, twice attempting to take his own life.

Carmen handled this complex situation amazingly well. She loved her husband very much, and his need for her was obvious. She felt lucky to have the stability of her work at the Center, even though she knew her job was a serious source of irritation to Federico. From a cultural perspective, it was the man who was supposed to go out every day and earn the living, not the woman.

Carmen: Federico isn't working. That is one of the problems that our family faces, because . . .

Robin: Is it a problem that all the men have? Or just some men?

Carmen: I think that here in Costa Rica it is usually the women refugees who can find steady work, while the men find it difficult just to get a temporary job. The international projects that are financed here are almost all agricultural cooperatives out in the country. And since my husband has a university education, he finds everything more difficult. There are no projects suitable for him.

And as you can see, almost all of the women who work at the Center or elsewhere have this same problem. None of our husbands can find steady work. So it is the responsibility of the women to make a living. We are the ones who provide for our families. And that, whether you like it or not, is a problem. Well, even though so much has happened, the Salvadoran man still has the "macho" mentality. He was raised with this idea, so for him it is traumatic when the woman is making the living. And whether you like it or not, this . . . this makes him stagger a bit, really.

Well, Federico actually does have a job, but only on Saturdays as a technical advisor to various agricultural projects outside of San José. But this job doesn't allow him to feel as if he were getting anywhere.

And now we have three children. So the problem is serious, even though we try to overcome things peacefully and with strength, little by little. But all this has caused in him . . . well . . . he has problems. And he has not seen his mother for eight years, since the time that he left his country. So when he doesn't receive a letter or get news from El Salvador, well, after two or three months go by, he starts imagining that bad news is going to arrive. Men seem to be more susceptible. They are weaker than women in this sense. He becomes . . . well . . . he becomes unstable.

And this interferes heavily in his relationship with me and also with his children. But with all our strength, we try to help him pull out of it. But when a married couple is not successful . . . is not able . . . how can I say it . . . to get stable work, with the economic situation the way it is in Costa Rica, this is a serious problem for the family. It really is.

Robin: Is it always the man who has the job in El Salvador, or do both the man and the woman hold jobs?

Carmen: Well, back home it is the man who carries the economic burden of the family. The woman can contribute, and the man allows this, especially in the middle class. She can help, but her collaboration is usually only part-time. She is the one who takes care of the home, takes care of the man and the children. If he didn't earn the living, then he would be considered, back there in El Salvador, something like a bum, a playboy, someone who is just taking advantage of others.

This is how we feel in our society. We believe that the man should support the home and his children, and if the woman wants to help him, she can, but only in the form of assistance. Here in exile, we have a different situation.

Robin: What is Federico able to . . . ?

Carmen: He helps at home, he contributes. But what is it really that enables us to survive in Costa Rica? It is my salary at the Center, whatever I get out of this project.

And so we really feel the conditions here, because for us it is very hard to better ourselves. Federico has had to resort to the care of a psychologist, because . . . because . . . he has something that, well . . . he cannot get better since I am the one who leaves the house every day, while he stays home. Sometimes he gets work selling books or things like that, but the truth is that this doesn't really help.

Caring for the children at the Center was, for the women, one of the most positive aspects of their refugee life. The work was often both physically and emotionally exhausting, but the rewards were incalculable. The children needed love, but offered love as well. Hugs and kisses were plentiful, and everyone enjoyed holding a baby on her lap. Good healthy laughter rang out in the courtyard when the women sat down to watch the children at play.

Associated with these emotional rewards was the political solidarity created by working with the children. The refugees were not content simply to allow their charges to grow up. They had specific ideas as to how they wanted the children to turn out. They wanted them to be Salvadorans, not Costa Ricans. The hope of the adults was to teach the children the kinds of values that would encourage them to return home. The future generation was needed to restructure El Salvador along more humanitarian lines.

Carmen, who was trained as a teacher and had always known she wanted to work with children, expresses the hope and challenge of the Center in this regard.

Carmen: For me the children have been something very important, something vital in my own life, in addition to the humanitarian side of helping them. Being in constant identification with them gives a person renewed hope in life, and every day new faith, a new dream. Even if many people have died in El Salvador, new generations are being born both inside and outside the country, new beginnings, let's say. And our task is to see that these children have a place to feel some peace, some calm, something we didn't have. We didn't have it, and we want their lives to be better.

It is also a challenge for us to contribute, even if it is only a little grain of sand, in the building of the kind of life we have always wanted, a life of peace and tranquility and . . . a life of justice. The Salvadoran people have been fighting for this, really, for eight years, ever since I left my country. The majority of Salvadorans that we have met, well, they haven't lost hope about returning. They wish to return, but under different conditions, to a situation of change, and to a new life. We want a better life. We want a life in which there is something for everyone. Even if we have to suffer economically, we want at least to have peace.

Now that I am a mother, I don't want to pass on a world full of hostility to my children, a world full of repression, of death, of blood, the kind of life we have had to experience. I don't want my children to be raised under these circumstances. And that is what we try to do here. We want our children to love their country for its good things, for its many good things.

This war has strengthened us and has taught us much that is positive. And we would like to instill these things in our children, so that when they grow up, they will want to return home to their country. We want them to return with an active spirit, with a constructive attitude. Not just problems of war, but also economic problems—catastrophes like earthquakes and everything—have left our country submerged in crisis. So it is both our obligation and our right to contribute something toward the development of the new generation.

This gives me the strength to think that our situation here, even though it is difficult, is not as serious as that of the children in El Salvador, those who are abandoned, whose parents have died, and who will never experience the kind of peace that perhaps the children here at the Center have.

And that is what we try to get the children to feel, so that they understand little by little, so that they don't waste their food or destroy the things that they have here, and so that they are always thinking about what it is that they are tossing away, since there are many children, many families in El Salvador that might be needing it.

And I believe that this is important. Because if we recognize what our people are suffering, we will then feel the debt that we owe to our people, to our citizens. And this is the way in which we can collaborate for now. . . .

If I didn't have this job, we would have left for El Salvador. We could not have survived in this environment. My children also benefit from the project. All three of my children attend the Center. But I have a problem, because next year the two boys will go off to school, and the Center will not cover them. They will have to eat at home, and there will be transportation costs and everything. So now we have another worry at home, another tension, making it even more urgent that my husband succeeds in getting his resettlement papers, because if he doesn't, I don't know what we will do.

8

Rita

"I only wanted to cry and cry."

The relative calm of their new existence in Costa Rica gave the refugees time to reflect and to recuperate from the trauma of their experiences. Emotions that had been repressed for months and even years finally came to the surface, frightening the women anew. Psychologists and social workers were assigned to help the refugees during these early years, but the emotional wounds lingered. Many of the women were still consulting psychologists for "nervous conditions" when I arrived eight years later.

No one spoke in detail about her sessions with psychologists, yet I assume that the *testimonios* were an integral part of the healing process. The "testimony method" for the treatment of refugees was finally brought to light in the psychological literature during the early 1980s with the publication of Cienfuegos and Monelli's work with victims of the military dictatorship in Chile (Van der Veer 1992:150). However, it is likely that psychologists were experimenting informally with the procedure long before this, because of the high concentrations of political refugees throughout Latin America and because of the public interest in their *testimonios*. The idea of psychological therapy was certainly not lost on the Salvadorans; I often heard the women mention the therapeutic value of working with children. Furthermore, they expected to weep while reliving their experiences through their stories in interviews with me; they also expected to feel better after the session was over.

Rita, who had been chastised by her neighbors in El Salvador for not mourning over the deaths of her three sons, broke down completely as soon as she got to the refugee center. All she wanted to do was sit in a corner and weep. The psychologists treating the refugees pushed her to get out of the center and take walks. They organized excursions to the countryside. Even Rita's husband, who was also suffering severely himself, encouraged these outings. The communal living conditions of the refugee center may have exacerbated her distress, however, because Rita expresses considerable relief at finally finding a small house to live in alone with her husband.

Rita: We spent three months at the Fátima Refugee Center. But I felt as if I were going crazy. It was so horrible. I spent all my time crying. I was so damaged that I felt at the very edge of existence. The psychologist said to me, "Get out and take a walk. You have got to get out." I didn't want to go out and walk. All I wanted to do was sit alone in the corner of the room.

Finally my husband said to me, "Let's go to the market to see what we can buy." Only in order to show some attention to him, I went.

I had just gotten to the market when that huge feeling of desperation grabbed me—such desperation! I told myself that I would return home. I went on to the market, but I didn't buy anything. Suddenly I turned around for home, rather, for the refugee center. I arrived. And I saw a mouse. Such a feeling of desperation came over me that I fell down. I said to myself, when I was not yet there, I said, "I'll go back to shop where my husband is." It couldn't have been more than 300 meters from the market to the refugee center. I tried to return to the market. I was halfway there when that desperate feeling came over me again, and I no longer wanted to go to where my husband was. I came back. And I only wanted to remain . . . I only wanted to lie down . . . it was really so strange. I didn't feel like being in any place, I only wanted to cry and cry, nothing else.

The psychologists did a lot. There was one young woman that worked a lot with the refugees. She organized excursions. She took people out. But I did not want to go on these excursions, because going out, like this, from the towns, well, there I saw . . . uh . . . in the bushes . . . in the mountains I saw dead people everywhere. You know, at home I had never seen dead people like that out in the country. But on these excursions I did. I saw the army running after young men. I saw them. . . .

I said to myself, "When did I ever see this back there in El Salvador?" I did not see this. But here, I was seeing it. My head was going crazy. The suffering, ah, the suffering. . . .

Three months later, when we found a house, we moved. The house was little. It wasn't pretty, or anything. It was nothing more than a bunch of boards. But indeed, we felt better there, because now we were alone.

The uncontrollable emotions felt by the refugees during those first few months linger on. They appear in the form of nightmares or sudden fears over trivial things. Although I had a number of occasions to witness intense emotions at the daycare center, I was actually more surprised by the normalcy of life there. The women sat together, gossiping and laughing and teasing one another all day long. They encouraged the children in songs and games and even got down on the floor to play with them. As the *testimonios* indicate, however, the emotions are still rumbling underneath the calm of everyday life.

Although emergency aid for the Salvadoran refugees had long since dried up when I arrived, international funding of a different kind was still available, primarily from Sweden. In the early 1980s Dutch and Swedish groups were active in supporting the formation of grass roots projects that allowed the refugees to become economically independent. Although the Dutch had limited their funding of such projects, the Swedes continued in their support.

As my Swedish friend Tina explained to me, the idea behind the grass roots projects was to help the refugees work together to form cooperative businesses that would become self-supporting over the years. After screening proposed projects for their potential for economic viability and for social benefits, these international funding agencies provided full financial support for the first one or two years of the project. During this time the project was monitored closely by the international agency. Then the agency gradually began to withdraw its funding, each year requiring more and more expenses to be financed through the proceeds of the project. The agency continued to offer guidance and technical advice, however, for as long as the project required it.

Needless to say, the refugees have benefitted greatly from this well-conceived approach to their economic situation. In spite of the lack of mainstream jobs, the refugees have been able to create meaningful positions for themselves through a variety of grass roots projects. In addition to earning a steady income and learning new skills on these projects, the refugees have used the cooperatives to build a supportive and active community of Salvadorans in Costa Rica.

During those early years in exile, the Salvadorans gravitated toward the locally based Committee of Mothers [an offshoot of COMADRES], which served not only to struggle for peace and justice in El Salvador, but also provided a source of community life for the refugees. Initially, the Committee took an active role in helping the women adapt to their new surroundings. International relief agencies worked through the Committee, in an attempt to respond to the most urgent needs of the refugees. Through their Committee of Mothers organization, the Salvadorans were able to establish an internationally funded daycare center, which not only paid the women who worked there a steady salary but provided urgently needed care for their small children.

Rita: After we had been here in Costa Rica for two years, we had only found one job, over there on the little piece of land that my husband was paying rent on, and we lived on that. But at the end of the two years, we were in a meeting of the Committee of Mothers. A man was there. And I decided to do what he told us to do, to "present a project," as they say. "Let's do something," he said, "in order to have work. Let's ask Holland to help us with a sewing project." So the young woman who was there, she asked for the project, even to the point of sending a letter and everything. She asked for a sewing project for everyone who was working on the Committee of Mothers. But at the same time they also submitted a request for a daycare center project. And this was finally the project that was approved. It was supposed to be a sewing workshop, because this was what they were originally thinking, but later they thought of asking for a daycare center.

We were all happy, now that we were going to work with children. There were so many orphans. There were some who were left without anything, others that perhaps had someone in charge of them, but who were without parents. All of them were brought here by some agency.

So the project was given to us. And we started to organize the daycare center. We worked for three months, without even earning five *centavos*. We worked from eight in the morning to four in the afternoon. First we began to search for a house. We went in groups looking for a house. Some of us went in one direction, others in another, to look over the houses. Then later we cleaned the house we had found and began to make it look nice. We didn't have very much to work with. We didn't really know anything, and nobody was helping us except for a talk that somebody gave. It was Doña Ligia's husband who finally gave us talks about food . . . about what to eat . . . about nutrition. And then we were able to resolve things.

You see, we still had many emotions, but we also felt good. After starting out so sad—we had almost never gotten together, because we didn't want anyone to see us—now we had come to the point where we saw each other every day. My sister [Teresa, who has since moved to Canada] was also with us. There were about eight of us who went to work on the project. We spent our time during those first three months just hoping. We spent it hoping, I tell you, without earning anything, without any promises. We started to tell people about the project, to solicit for children, to look for people who had children they could send to the Center. And finally we began to work with the children.

It felt good working with the children. We worked hard. As I tell the others, we are earning good money now. We work now, but not the way we worked before. When the project first started, we worked harder and we earned less. I understand that now the women assigned to buy the groceries go by car. They work on a certain day, and then on that same day they go and bring back the groceries. Before, when we started the project, we used to get the groceries on Saturday and bring them from the outdoor market on our backs! Nothing to help us along, or anything, you see? We made a game of it, the director and I. I went with her almost every Saturday. I worked with the littlest children, with the biggest children, in the cooking, in the cleaning, in the shopping . . . what didn't I do!

But yes, I feel that we have come a long way. We have come from working with just a few children to working with a lot. We have more experience now. It has been very good for me—as I am saying now, as I have always said, and as I shall continue to say—the work at the daycare center has been very good for me. Thanks to this work I am no longer going crazy. I don't stay alone, locked up in the house. . . .

The three sons that Rita had lost to the war were her eldest children, and the family had sacrificed to see that they had a chance to go to school. Following the government's flooding of their farmland during the building of the Cerrón Grande dam, the family had picked up stakes to move to the resettlement community in order to allow the boys to continue their education. Now, with the boys gone, Rita began to concentrate her efforts more on her girls. Clearly the juggling of schooling and jobs remained a problem for the family, especially now that the girls were old enough to decide things for themselves.

Even though public education in Costa Rica is free, it was still a financial burden on the family to send their children to school. Uniforms were required; books and other supplies had to be purchased; and there were numerous unexpected daily expenses that arose when teenagers began to socialize with each other after class. Furthermore, a child who was studying was then not able to contribute financially to the family. The child's wages, while small, often meant the difference between having a roof over one's head or living out in the street.

Rita: My daughters were happy that we came. We put them in school as soon as we were able to. They had already studied for a year, but since we had not brought their school records, they had to repeat the year.

And they said to me, "How sad it is, to go to a school where they don't want you. The other students really don't like us because we are Salvadorans."

"Be patient, girls. There soon will be other Salvadorans here in the barrio."

I tell you, we suffer a lot. The Costa Ricans have never looked on us with favorable eyes. We have heard a lot of nasty things from the Costa Ricans. There are also nice people here, of course, who do indeed treat you well.

We have lived here for several years. By now I feel a little better, because now I have forgotten some of the things that we suffered back home. Lupe has grown up, the girl that was just fifteen years old when we came. Just imagine, when we arrived, she celebrated her fifteenth birthday here! [Lupe works in the kitchen at the daycare center]. Ever since we came, she hasn't had a chance to study or anything. She's been working.

I had a problem last year, or rather at the beginning of the school year when they were about to begin classes. I had to tell my two youngest daughters, who were both studying in evening classes, that I didn't have enough money to support their studies any longer.

And the older one told me that she didn't want to study. "Ay, Mamá," said Isabel, "I cannot go on studying in the evenings."

But the youngest one, Paula, who is, well, not very diligent about her studies . . . Paula said to me, "I am not going to study. I am going to quit school. I'm going to leave everything and go to work."

I thought it was noble of her. So I said to her, "I don't want you to leave school, I want you to study."

"Ay, no," Paula said, "I don't even like to study."

Then Isabel said, "Well, yes, I really do want to study. I want to have a career, whatever it may turn out to be. But you do not have to go to work, Paula, just so that I can get along in my career."

Well then, I told Isabel, "Yes. If you want to study . . . if Paula works, then you can study."

But later the older one got a job in a supermarket. Isabel said to me, "They are even going to give me a job as a cashier. But what should I do? I have two possibilities. One is to work as a cashier, and the other is to continue my studies. But how can I work in the supermarket? If I work all day in the supermarket, I cannot study because I leave work too late at night."

"Look," I said to my daughters, "now you can see what you must do."

"Ay, no," Paula, the younger one, said to me, "it is I who shall go to work in the supermarket." But she would not be able to tell them she was only fifteen years old.

"I would have liked," I told her, "your older sister to have gone instead."

"Ay, *Mami*," Isabel then said to me, "ever since you told me about our money problems, I have felt a pain in my chest. I feel like I'm in a blind alley, without being able to leave! I would like to go to work at the supermarket. But I also want to study. What should I do? How do I resolve this? Do I go to work, or do I study?"

"I do not know," I said to her. Look, she was almost crying because she didn't know what to do. My eldest daughter Lupe told her, "I won't open my mouth, since I don't know how to help. I know you want to study."

So Paula said, "I'm the one who is going to work at the supermarket."

"You are not going to be able to handle this cashier's job," I warned her. "I see more talent in Isabel than I see in you."

Then Isabel said, "No, Mamá, look at how intelligent Paula is, how good she is in math. You see her as very informal, all clown, but really her work is very formal. You think that because she is a clown that she should not be allowed to work in the supermarket. She can surely handle the work there. You have to let her do it. She wants to work, and I want to study. So now you see what should be done. Paula is not really interested in studying, but I am. She should go to work and I should continue studying. I can even go to day school."

Paula agreed, "You study, and I will go to work." Then she said to me, "Don't worry, I will show you. I will show you that I can go out and work as a cashier. You'll see how good it will be for us."

She is now training at the supermarket. But I am worried about her being so young. She goes to work at eight in the morning and leaves work very late, after six in the evening. And she is so young. I don't know, but I feel bad, because . . . see . . . she works until so late. But well, you cannot do anything about it.

The subsequent marriages of Rita's daughters created continued anguish over money. Now, even though the girls were working, their money no longer could be shared with their mother. What little money they earned belonged to their newly established households. Rita felt the added responsibility on her own shoulders, even though she wished the best for her daughters.

Rita: When Lupe was single, I found it good, because we both worked at the daycare center. And between the two of us, we helped each other with our salaries. But soon she got married and left me alone. "Ah, well, now I am leaving . . . ," she told me.

Later I said to Paula . . . to my youngest daughter I said, "Now you are going to help me." Earlier they had both had jobs. They had worked in people's houses. They had earned very little, and I had said, "Don't let anyone take any of it from you. We will use your money to buy you the things you need. And I'll let you buy me the umbrella, if you want."

Ah, well, then my youngest daughter went to work at the supermarket, but before she went, Lupe got married. So I told them, "Well, we are going to have very little money, but we shall see what we can find to help us." And five months later Paula, my youngest, was preparing to get married too. See, they left me, really, working alone at home. My sister said, "So if she gets married, she gets married."

It is sad to have only one person, no more, doing all the housework. Who would have told me when I was younger, "Look, when you are older, when you no longer even have any energy, you will have to take care of the whole house."? I wouldn't have believed it. I would have said, "How can I do it?" Well now, indeed, I am doing it.

But I tell you, perhaps this will be the last year that I work, I mean, at home. "Because if I live through this year, it will be enough," I tell them, "since anyway, I feel sick." They don't like it when I talk like this, that now I am going to die. But I say, "How is it that you don't want me to tell you that I am going to die, if I feel it? I feel that I am being consumed by my illnesses."

But they say, "Mamá, don't talk like that."

"No," I tell them, "you are the ones who have to watch out for yourselves. Watch out for yourselves, because you have your lives in front of you, I don't. I have used up my life, good or bad, but I have already passed the time when I could take care of things for everybody. Now is the time you must take care of yourselves."

They don't like me to talk this way, but it is the truth. As I tell them, "Now it is you who have to watch out for yourselves, because you are just beginning to live."

9

Alicia

"So we go on alone."

On Sunday my daughter and I go to visit Alicia, as I have promised. She and her children live in a small village that houses a number of Salvadoran refugees. Their house is in a row of small narrow units, which share walls on both sides with the houses next door. The place is kept from looking grim by the ubiquitous Costa Rican vegetation.

Inside, the house is poor, but spotless. My nine-year-old daughter Jessica, who has come along in the hopes of finding a playmate, sits on the couch in astonishment, watching Alicia's eldest daughter (also nine years old) diligently mop and wax the floor. The younger children watch television and tickle each other in an attempt to get Jessica's attention.

Alicia calls me into the bedroom as she takes out her hair curlers. She remarks about our promptness even though we have arrived half an hour late. While we were driving around on the wrong road, I had worried we would be too late for the Salvadoran mass that Alicia invited us to attend. I need not have worried, however, since Alicia is even more behind schedule. She talks about Ligia and the daycare center as she fixes her hair. Alicia did not really expect me to come today at all, because of the tension caused by her request that I not give her story to Ligia. Alicia is obviously delighted to be able to give me her side of the controversy.

According to Alicia, Mirabela had initiated the problem. Mirabela had interpreted my conversation with Alicia in the kitchen as an accusation that Ligia was attempting to "sell" the documents for her own personal benefit. Not only am I dismayed to find myself inadvertently involved in such a conflict; I am also discouraged to discover that Mirabela has sided with Ligia against Alicia. Does she, too, think that Alicia is going to take advantage of me? Or that Alicia is a liar?

Alicia says something else to me that day which is even more
distressing. Apparently after I left the daycare center on Friday, Ligia
called a lawyer over to the Center for a meeting with the entire staff.
They discussed Alicia's alleged accusation that Ligia was planning to sell
the *testimonios*. According to Alicia's account, there was a quarrel at this
meeting with people shouting at each other and threatening to smash my
tape recorder and rip up all my tapes. Luckily for me, the lawyer was
firm. He said that the Center had no rights over the tapes even if they
were made on the premises. Alicia was vindicated, but I had a sinking
feeling about the status of my research.

The manner in which Alicia tells me this story implies that she
was on my side during the whole conflict. While others had shouted
about destroying my tapes, she had not. She clearly wants me to align
myself with her. I equivocate, however, saying that I have to treat
everyone at the Center in the same way, if possible, for the purposes of
my research. Like Ligia, Alicia tries to understand, but she would rather
have me take sides.

As soon as Alicia finishes her preparations to attend mass, Jessica
and I set off with her down the road. Her children do not accompany us,
making my daughter somewhat uncomfortable. The little ones all stay
home to clean the house and watch television. The Salvadoran mass is
being performed by refugee members of the liberation-theology Catholic
Church from Guatemala and El Salvador and is held outside in a
charming meadow by the river. The service itself, with its interaction
between the priests and the congregation, follows the same format I have
already observed among the Salvadorans. The hymns and the prayers set
a revolutionary tone. The priests lead discussions based on biblical texts
whose messages seem relevant to the lives of the refugees, calling upon
the members of the congregation to respond with their individual
interpretations of the texts.

The congregation consists predominantly of women, several of
whom I recognize as mothers of children attending the Center. During
the discussion the women speak up. Alicia is the most active participant,
however, delivering her interpretation of the passage with the same
eloquence that I have seen her use in her *testimonio* to me.

After the mass Jessica and I hurry back to Alicia's house in the
hopes that Jessica can play a little with the children. Alicia stays behind
to chat with the other refugees. For most of an hour we wait for Alicia
to return, the children insisting that their mother will be along soon.
When she does not come, we leave for home still wondering about the
appropriate behavior for this social occasion. Alicia says to me the
following week that she was expecting us to stay for dinner and sorry that
we had left, but since she did not specifically invite us, I am not sure.
My interpretation of her behavior is that, although she was "supposed" to

have us over for dinner according to her own cultural norms, she was not really prepared to have us accept the invitation.

After this visit to Alicia's house and her unnerving story involving my research, I am unsettled about my future relationship with the Center. For my own peace of mind, I go to talk with Ligia the next day. She has already set up my last two interviews for me. When I arrive at the Center, Ligia is working with Rita in the room that houses the smallest babies. She says she is filling in for María, who is absent from work that morning. Ligia is upbeat and cheerful, asking that a chair be brought from another room for me to sit on while we talk. Normally, the only furniture in this room are two playpens and a diaper-changing table. As I perch on the tiny chair, Ligia tells me her solution to the problem, which is that I should hold all future interviews outside the Center. This plan suits me fine. I do not enjoy the feeling of being pressured into giving Ligia copies of the *testimonios*, when others are unhappy with the idea.

Following this incident, the focus of my fieldwork shifted. Although I was still interested in examining how individual refugee women were adapting to their new lives in Costa Rica, I found I had to broaden my research to include an examination of the interpersonal relationships among the staff members at the Center. If I wanted to work more closely with Alicia, which I did, I needed to be careful not to offend Ligia. Ligia was, after all, the key to my access to the Center. Now that I had committed myself to studying this group of Salvadorans, I did not want to make an error in judgment that would cause me the loss of my project. I was emotionally involved with these people; my position was vulnerable.

One decision, in this new cautious state of mind, was to put a damper on my relationship with Alicia. This was difficult for me to do. In the first place, Alicia was friendly and aggressive, seeking me out when I came to the Center and drawing me aside to talk. Always, I felt that the others were watching us; my smiles became unnatural and our conversations subdued. An even greater problem for me, however, was my own interest in Alicia, whom I found fascinating. Her *testimonio* was an incredible story, not only for what had happened to her, but also for the manner in which she described the events. Moreover, Alicia's problems at the Center intrigued me. I could not easily comprehend why this complex and engaging young person should find herself so ostracized by the others.

Instead of actively pursuing my research interest in Alicia, I pretended not to care, but this took all my strength. I felt that avoidance of Alicia was necessary to the preservation of my research project. Moreover, I hoped to protect her from the others, who might be angered by my attention to her. Alicia, of course, did not understand my motives and was hurt.

Another decision I made following this incident involved a change in the nature of my visitations to the Center. During my initial interviews, I had only visited at the appointed hours set by Ligia. Now that I was no longer interviewing the staff on the premises, I had to devise other reasons for coming to the Center. If I lost access to the Center, I would ultimately lose contact with the women I wanted to study. I needed to establish a comfortable and easy relationship. I asked Ligia if I could come and observe during daily activities and perhaps help out. She agreed and said we should set up a schedule for my visits. As the weeks went by, however, and we had not yet determined my appointed hours, I simply fell into the pattern of dropping by whenever I found the time. Soon everyone became accustomed to my comings and goings. Even though I was always treated as something of a guest, the women learned to go on with their work while I was around.

The main concession made to my presence was to include me in Center activities. When the babies were lined up in their highchairs, I acted like the others and fed a row of open mouths all with a single spoon. I sang songs and played hand games with the older children. I read books to the lovely little girl who shyly pushed books into my hand. I went to holiday celebrations and cried in sympathy with the women who were homesick for El Salvador and the lives they had once lived. I watched with anxious heart as the children played in the tiny yard, while the child in the swing missed the child on the seesaw only by inches.

Shifting my research focus from the stories of the individual women to their relationships at the Center made me aware of the significance of the *testimonios* in their lives. The idea that Ligia might sell the stories, even if for the benefit of the Center, was a threat to the solidarity of the group. The sale of a *testimonio* implied a commercial transaction which could degrade the political goals of the refugees and might cause certain individuals to gain at the expense of others. Ligia's fear about Alicia was similar. Alicia might use her *testimonio* to manipulate me into offering her personal favors, thus giving Alicia advantages over the other women.

To some degree, it was considered legitimate to use the stories in this way. The *testimonios* provided the women with an effective means of gaining sympathy from others—useful as leverage in the solicitation of relief funds or medical aid. Most refugees lived on an economic precipice; a single unforeseen expense in their daily lives could mean that the family did not survive the rest of the month without begging for help. Most of the begging was done privately through friends, but when these sources were exhausted, the refugees had to resort to local and international aid programs. They found the *testimonios* to be indispensable when dealing with strangers.

Clearly, however, usage of the *testimonios* for personal gain was strictly limited by group pressure. The motivation for giving the stories to me was primarily political, and such efforts were considered collaborative. I was supposed to do my part by disseminating the stories, while they were to do their part by giving, not selling, the stories to me. Undue commercialization of the process by individuals would only contaminate the message.

The conflict between Ligia and Alicia over the extent to which the *testimonios* could be used for personal gain demonstrates the refugee awareness of the inherent contradiction of the *testimonio* as a means of oral expression. These stories were not simply oral life histories of individuals; they were activist statements on behalf of a collective people. Whereas a life history is "authored" by an individual, even if indirectly, and can therefore be negotiated by the individual, a "*testimonio* constitutes an affirmation of the individual self in a collective mode" (Beverley 1992:97). Thus, any monetary gain arising from the *testimonios* had to be of benefit to the group. Relief aid for individuals and international funding for the Center both served to support the refugee community, but personal gain for the individual "authorship" of the stories remained an unacceptable manipulation of others and constituted a misuse of the *testimonio*.

Back in El Salvador, Alicia needed to get out of the country, but she didn't have the money to pay for the passage. She felt responsible for the safety of her entire family—including her three children, her brothers and sisters, and her parents—partly because she was the eldest daughter, but also because it was her husband who had been killed by the authorities. The family had spent all its available money in getting her mother, Ana, off to Costa Rica. They had felt compelled to send Ana away, because her unstable behavior was threatening all their lives. Once in Costa Rica, however, Ana apparently pulled herself together and got a job picking coffee. In spite of her bitterness at being sent into exile alone, Ana managed to arrange passage to Costa Rica for the family through a U.N. relief agency. She helped to book the flight and told Alicia that she would meet them at the airport.

Alicia: When I got to Costa Rica, there was another surprise for me. I came here on the twenty-seventh of November. I got to the airport with all my children and my younger brother and sister. I got here at noon. We left from there at almost eleven-thirty, and at twelve we were already here at the Juan Santamaría airport. I had never traveled in an airplane. I didn't . . . what I mean is . . . I was afraid of Costa Rica. I kept saying, "Will there be land there? Will there be this, will there be that?"

What the people said, more than anything else, was that there wouldn't be any corn flour to make tortillas. That they only ate rice over there. "Oh, dear God, how can that be?" I said to myself, "What am I going to do?"

Well, I decided to come. When I arrived at the airport, I didn't see anybody. I had this terrible urge to cry, because I didn't see anybody. I had never been to Costa Rica, or anything. Finally, when I saw my mother, well-dressed and wearing a watch, stockings, and high-heeled shoes, which she had never used before, I thought, "How strange!"

From the time my mother arrived, she had gone to pick coffee. She had saved her money and had bought herself some things. She came up to me and said, "You came?"

"Ah, yes, we came." I had my little baby boy in my arms still, because he was only eight months old.

Then she said, "Well, now that I have gotten you out of danger, you are going to have to find a place to stay."

And she left me at the airport, taking with her only my younger sister. Look at that! I wanted to go right back to El Salvador! How could she just leave me there! And what was I going to do, never having been to Costa Rica before, without even a *centavo* in my pocket! I was there with only my children, no more, and my younger brother and sister. Well, as I said, the only one that she took with her was Julia, my sister. That's the only one she took. She left Pablo, my brother, with us.

I didn't want to start to cry, so I said to my brother, "You watch the children for me here. I'm going to talk to those people who brought me."

I went to the office, and I said, "Look, I want to return to my country."

"*Señora*," he said to me, "we are authorized to get you out, but not to send you back. We don't send anybody back. It is our job to get you out of danger, not to send you into danger."

I started to cry right then and there, sitting in the office. "Then, who? Where am I going to go? My mother came and got my sister, and she left," I said. "It would be better if I'd never come. I should have stayed there. But it doesn't matter."

I wanted to go home. I was sitting there crying, when I noticed a Salvadoran man who was from the same place I come from. He came over to me and said, "Did you bring any Salvadoran money, Alicia?"

He could see that I was crying, and he came over to ask me if I had any Salvadoran money! "No, *hombre* [man]," I said, "I don't have a *centavo*."

The thing was that at that time Salvadoran money was worth something, and when a person came from El Salvador, people would come up to him at the airport to buy the money. "*Coyotes*," they are called.

So he said to me, "Didn't you bring anything?"

"No."

"And Ana?"

"She came and took my sister," I said.

"And she left you here? That can't be! Your mother couldn't have just left you here."

"Yes," I said, "she left me here, and I don't have anywhere to go."

Then he said, "Ana couldn't have done that to her daughter and to her grandchildren! She couldn't have left her son with you here! It can't be!" Then he went to look for her, but he didn't find her. "Well," he said, "Don't worry. I'll help you."

Before he left, he asked again, "You didn't bring any money?"

"No," I said, "I didn't even bring five *centavos*."

So he said, "I'll arrange for a taxi."

He went and brought a taxi and put us in it, and we all took off. I cried and cried, with my little baby boy in my arms and my two children and my brother beside me.

The man asked me, "Didn't she say anything to you, not anything?"

"No, she didn't say anything. She only told me that she had gotten me out of danger, and then she left me there," I said.

There was a refugee camp in Heredia, but no one had told me about it, not even when I arrived. So the man said, as we were riding in the taxi, "Look. I'm going to take you to where Jorge is. Jorge lives in a good-sized house. I think he would let you stay with him." And he took me there. It is in Heredia near the cemetery.

The man said to him, "Look, Jorge, can you imagine? Ana left all these children at the airport. She told them she had gotten them out of danger, and then she left them there. This woman doesn't even have a penny. And look how they've come. Couldn't you give them a place to stay here?"

"I don't have any bedrooms," he said. "There is this little tiny living room, if she can fit into that."

Then the man said I should put my things over there in the little room. I brought in the small pillows for my little girl, and I brought in the milk to give her, and I brought in my little gas stove and the tank of gas. I brought in all my stuff. Then I unpacked everything and settled myself in.

In the night I put on all the baby's clothes, and I put him to sleep with my brother and my little girls. And I stayed up, sitting back in the corner. There was a tape recorder and some tapes of music. I put on the tapes with the music, and I cried. The whole blessed night crying! Sitting, listening to the music, with my children fast asleep.

In the morning everybody in the house got up early, because they were all going out to pick coffee. The woman came with a little hot food and said to me, "Alicia, eat something."

I said to her, "No, thank you. I don't want to eat." Then I said, "I'm very grateful to you, but please give it to my children."

"No," she said, "I am going to serve the children in there. You eat this."

"No," I said, "I'm not hungry." And she took it back.

The children ate in the other room. And when I saw that they were eating and everything, I gave the family the milk and all the food. Then everyone left.

"I'm going to stay to make lunch," said the woman.

I said, "No, you go on. I will make it. Just tell me what it is I should prepare, and I'll do it. I've got to do something around here. Otherwise, I'm going to die in there, crying."

And she said, "You are right." So she left to pick coffee, and I set about making lunch.

When they came home, they said, "Alicia, come here. Eat."

"I'm not hungry."

Three days went by without my eating, without my drinking water, without anything. Think of it, what desperation! I suffered such resentment toward my mother, something I never, never would have imagined.

My children were eating and everything. Don Jorge said to me, "Alicia, don't you want to go to mass?"

"Yes" I said to him, "I want to go."

He said, "Leave the children here with . . . with Gabriella." Gabriella is his daughter.

"We will go to mass," he said, "so that you can get to know Heredia."

We went to Fátima Church, where they were holding a mass commemorating the deaths of the FMLN. Father Enrique was giving the mass. When I arrived, I started to pray with such devotion. I said to myself, "What am I going to do? My God, I owe so many favors to these people."

After the mass was over, I felt different. After I went to the mass, I already felt so different, as if I had strength. I no longer felt defeated, but full of strength.

Don Jorge said, "Alicia, let's go over to where Enrique is."

"What for?" I asked.

"Let's go," he told me, "It's that he is supposed to help the people who come. And especially you, since you have children. And you came without anything. He has to help you."

"Enrique?" I asked. "Is that the Father who is over there?"

"Yes."

"And what is his name again?"

"Enrique Flores."

"Enrique Flores?" I said. "He is a member of my family! Is he the man that went over there?"

"Well, yes," he said, "Don't you know him?"

"Yes," I said, "I know him, but here at mass, I didn't recognize him."

Then I went over there to the secretary's office that he had, and he acted as if he didn't know me. "I don't know you," Father Enrique said to me.

Robin: But he is . . . ?

Alicia: He is part of my family, yes.

Robin: But in what way? Uncle, or . . . ?

Alicia: No, no. We are cousins. Cousins. But when he held mass in Santa Teresa, he came to the house to sleep. And there we gave him food and everything. And here he acted as if he didn't know me.

So I said to him, "Ah, yes, here you don't know me. Remember when you carried off my cousin?" Because he carried her off. He stole her, and him a priest!

When I said this to him, he said, "No more. I'll give you 500 *colones* [$58]."

These 500 *colones*, when I gave them to Don Jorge, all of them, he said, "No, Alicia, why do you think you should do this? Buy something for your children."

But I said, "No, you have given me so much here. I haven't helped you in anything, not even with the electricity, not with the food. No."

"No, Alicia," he said, "No. Now it is you. Another day it could be me. It's all right. Buy yourself something over here for your children."

Well . . . "Besides," he said, "you need to travel to San José. Because you have to go to the relief office to present yourself. You have got to go and appear there. I can't take you now, because we are picking coffee, but tomorrow we'll go. Tomorrow I won't go to pick coffee. I will lose the day taking you, so that they will give you some help."

So Jorge lost a day of work to take me. We were there early, at about eight in the morning. I was the first person to pass through to see the High Commissioner. He then sent me to the Red Cross, because at that time it was the Red Cross that helped the refugees.

I arrived at the Red Cross, and they told me, "Well . . . you don't fit any category of aid, because you are responsible for too many children."

Then I said to Jorge, "So they are not going to give me anything?"

"It can't be, Alicia, that they won't give you anything! If they have helped vagrants," he said, "why are they not going to give to you?"

Then he said to me, "Let's go. I'm going to take you back over there." So I was given another appointment with the High Commissioner. I told him that I had gone to the Red Cross and that a woman had said to me this and that. That she had told me that they wouldn't give me any help, and that here . . . The High Commissioner told someone to write a letter. "Go back there," he said to me. "Knock on the door, and give this letter to the woman." It was a black woman, see. I arrived, knocked, and she was . . .

"I am busy," she said.

"But just a moment. Here, they sent this to you," I said. I put the letter on the table. Well, I've always been proud. Why am I going to tell her anything? I don't like to beg. When they humiliate me, I do it right back. I don't just let it go.

So I left the envelope there, and I made her open it. She stopped doing whatever it was she was doing, and I made her open it. When she saw where it was from, she said to me, "*Señora*, you told them that I had forced you to . . . ? You didn't have any reason to go over there. It's here . . ."

"I came here," I said, "and you told me that you wouldn't help me because I have a lot of children with me."

She said to me, "You don't have the right to go and accuse me over there." Who knows what they said to her in the letter. I didn't know because it came sealed.

Immediately she said to me, "Come here. Give me the data!"

And they gave me 1500 *colones* [$175], 1500 *Tico* [Costa Rican] *colones*. With this, I said to myself, I can look for a house. I found a house for 700 *colones* [$81]. The rest was left for food.

"Yes," I said to Jorge, "I'm not going to pay you for this favor you did me." He said, "No, Alicia. We were here to serve you this time."

Well, my mother later had a problem, and she came to live in my house. Back in El Salvador, in the little house that I paid for, she and my father had fought with each other, and well, now she had a problem. I already felt bad leaving my father in El Salvador. I didn't want to leave my mother, too, all alone and abandoned at her age. So I brought her to live in my house.

From this time on . . . well . . . it was like . . . I started to work here with people from . . . well . . . with . . .

Robin: In the daycare center?

Alicia: I am one of the founders of the daycare center.

Robin: But did you do that right away? Or did you have another job first?

Alicia: No. Or rather . . . I first started to work . . . I never got a job working in someone's house or anything like that. I began by working in organizations that help in the struggle. They began to know who I was. They said that our work was for El Salvador.

I worked with the Committee of Mothers back in El Salvador, after they had helped with my eye operation. So I began to work with them again here. I walked around everywhere with my three children. And they soon saw the necessity for a daycare center. Not just for me, but there were lots of people who had children and who had the same kinds of problems. At school they called the Salvadorans "guerrillas." Or if they called them Salvadorans, they didn't give them any attention at school. There was always discrimination against the Salvadorans. For this reason a daycare center would be good. So we had a meeting and examined our needs.

The daycare center was necessary. We wanted it so that the children could regain the values of our country, everything that it is, everything that it has, and where we came from and why we are here, and all that . . . our identity. We had a meeting, and we planned the project.

Robin: Where?

Alicia: In Heredia we did it. Well, we did it in various places, one part here, another part in the Sabana, well, wherever we got together. We noticed that we were attracting attention when the Costa Rican representative of CNK [sic: NCK, a Dutch relief agency] came to a meeting. He had come to Costa Rica to examine some other projects funded by the group.

A group of Costa Ricans offered to be our sponsors. We found out, however, that these Costa Ricans were very corrupt, even though they were close friends with some of the Salvadorans. When we got a little funding to set up the project, they took charge of the money. But the project didn't move forward.

Then we asked Higinio Alas to help by representing us as the rector of Fátima Church. And he agreed. In order to present a project, we had to have a responsible official or organization to back us up and see that the project went forward. In case things failed, it was the organization or agency that took the blame.

So we asked Father Higinio. He didn't say "no." He said that he would be happy to collaborate with us on the project. We then made an appointment to talk with the representative of the Dutch agency, and we went.

I was pregnant at the time. My new boyfriend got me pregnant. I feel better this time [Alicia is referring to her current pregnancy], but I felt very sick then.

When we got there, we presented our project. The man read it and looked at it and analyzed it. Then he said, "Well, I'm going to be honest with you. We cannot finance the project in its entirety. All we can finance are the materials and the immovable items. In other words, we can help you with the teaching materials, the housing of the project, the furniture, and everything . . . minus salaries and food. We don't finance meals."

But we said to him, "Look. We are women alone. We belong to the Committee of Mothers. We are women. We cannot pay for the meals of a daycare center. As mothers here, we are given money that barely serves to pay the rent, much less enough to support meals. And here we have a situation in which 100 percent of the children are undernourished. They are full of parasites. We have to get rid of the parasites. That is the goal of the daycare center. We don't just want a place to toss our children."

"Well," he said, or rather he had an interpreter there also, because he spoke very strangely . . . Italian, or . . .

Robin: What country was he from?

Alicia: From Holland. Then he said, "I'll take your proposal with me. Housing, furniture, and other materials can be financed for sure. When I get to Holland where they are having a meeting of all the Dutch relief organizations, I'll talk about your concerns. But don't expect anything. Don't expect us to finance the whole project."

"Fine. Do what you can. Let us tell you our concerns."

Everyone talked to him. I told him about how I had arrived in Costa Rica, what the situation was that forced me to leave El Salvador, and all that. The other women did the same. So he carried with him our concerns.

That was at the end of 1982. It took a long time, six months from the time he had been here. After exactly six months, in 1983, the first check came. When they finally responded to our request for a project, they sent us the money and told us to order the furniture and look for a place to rent immediately. And they said that the meals for the Center were being financed after all. There were going to be no problems.

Soon I was left alone to run the Center, because the women from the relief agency were told that they had to leave the country. They had to go to Nicaragua from here. The only person that was left was me [Alicia is exaggerating here].

And I said to them, "Ay, how am I going to do it?"

They said, "Alicia, you have to. Look for someone here to help."

I went to Father Higinio, and I told him that he was responsible for the daycare center, and we hoped that he would help us. I had never worked in a daycare center before. I didn't know what I was supposed to do or anything. Well, I had studied up to eighth grade, but I didn't have the faintest idea how to do it. I felt bad and I said, "Ay Diós, I'm going to fail at this . . . !"

Then I met a man who was a teacher in El Salvador and who had set up a home-school project for adolescents. I asked him for help. I wanted him to come work with me. But he couldn't give me a lot of time, only one quarter time, no more, but I learned a lot from him.

Father Higinio also helped me a great deal in other things. We were supposed to write up a narrative report telling how we had spent our money and all that. I was in charge of the management of the project, what was happening in the way of meals, what was being spent for furniture, and what was happening in the office. That is where I began to work. It was hard, because it was simply another thing I had to do, one more responsibility in addition to my children.

I always had the idea of studying. Always, that was something I wanted to do. I began to earn 3000 *colones* [$349] in the daycare center. I got 1800 *colones* [$209] from the Red Cross also, but after seven months of working in the daycare center this aid was cut off. Just because I was working in a project. Even though the daycare project is not recognized by the Red Cross since it is not financed by any institution from here, but rather by other . . . other . . . nations. They cut off my aid, and I was left with 3000 *colones*. But I had the advantage of living right in the place. I took care of the place and the children. Sometimes there were problems. The parents didn't come to get the children. No one came, and I had to take care of the children until seven at night. I was often left there alone.

I talked with my mother one day when she was there. I asked her to watch over the children. I arranged with her that if she would take care of the children for me, I would pay her. She didn't have to pay rent anyway, only the food. I would pay her something, so that I could continue studying. She said that, yes, that would be fine. She took care of the children, and I went at 6:20 p.m. to go to school. I finished ninth grade; here they call it the third year of secondary school. The director of the school was happy with me. But there were dances and other activities that I couldn't attend, and this lowered my points. So I told the director that I couldn't participate. I had children, and I had left my mother taking care of them.

"Yes, that's all right, go on home. But just you alone. Don't tell anybody. Because if you do, all the students will be after me to excuse them, and then what . . . ?" he said.

See . . . I used my children then, in order to be able to come home. So that my mother could go to her house. After I had finished ninth grade, the director said to me, "Alicia, keep on studying. I'll give you the matriculation fee. I'll help you. I can see that you are doing well here." The director has surely died by now.

But my mother said, "No, child, I cannot continue helping you."

So I was left with ninth grade, with the third year of secondary school. I said, "Ay, such sacrifice . . . ay . . . no, *hombre!*"

Then about half a year later I said, "Mamá, I want to go on studying. Can't you help me again?"

She said, "Look. Not to go to secondary school, no."

"No, I want to go to the Richard Nixon," I said.

Robin: Is that a school?

Alicia: Yes, it's a private school. Then she said, "How are you going to get the money to pay for that?"

I had talked to the girl who works with the funding of the daycare center. At this time it was no longer the CNK [sic: NCK], but the Swedes of the Cecamuresa [a branch of DIAKONÍA]. I talked with this girl, and she said, "Alicia, I can help you. If your mother helps you, I will help you to get through the course here." She could see that I had good grades.

So I told my mother that the girl would pay the course for me there and that I only needed my mother's help. My mother said, "All right."

In one year I completed the course in typing. It is the only one I did. I know that I am in debt to the Swedes, because they were the ones that helped me. And to my mother, who in the final instance also helped. If she had not taken care of the children, I would not have been able to go on studying.

So I completed it. It was the only course I got . . .

Robin: Are the majority of the Salvadoran mothers here alone, or do they have their families with them in Costa Rica?

Alicia: Well, of those that work at the Center, right now there are three of us alone. Alone with children. And from there, well, others, also women, have a husband here. And of the children, many of the children are alone with their mothers. They do not have fathers. There are others with stepfathers. But it isn't the same. A stepfather is never the same as a real father. The way I am too. Now I am with another man, imagine it. Looking for support, I found another. No, but the way it is going, it is terrible.

Robin: Is he a Salvadoran?

Alicia: He is a Costa Rican. But it is all the same to me, because I don't have the strength to go on alone. And with another child, it will be five.

Robin: Is that the way a woman alone here has to live?

Alicia: It's terrible. Because sometimes a person thinks that perhaps this one will be the *compañero* [male companion, common-law husband], the right one. A person has the illusion that, even though he isn't the children's real father, he could provide support. It's terrible. But that's the way it is. So we go on alone. *Echando pellejo y echando pa'lante* ["Wearing out your skin and going ahead," "Going ahead even though life is hard"].

I am watching the women make tortillas in the kitchen when Alicia comes up to me.

"Robin," she asks, "Would you please translate an article for me?"

"From English into Spanish?" I ask her cautiously. "How good a translation do you need?"

"Oh, I just want to hear what it says," Alicia answers.

I respond, "Then I'd be glad to."

The next morning Alicia brings me a feature article from an English-language newspaper. I peer at the photo and recognize Alicia immediately, standing under a tree with two of her children. I take a minute to read the article to myself, and then I translate it for her. The feature summarizes Alicia's escape from persecution in El Salvador and tells how she is now struggling to make ends meet as a widow and refugee. Also outlined in the article is the story of Ligia's husband Marco who fled to Costa Rica because he was accused of providing medical help to "subversives" in El Salvador.

At the end of my translation, Alicia looks at me expectantly. I am not sure what she hopes from me, so I ask a neutral question, "Did you just recently receive this article in the mail?"

Alicia responds, "No. I've had it for several months. Someone translated it for me once before, last year."

I suddenly realize that Alicia has requested this translation as much for my benefit as for her own. She wants me to know that she has been interviewed by reporters and that the news of her plight has reached my country. I try to imagine what this means to her. Almost everyone likes the idea of appearing in a newspaper. And being the central figure of a feature story in a U.S. newspaper must be quite an experience for a young peasant woman from El Salvador.

I wonder also if Alicia isn't proud of appearing in the article alongside a prominent physician. From an international perspective, her story is clearly at least as important as that of Ligia's husband.

Alicia was undoubtedly given some money for her willingness to grant the interview for this article. She told me later that a U.S. reporter periodically sent her checks to help support her children. All the women were made aware of the potential monetary value of their stories through incidents such as this. The tension at the Center about keeping the *testimonios* on file was a direct result of such awareness. The pertinent questions for all of them were: Who has the rights, not legal but moral, over the *testimonios* when they are considered a valuable commodity? And how does the acceptance of money for a recorded *testimonio* affect the group's political efforts?

10

Mirabela

"Robin, when will you let me talk with you again?"

Although the *testimonios* were given to me privately, there was considerable group pressure as to their form and content. Numerous encounters with reporters and relief agencies had informed the women regarding the significance of their stories to the outside world. They had heard of Rigoberta Menchú, who at the time had not yet won the 1992 Nobel Peace Prize for her *testimonio* and other work as a Guatemalan Mayan Indian activist (see *I . . . Rigoberta Menchú; An Indian Woman in Guatemala*, edited and translated by Burgos-Debray, 1984), but who was becoming increasingly well known in Latin America.

It was on the basis of such awareness that the refugees were able to critique their own *testimonios*, openly judging the stories for their potential public impact. My informal conversations at the Center revealed that, for the refugees, the degree of personal tragedy inherent in the story was the most important element. They felt that María's experience of rape, violence, and murder was essential to my research. They were aware of Alicia's exceptional talent as a storyteller and hoped that I would be touched emotionally by her *testimonio* (even while they feared I might become overly influenced by her strong personality). Of importance also was the obvious linkage of the story to the political struggle; thus, the political rhetoric of Mirabela was considered another appropriate form for the *testimonio* to take.

Part of the inherent strength of the *testimonios* lay in their association with other local forms of oral traditions. Indigenous groups in the Central American region have long depended on improvisational performance to pass on cultural values and traditions (see Bricker 1973). A northern extension of this tradition can be found among Hispanic women of the United States in El Teatro Campesina, which was founded in 1965 as a vehicle of Chicano political activism (Broyles-Gonzalez 1990). This latter is a theater with emphasis not on individual performers (as in the U.S. mainstream theater), but with focus on the group. Because of its activist purpose, it is centered around oral improvisation and a flexible response to changing political climate, rather than on a written script that can become politically outdated. The refugee women show their familiarity with this dramatic tradition both in their religious and political celebrations involving improvisational theater and in their impromptu dramas enacted with the children at the Center.

The *testimonio* is not usually viewed by outsiders as oral performance, since by the time it reaches the majority of its "audience" it occurs in written form, having gone through the various processes of transcription, translation, and editing. The *testimonio* is more often spoken of as "resistance literature" (Harlow 1987) or as an "outlaw genre" (Kaplan 1992:119), which begins in oral form because of the assumed lack of writing ability on the part of the narrator, a person that has to be "represented" by a professional writer (Beverley 1992:97). In the case of the refugees, I felt that they believed in the theatrical dimension of their stories, not fully realizing, perhaps, that much of the emotion and drama of the interviews might be lost in the written version.

Nevertheless, the women had a sense of the flexibility of the written version; they knew that my understanding of their situation was significant to our collaboration. Mirabela and Alicia both worked hard to influence me in this regard, recognizing that my personal feelings about them could affect my later presentation of their *testimonios*.

Mirabela, whose initial interview had been interrupted by a broken tape recorder, had more opportunity than most to respond to my reactions as a listener. In the first place, she had to repeat her story so that I could tape it again. In the second version, I noticed that she had made a subtle switch toward a more personal angle—giving added details about her husband and parents and reconstructing her conversations with people—even though she retained her original political rhetoric throughout. She must have been sensitive to what interested me most in her story.

By the time Mirabela insists on talking with me a month later, she clearly wants to relate to me more personally. For my part, I am delighted to have a chance to break down her political facade and find out what she is really like. We arrange to have her come to my apartment at the end of her workday on a Monday afternoon.

I walk over to the Center at four o'clock to pick Mirabela up, so that we can walk back the few blocks to my house together. I am nervous about inviting her over, because I am aware that she might find my apartment very luxurious in comparison with her own. At this time, both my daughter and I sleep on mattresses laid on the floor, and our livingroom furniture consists of only two chairs, a rug, and a few plants. Most of this is on loan from friends. Nevertheless, I know that our two-bedroom apartment will seem very spacious to her. There are only two of us living in it, and each of us has a separate bedroom.

Mirabela has described her apartment to me as poor and shabby, not worth the 3000 *colones* ($42) that she is paying monthly for rent. The roof leaks badly, and the kitchen and bathroom floors are unending pools of muddy rainwater. Her landlady is trying to raise the rent and definitely not considering the idea of repairing the roof.

In the process of trying to find a better house, Mirabela has experienced considerable prejudice because of her refugee status. "When you are out looking for a house to live in, they ask you questions about whether you are a Catholic, and why you came to Costa Rica," Mirabela says. She says the landlords always want to know about her husband. In her answers to these questions she tries to imply that she and her husband are separated for personal reasons. She is afraid to tell them that he is one of the "disappeared" in El Salvador. Such an answer could brand her as a guerrilla and a subversive, thus making it impossible for her to find a house.

So I am prepared for the questions she asks. She wants to know what I pay in rent, where I have gotten my furniture, and why I do not have a television. I have decided to answer all her questions openly and deal with the consequences later. Mirabela's *testimonio* has given me the feeling that she is intolerant of any display of wealth, but I am not yet sure what she might consider a "display." Surely it does not help that I am paying 14,500 *colones* ($200) in rent, more than the total of her monthly salary.

As it turns out, Mirabela is sympathetic about the rent I am paying. She confides to me later that she can find me a three bedroom house in a little village for half that cost. She does find one aspect of my house most attractive, however. This is the security of the several locks on the doors and the bars on all the windows. Even the poor have trouble with thieves in Costa Rica.

When I thought about it later, I realized Mirabela must have found my apartment dreadfully sparse and lonely looking. Most Central Americans are used to living in close quarters, surrounded by their large families and their possessions. While they might envy my freedom and my apparent riches, they do not envy my lifestyle, traveling to strange lands and living far away from my parents and other comforting relatives.

As we sit in my sparsely furnished livingroom, I ask Mirabela the questions I have prepared after reading through her *testimonio*. My assistant Judít has transcribed Mirabela's tape for me, and I hope to clear up certain words and phrases in the recording. I start with these. Then I go on to ask about her husband and her father, hoping she will open up a bit. I do not tape this session, taking notes instead. Mirabela seems like a different person to me. Gone is the strident tone and the political rhetoric of her *testimonio*. Mirabela is talking to me as a person, as a woman, even lowering her voice sometimes in conspiratorial whispers.

Although Mirabela's story remains highly politicized, there are contrasts, even inconsistencies, between her taped *testimonio* and this more informal interview. For instance, Mirabela had indicated in her *testimonio* that her conflict with her father arose due to political differences between them. Mirabela's resentment towards her parents' conservative political position began when she was a small child, though her opinions didn't surface until she was married. Her husband's union involvement and his subsequent problems with the Salvadoran authorities finally gave her the courage to oppose her father openly.

In her *testimonio* Mirabela had depicted her father as angry, unreasonable, mean, and arrogant—a tyrant. When she had spoken of her parents and their political opinions, she had said, "If they were to die while I was here in exile, I believe that they would die wrong. . . ." Not surprisingly, she had chosen these words for a particular effect, to impress upon me the contrast between her own "correct" political viewpoint and the conservative perspective of her parents. The implication of this statement, however, had also been that her parents were both alive, which was no longer true at the time she had given me her *testimonio*. Her father had died the previous year, in 1987, of a heart attack. Now, only in answer to my direct questions does Mirabela tell me the truth about his death.

According to Mirabela's unrecorded story, her father's heart became weakened by two violent incidents, the first of which happened two years prior to his death. Her father kept his guns stored in the two guardhouses that flanked the drive to the house. A group of men—not clearly identifiable as either military or guerrillas—arrived to appropriate the arms. Mirabela's father tried to fight them off with his bare fists, getting badly beaten up in the process. The second incident involved the loss of his favorite son. The son was ambushed and killed as he rode down the avenue from the house. Again it was not known who was responsible, the military or the guerrillas. After the murder, her father's health deteriorated quickly, leading finally to his heart attack. Information about both these incidents came to Mirabela in Costa Rica through the infrequent letters from her family and through Salvadorans who maintained contacts in her native village.

After hearing the story of her father's failing health, I could see why the information had been left out of her *testimonio*. Mirabela was hesitant to portray her father as a complex and possibly sympathetic human being. For Mirabela's political purposes he needed to remain a tyrant, even though on a personal level she was able to reveal to me the complexity of her real feelings toward him.

Although Mirabela did not agree with her parents, she found herself in political agreement with her husband's mother. Her mother-in-law, though not at all sophisticated, was a determined woman. She first enlisted Mirabela's help in locating her eldest son, who was one of the "disappeared." Later, as members of the newly founded Committee of Mothers, the two worked together to search for Mirabela's husband and others. The elder woman's own daughters had abandoned her, probably because they felt that the search for their brothers would endanger all of them. Mirabela, in exile, still felt closer to her mother-in-law than to her biological parents.

Mirabela: My mother-in-law has four sons lost . . . two sons that have disappeared and two sons killed. A peasant woman who can neither read nor write, who doesn't even know the city. I had to walk around with her . . . in this direction, in that direction . . . and such a fighter.
She is still walking around. She went to stay with one of my sisters. She is probably still there. Because her children, my mother-in-law's other children, have turned their backs on her, because of what she was doing, for the work she was involved in, for requesting freedom for her eldest son who had disappeared. They rejected her. So there she is, staying with one of my sisters, and wandering around.

Robin: Where is she now?

Mirabela: Back there, in El Salvador. In 1982 I went around trying to find out if I could bring her here. But since she doesn't have a birth certificate and doesn't even remember where she was born, or the date or anything else, I haven't been able to do anything about bringing her. But I know she is there wandering about suffering, staying with friends, and trying to pass the time . . .

Robin: How is she able to eat and sleep?

Mirabela: They give her something where she stays. They give her food and a bed.

Mirabela's political life continues to affect her personal relationships even in Costa Rica. Although she no longer has much contact with her extended family, she is now the mother of three school-aged children. Because of her activities in Salvadoran politics, which often keep her occupied until late at night, her children have to cook for themselves in the evenings and put themselves to bed. Mirabela expresses her concern about leaving them alone so much, but feels her efforts towards Salvadoran solidarity to be essential.

Robin: And of all your family, only you and your children are here? No nieces or nephews? No one else?

    Mirabela: No one. I am here alone with my three children. But sometimes I start to think, and I say, "Well, for the children, really . . ." because there are times when I want to leave, and I see my husband say "no," so I don't leave. There have been times that I have even decided, "Fine, I will leave you all behind and go. You stay here, but I don't feel—how shall I put it—tranquil about being here and knowing that one is truly needed elsewhere, do you understand?"

    Mirabela's motivations to continue her political activities stem largely from the inspiration of her husband, Hernando, who disappeared in 1980. Now she can only rely on the memories of that relationship, but the childhood sweetheart that she had married at age twenty-six had been a close friend and political confidant, and her feelings for him still guide her actions in Costa Rica.

    Mirabela: I can also do things here, the same way I did back there. My husband told me, "Once you are outside the door, don't count on me. Count on me only inside the door. Because the day that I leave and don't come back, you know what you are supposed to do. Go on in the same way, and explain to the children why their father is not with them."
    And even though it hurts me to tell them why they are not with their papá, at the same time it makes me strong. I tell them that he died for a just cause, for something that he was hoping would happen in El Salvador. [Mirabela does not know for certain he is dead; he is among the "disappeared."] He wanted his children, and everybody's children, to live in a just society. All these words come to my mind and make me dedicate myself to my work. And even though I leave the children alone, I know I am not doing the wrong thing. I am doing it as part of my work, for all the people who want to be free, for us who want to be free. . . .

    Mirabela and I work for a couple of hours in the livingroom, editing and discussing the details of her *testimonio*, while my daughter entertains herself by reading a book. Finally, Jessica emerges from the bedroom and insists that I give her something to eat. The three of us sit down for a simple macaroni-and-cheese supper in our small dining area off the patio. After we serve her, Mirabela says she cannot eat much cheese; the oil makes her ulcers act up terribly. I promptly give her something else to eat, but the subsequent conversation is revealing. Mirabela reviews for me all the possible causes of her ulcer, one of which understandably includes the stress of civil war. Others involve the general problems of being a refugee—lack of money, poor housing, job insecurity, and the instability of interpersonal relationships. The focus of Mirabela's frustrations during this conversation, however, centers around her fellow worker Alicia.
    Mirabela came to the daycare center in September of 1987, a little less than a year before I met her, but long after her arrival in Costa

Rica. She was hired to work in the kitchen, cooking and washing dishes. At first, she and Alicia had been on good terms. As evidence of this, Mirabela tells me about a small party that had been given on her birthday soon after she arrived. On birthdays at the daycare center, each person is expected to offer the birthday celebrant a verbal compliment. At this party Alicia had declared Mirabela to be a wonderful friend, one for whom she would do anything. Mirabela felt that the compliment was sincere at the time.

Later that year Mirabela became sick, part of it due to bad feet, and she was ordered by the doctor to take a month of sick leave. Mirabela says that there was considerable angry murmuring about her month's leave because she had not held her job at the Center very long. When she returned to work, she was transferred to the preschool section to help with the older children, a task that would allow her to stay off her feet. It was during this period that Mirabela's conflicts with Alicia began.

In December the Center had a Christmas party to which all members of the staff were invited. Names were drawn for a gift exchange, with Alicia getting Mirabela's name. According to Mirabela, Alicia's sarcastic response was, "Guess whose name I drew! And now I have to buy her a present!" Since that time the two have not been on speaking terms. Alicia and Mirabela rub shoulders every day, passing in the narrow hallways of the Center and not saying a word.

Some time after this Christmas incident, Alicia became threatened with the possibility of a miscarriage. Mirabela was still working in the preschool section because of her problems with her feet; Alicia was doing the cleaning. Because of her pregnancy, Alicia's doctor decided that she should not be doing such heavy work and ordered that her tasks at the Center be lightened. Alicia was then shifted to work in the kitchen, forcing Mirabela out of the more desirable preschool position and into cleaning. Later illnesses caused still more task exchanges. Each woman constantly had to accommodate herself to help the other, and both resented the imposition.

When Mirabela starts talking about Alicia, she returns to the strident tone I have heard during her *testimonio*. Her gestures become intense. Not only is Mirabela angry because Alicia will not speak to her; she says that Alicia creates problems for everyone at the Center. Moreover, Mirabela cannot understand Ligia's patience with Alicia. If Mirabela herself were the director, she would . . . ! I suggest that Alicia might be under psychological stress because of all she has been through. (For the purposes of this conversation, I decide to accept Mirabela's premise that Alicia creates problems for everyone at the Center.) Mirabela's response is that every one of the women has had terrible experiences, and none of the others show such psychological symptoms.

I then suggest to Mirabela, as I had earlier to Doña Ligia, that

Alicia might be causing problems because she is pregnant and has already
been abandoned by the child's father. Mirabela's response to this is that
Alicia has no principles, referring to her sex life and the fact that the new
pregnancy will be Alicia's second child out of wedlock. Mirabela sees
her behavior as indicating a lack of commitment to the political struggle
in El Salvador. Alicia does not show the proper discipline.

For Mirabela, the editing of her *testimonio* included pressuring
me toward a bias in her favor, and against Alicia. She obviously thought
she was a better representative of the political goals of the group. Even
though I tried to remain sympathetic to her approach, I still felt the need
to hold back my judgment. It was a delicate balancing act.

It is getting late, and my daughter needs some help with her
homework, so we all run out to the car through the rain to take Mirabela
home. The windows of the car are all fogged up, but Mirabela directs me
slowly to a side street on the edge of Heredia. Her house is a small
place, not much more than six feet wide along the front. The door opens
onto a tiny room with a small couch facing a television set in the corner.
Mirabela's two young girls—ages ten and thirteen—greet us from the
couch as we arrive. They have supper all prepared and have apparently
been waiting for their mother to come home. I am surprised that
Mirabela has not mentioned they might be waiting. She replies that her
children are accustomed to her coming home at all hours of the night.

Mirabela shows us down a long, dark corridor, past a small
bedroom or two, to the kitchen at the back of the house. We see where
the rain comes down into the kitchen. The floor is wet on one side of the
room. Mirabela asks us if we would stay for a bite to eat. I know by
this time that Salvadoran custom requires her to offer us something to eat.
I also know that we can refuse her politely without causing offense. So
I thank her instead for all her help, and my daughter and I take our leave.

Because of their strained relationship with one another, I found
myself constantly comparing Alicia and Mirabela in order to understand
them. Both were widows of the Salvadoran conflict whose husbands had
been killed because of their union activities. Each had adapted in
different ways to the struggle in El Salvador, and each was now taking
a separate path in her new life as head of a family in Costa Rica. Alicia
was searching for a new husband, and Mirabela was helping in the
political struggle. They provided an interesting contrast in personality.
Moreover, each of their *testimonios* offered a uniquely powerful
statement. While Alicia's story maintained its strength through poetic
drama, Mirabela's story indicated political conflict everywhere, even in
her most intimate personal relationships.

11

María

"'Lady, I thought you were stupid.'"

Celina, a young Spanish-speaking student on vacation from Bryn Mawr College for the summer, has been volunteering at the Center for about a month, helping with fund-raising activities. She has been on the phone, setting up appointments with various relief agencies in Costa Rica in the hopes of getting international aid. She has also arranged for the preschoolers at the Center to perform a show of Salvadoran songs and dances at local private schools, where the wealthy parents might be persuaded to donate used clothes and toys for the Center. Celina's time in Costa Rica is limited, however; everyone knows she will have to leave many of these tasks unfinished. The women at the Center plan to carry on with her efforts after she returns to the United States.

Having heard about my work and the *testimonios* I have gathered, Celina comes up to me a few days before her departure and asks me to help her set up a group session with the women, which she can then record.

"What do you hope to do with the stories?" I ask.

Celina answers, "I will give them to my father for a newspaper story. He is a reporter. If he doesn't use them himself, he knows other people who can."

Even though I am nervous about this duplication of my data, I am grateful to Celina for inviting me to participate. The meeting is arranged. Except for Carolina and Eduardo who are reluctant to join, the Salvadorans are clearly eager to have another opportunity to express themselves. At the appointed time everyone crowds into Doña Ligia's office. Things are relatively quiet; it is naptime at the Center. Eduardo and Carolina have been assigned the duty of watching over the children who are resting on mattresses in the other room. In spite of their hesitancy about being part of the meeting, the two teachers peek in periodically at the door to see how things are going.

The women chat together in excited anticipation. There are not quite enough chairs in the room, so Mirabela and Carmen bustle around to find more. Finally, everyone is settled, and Doña Ligia asks who wishes to be first. Carmen suggests, "Mirabela, why don't you start?"

Celina and I each turn on our tape recorders and wait for the women to begin. The session, emotional as it is, does not evolve as planned. Mirabela begins with her usual courage, yet I notice she does not include any of the intriguing details about her life that lend credibility to her story. Then the focus is on María, whose intensely personal story is so crucial to their political message. But María looks up at the circle of women, tries to speak, and bursts into tears; everyone is depending on her, but she cannot utter a word.

My heart goes out to her. Her tormentors are still with her; the demons will never go away.

María's traumatic experience of rape and murder has profoundly influenced her attitude towards men. Even though she says in her *testimonio* that she "forgives" the soldiers who committed these atrocities, since they were only acting on orders from superior officers, it is probable that she will never be able to respond positively to any man again.

Robin: Is your husband still back in El Salvador?

María: No. Well, yes. He was killed, too . . . after I came here.

Robin: You say you would like to go back to your country, you and your three children. Would you be able to start another family? Or is this not possible for a woman who already has children?

María: Oh, no. No. I would stay alone with my three children. Because . . . it's just that . . . I don't know . . . see, now that this has happened to me . . . well . . . I feel a . . . disgust for men. I don't know . . . after everything that happened to me . . . well . . . I feel a great tenderness for my children, and for my sisters and brothers, as you can imagine. But . . . to look for a new husband? No. I feel something like hate, you understand? What I feel is disgust. And hatred.

Robin: I see . . . Do you have a house here alone with your three children? You aren't living with other people?

María: With my brother. He lives with us. I feel that he supports me . . . in whatever . . . that he has some respect ["respect" is a discreet way of saying that he doesn't abuse her or her daughters sexually] . . . since now I have a . . . my daughter is now fifteen years old, and . . . well . . . I feel that he supports me, and that he shows respect. . . .

Cultural notions of masculinity and femininity among Salvadorans follow the general pattern for the Latin concept of *machismo* (for discussions of *machismo* see Pescatello 1973), where men are viewed as being the possessors of women and take the active role in any male-female relationship. If their behavior becomes uncontrollable, this is only a reflection of the degree to which their instinctive nature has developed. Women, on the other hand, are viewed as being dependent on men by nature and are assumed to be fulfilled only by the bearing of children. Women are not supposed to enjoy the sexual relationship with a man. For them, sex is a very private, secret, and even shameful act; for men, in contrast, sex is a way of proving one's manhood.

Although a man is expected to be the wage earner and the authority figure for a family, there is considerable societal toleration for irresponsible male behavior. Men are often absent from home, sometimes for legitimate reasons such as earning a living, but other times for socializing with other women; and the physical abuse of a woman, while it is criticized by others, is also seen as part of a man's nature. Thus, María's "forgiveness" of the soldiers who raped and tortured her, while extreme, fits into the context of her culture.

In El Salvador traditional patterns of authority based on *patronismo* [paternalism] run parallel to and interact with accepted views of male-female interaction. Not only are males supposed to be heads of their households, but there exist hierarchies of male authority. Within the family, fathers exert control over sons, and elder brothers over younger ones. Outside the family, men still rule, but it is the rich who have power over the poor, the landed gentry over the landless peasants, the factory owners over their workers, and the military or government officials over ordinary civilians.

Traditionally, the wealthy and powerful are also supposed to be responsible for their underlings. They are supposed to protect them and watch out for their welfare, just as the male head of the family is supposed to take care of his wife and children. Under the best of conditions, for instance, the factory owner listens to his workers and tries to make them happy, knowing that a happy worker is more productive and less likely to cause trouble. But just as there is considerable toleration for a husband's irresponsible behavior toward his wife, there is also societal toleration for the irresponsible actions of those in authority. In the same way that a woman in this society finds herself forced to concur with the wishes of the men around her, the poorer in the society have traditionally found themselves in a similar position with regard to the wealthy.

Thus, confronted with public officials who reversed their policies with regard to her economic situation, María was hurt and confused. Early in her refugee experience, María had been overwhelmed with emergency relief aid. Because of the injuries she had received at the hands of the Salvadoran army, she and her children remained under total emergency care for many months. During this period she was led to believe that her situation was special and that she deserved unlimited long-term benefits.

María: I still go to OAR-CASPRE [relief agencies] to get help from them, for my children, so that . . . but they said "no" to me. They made me fill out medical forms and all that. Even the other doctor did. They did not want to help me.

"Why are you asking for so much? We are not going to look at your case anymore," they said to me. As if they had never told me that they were going to consider my case to be special.

I even went to see if they could give me a sewing machine for my daughter because she is learning to sew and to make candy. But they did not want to do this either. I do not know why it is that they cannot look at individual cases.

But no. Never. Better not. They no longer want to give to me. They have only said that I should fill out medical forms. They would not do what they did before and help me with anything. Soon you see that they are deceiving you.
. . .

In spite of her confusion over her inability to influence public officials, María demonstrated considerable presence of mind in matters of greater urgency, such as the protection of her children. María's ramshackle shelter built onto the back of someone else's house may have been substandard housing, but she knew it was better than living in the streets. So when the landlord tried to kick her out in order to get higher rent for the place, she was strong enough to fight him back.

María: Where we live the landlord gave us notice, which means you have to get out of the house quickly [Costa Rica has tight restrictions against landlords in favor of the renter, but perhaps the landlord felt he did not have to follow the law because the refugees were not legal citizens]. But I had all the receipts that he had given me each month for the rent. I went to show them to a lawyer.

My landlord is the director of the university. I said to him, "Look, if I didn't have any children, I wouldn't care if you threw me out of the house at any time. I could stand it for a while living on the street. But I have children, and they are in school. Since you are this way . . . a person pays you every month. There are times when she goes without something so that she always has enough to pay the rent. She does this because she is afraid, well, that she will be thrown out of the house. Every month I am supposed to be paying you. So I pay you every month. And here are the receipts." I showed him all the receipts.

Then he said to me, "Lady, I thought you were stupid." That is what the man said, the director of the university, whose rents are so . . . !

María's psychological and physical wounds are evidenced in her listlessness and pessimism about the future. Like the other women, she worries about her continued family responsibilities and about the security of her job at the Center, but for her the work provides an escape from the mental torture she still feels.

María: The best thing here is to work. I went to a psychologist earlier, but I stopped going. My work has acted as my therapy. I try to concentrate on my work. I think about my job. I think about my children. Only these things. Sometimes I remember what happened to me, but I try to leave it aside. Sometimes I cannot . . . and I start to cry. Then my children . . . they tell me to be brave, that I shouldn't cry, and that someday we will return to El Salvador . . .

I feel good about my work here. But if they take away the funding . . . those people who are financing the project . . . then what am I going to do with my children? How am I going to survive? How am I going to endure it?

12

Rina

"My husband abandoned me . . . just when I needed him most."

After the arrival of the Salvadorans in Costa Rica, the Swedish agency DIAKONÍA offered classes to all the refugees. Courses in nutrition, sewing, and business management were all well-attended. At one time during the initial years, the Swedes also offered a class in feminism or women's liberation, which they felt would be useful in helping the women to become self-sufficient. I do not know the exact title of the course, but as my friend Tina explained it to me, the class was intended to focus on the power relationships between men and women, with an emphasis on the cultural notion of *machismo*. The Swedes at DIAKONÍA were surprised to discover, however, that the refugee women were not particularly interested in becoming "liberated," at least not in the sense that the Swedes understood.

One reason for refugee indifference to such a class came from the greater urgency the women felt concerning their day-to-day survival, a more crucial issue than the minor irritants of *machismo*. Instead of struggling against dominating husbands, these women wanted practical lessons in coping by themselves in a new environment. The civil war and the refugee situation had made them acutely aware of the vulnerability of the men in their lives. The women had to work on issues that helped the men as well as the women.

Attitudes of the Salvadoran refugee women were bolstered by the relatively high legal status of women in Costa Rica. Although the cultural notion of *machismo* has a strong influence on interpersonal relationships in Costa Rica, the laws are explicitly supportive of equality between the sexes, especially in regard to business (Biesanz 1982:107–18). Sex discrimination in hiring and salary is forbidden by law, and women have the right to make contracts, borrow money, and form business corporations. Moreover, the special needs of women are taken into account by law, which gives women the right to maternity leave and time off to nurse their babies once they return to work. Although upper-class Costa Rican women are more "liberated" than lower-class and middle-class women, the refugees are conscious of the relative freedom of women on all levels of their adopted society. All the refugee women were influenced by this progressive cultural attitude toward women, even when they occasionally felt threatened by it as upsetting to their own cultural norms.

Related to the cultural notion of *machismo*, often referred to as the reverse side of the same coin, is the concept of *marianismo*. Having strong roots in the Marian cult of the European Catholic Church, in which the Virgin Mary is worshipped, it may also draw from such indigenous traditions as the worship of the goddess Tonantzin ["Our Mother"] in Mexico (Stevens 1973:91–94). The secular variety of *marianismo* is the belief in the moral and spiritual superiority of women (as opposed to the intellectual, political, and economic superiority of men). Under this notion women are admired for their capacity for humility and self-sacrifice. They are praised for submission to the excessive demands of husbands, sons, fathers, and brothers and for infinite patience in the face of man's infidelity and childishness. These feminine qualities are viewed as saintly; the woman who lives up to them is staunchly supported by her family and society (Stevens 1973:94–96).

Although such a concept mirrors *machismo*, I cannot say that I often saw the refugee women acting in a humble and submissive manner. When Rina gave me her *testimonio* in her home, after I had interviewed most of the other women, she told me she had to ask for her husband's permission first. However, this appeared to be merely a formality, a politeness. There was never any question that he might refuse to allow her to talk with me. As a matter of fact, although I saw Rina's husband later on a number of social occasions involving large groups of refugees, he remained very much in the background during my interactions with Rina. This is not to say that the refugee women felt free to do anything they wished. If I had been a male researcher, I probably would not have had permission to speak with any of the women alone.

Another aspect of *marianismo* more relevant to the refugee situation is the underlying assumption that women are supposed to fulfill their roles as wives and mothers. In a society where a high value is placed on families, these traditional roles are clearly a source of pride. Motherhood, especially, gave the refugee women a sense of well-being and warmth, even when the responsibility of having children was often overwhelming. Cultural support for this essential role lent the women a self assurance that extended well beyond the home. Not only did the women exhibit confidence in their work with the children at the Center;

they had all demonstrated courage in the face of personal tragedy, as evidenced in their *testimonios*.

Rina, for example, was a strong-willed young woman, who knew clearly what she wanted. Her decision to emigrate to Canada to be with the rest of her family was a conscious choice, one she herself worked hard to accomplish. Rina's mother Teresa, also a vigorous woman, had taken charge of her large family and had significantly contributed to the Salvadoran refugee community during those early years following her exile. Everyone praised the courage of this older woman who had first helped to found the Center and then later emigrated to Canada. What I discovered about Rina and her mother, as well as about many of the other refugee women, was that they were the guiding force in their families, even when there were men around to help. This seemed to contradict what I had heard about *machismo*, even from the women themselves.

One significant strength demonstrated by Rina and the others at the Center was the ability to support and raise their own families. This was not an aspect of their lives unique to being a refugee; many of them would have had similar experiences back home. In the 1970s and early 1980s in El Salvador, there was a distinguishable change in traditional family ties. For example, in 1974 the marriage rate for El Salvador was only 4.24 per 1000 inhabitants, as compared to the 10 per 1000 that was considered normal, and in rural areas, where many of the refugees were from, the marriage rate went down from a low of 2.48 per 1000 in 1976 to an even lower 1.98 per 1000 in 1982 (New Americas Press 1989:119).

These figures were undoubtedly matched by the large numbers of women who lost their husbands in one way or another to the conflict. Men went into the army or became part of the guerrilla movement. Some were kidnapped or killed. Many had to travel across the country to find work, in some cases because there was nothing available nearby and in other cases because they needed to hide from the authorities. A certain percentage of the men emigrated abroad in search of jobs or safety.

In spite of the low marriage rate and other negative influences on the family, as I observed among the refugees, Salvadoran men and women often lived together and even had children as a common-law couple. Rina, for example, had never married the father of her first two children back in El Salvador, and, as her *testimonio* reveals, her marriage to the father of her third child was accomplished quietly in Costa Rica and only when circumstances forced the couple into it. As the refugee women told me many times, in the final analysis, it was the woman who had to look out for herself and her children.

Rina: My *compañero*, the father of my two daughters . . . he is back there in El Salvador. He abandoned me because he was afraid; my family was very much under pursuit. While I was pregnant with my second daughter, I was living with my father-in-law, with his father. But my husband abandoned me when I was eight months pregnant with Elena, just when I needed him most. Back there it is fear that destroys a person. Anyway, he abandoned me.

I came alone to Costa Rica. Well, actually I came with my family, with my mamá and my brothers and sisters, but this isn't the same as coming with your husband or your *compañero*. The girls' father stayed home; I never heard a word from him again. [Rina told me later that her common-law husband had taken over the house that her father had built in the resettlement community back home.] It was cowardice that made him abandon me when I was eight months pregnant. He didn't want to be with me because . . . because, as he said, they were out to kill me.

Robin: And the man you live with now . . . ?

Rina: I knew him from school back in El Salvador. I met him again here, and we got together. We have been living together now for six years. He is the father of my little boy. And two days ago, we got married in a civil ceremony.

Robin: You did? Congratulations!

Rina: Well, we got married legally because . . . we were living together and decided that the children needed a name. And since the little girls' papá didn't want to recognize them, this other man gave them his name. So the girls belong to him, for all practical purposes, since he has helped me to raise them and get them educated.

Robin: How is he doing here? Does he have a job?

Rina: He . . . we are having such a difficult time right now because he is not supposed to be here. They are not allowing him to remain. They don't want to give him permission to work, and they don't want to give him refugee status either. In 1985 he had to leave Costa Rica to return to El Salvador to visit his mother. She was seriously ill, and he hadn't seen her in five years, not since he came here in 1980. He was desperate to see her again, so he left Costa Rica. But when he tried to return, they wouldn't let him in; he had lost his status as refugee.

I sent him the money to come, because I was all alone here. I had been staying with my mother, but two months after he left Costa Rica, she went off to Canada, leaving me alone. I was alone with my own family, my three children, nobody else. So I called him on the telephone. He told me that he would like to return, to come and help me out, but he couldn't figure out a way to do it. He couldn't get into Costa Rica, because the government wouldn't let him in. He finally came in as contraband . . . he was smuggled in.

Robin: On foot? Or how?

Rina: In a trailer truck.

Robin: In a trailer truck? Hidden in the back?

Rina: No, he came as a transporter, as part of one of those shipments hauling merchandise, market products, or clothes, or . . . he came in a trailer truck full of eggs. Eggs were scarce at that time, so they were being transported here. He arrived as if he had never been in this country before. But when he tried to arrange for his documents, when he tried to get legal resident status, the doors were closed to him.

At first we couldn't find any way of getting documentation under such circumstances. Even worse, he got into an accident that made him unable to work; he lost most of his hearing in both ears. Now we have a lawyer. We have to pay the lawyer's fee, and we also pay for his legal right to be here [I got the impression this latter payment might be a bribe]. We are still involved in this situation. And these days I am waiting for an interview with the Canadian Embassy, so that, if God wills it, we can get out of here . . .

Robin: Does your new husband also have an interview with the embassy? Is it for the entire family?

Rina: Yes, he has one, too. [Rina told me later that one of the reasons they had finally decided to marry was to allow him the opportunity to go to Canada with them, since men without families are not usually chosen as immigrants.] So we are waiting. The days seem very long to us, especially since he only has permission to stay in Costa Rica until the end of this month.

Robin: And what can you do after that? Can you renew his permission?

Rina: We start the battle over again, to see if the lawyer can get it for us for another few days. Right now he comes under the rule of "protective shelter" [*amparo*], as they call it, which is only temporary. He doesn't have any secure permission. He went to request a work permit from the *Ministerio de Trabajo* [Ministry of Labor] and was rejected. They said that, no, he couldn't work here even though he has a son who is a Costa Rican; that doesn't mean anything. They didn't give him the permit.

He keeps going to the Immigration Office, and they tell him he cannot work, and if they come and catch him working they will fine him or deport him at once.

In spite of the strong moral code promoting marriage for women and virginity prior to marriage, *hijos naturales* [natural children; children born out of wedlock] are prevalent both in El Salvador and in Costa Rica. In the Salvadoran census of 1971, a third of the fourteen-year-old girls had already been pregnant at least once (Thomson 1986:34). Likewise, during the 1970s in Costa Rica, 38 percent of all births involved illegitimate children, and 20 percent of all births listed the father as "unknown" (Biesanz 1982:88).

At the Center, Alicia was criticized for her fifth pregnancy, not so much because the child would be illegitimate or because Alicia already had too many children, but because of her undisciplined choice of a father. Her latest man was neither a Salvadoran nor was he honorable. He had left Alicia to have the baby alone, just as the father of her fourth child had done.

Rina's situation was much more admirable in the eyes of the others. Her men were true *compañeros*; they acted as fathers as far as they were capable. Her first man had turned out to be a coward in the face of the threats against her family, but Rina was not held accountable for this. And the father of her third child had finally legitimized a long-standing relationship.

When faced with the issue of family planning and birth control, the refugee women expressed ambivalence. While at times they envied me for having only one child, they would have felt lonely under my circumstances. They loved being surrounded by their children.

Their attitudes were influenced by a number of competing factors. Birth control in El Salvador was viewed negatively by many of the citizens, as much for political reasons as for religious ones. Because of the intense overpopulation, the Salvadoran government developed a family planning program that included forced sterilization of women, in which medical personnel were pressured to fill quotas on the number of women converted to contraception (Thomson 1986:36–38). The Popular Church opposed the program, promoting instead informed choice for women regarding contraceptives and encouraging responsible attitudes about pregnancies in both men and women. There was a general negative suspicion that the program was designed to help the rich and hurt the poor. Poorer families resented the practice because they saw it as an erosion of their social and economic network. They believed it helped employers to keep wages low, since a man with a large family would be more desperate in his demand for a pay raise, while a man with only one or two children could be forced to live with less.

In Costa Rica, however, the refugees found family planning to be a popular idea. Many people, though devoutly Catholic, did not follow the official Church line. Although as recently as 1968 a person could be strictly punished for advocating birth control, Costa Ricans began practicing family planning anyway, and by 1974, 64 percent of married and common-law couples were using birth control (Biesanz 1982:92–94).

In spite of lingering resentment over the enforcement of birth control by their own government, the Salvadoran refugee women were beginning to see the advantage of having smaller families. They could appreciate the fact that it was less costly to educate and feed fewer children. More education for each child could lead to better jobs, and thus fewer children could provide sufficient support for the parents in

their old age. But in many ways birth control was a hypothetical issue
for the refugees; they were, after all, planning to return home to El
Salvador one day.

13

Carolina

"Feeling much stronger because we were together . . ."

Carolina, who had been hired later at the Center by Ligia, was reluctant to give me her *testimonio* until I assured her that I would use it only to understand the life of a teacher in El Salvador. As a consequence, she used the *testimonio* as a relatively impersonal political statement, avoiding details about her life and stressing the commonality of the refugee experience. Her political opinions and her description of the conditions that helped form these opinions are typical of the entire group.

Carolina: When we first came to Costa Rica and stayed at the refugee center, we had to sleep on sheets of cardboard. They gave us a little blanket and some cardboard boxes for sleeping. Just imagine it, with all my children. . . .

We stayed there in order to be close to our fellow Salvadorans—living in poverty, all of us, but feeling much stronger because we were together. Somehow we had the confidence that God would watch over us.

We began to work, going to pick coffee and working as servants in houses. They treated us very badly. People said, "You are communists, go ahead and starve to death." It was hard.

If we had an umbrella, the *Ticos* [Costa Ricans] wanted to snatch it away. One of my friends was carrying a little umbrella that she had brought from El Salvador. It was raining, and a Costa Rican woman said to her, "Look, lend me your umbrella, give it to me. Anyway, it was my government that gave it to you in the first place."

"No, *señora*," my friend answered, "make no mistake. Your government didn't give me this umbrella. On the contrary, you people are getting things from me. I am a refugee, and I have my rights. But you people are using me, you are taking advantage of all of us."

What a courageous woman!

This kind of treatment was humiliating, but what could we do? Nothing. We spent that entire time being poor and humiliated.

The women seemed to agree that they had common political goals; this was assumed in their notion of *colaborar* [collaborate]. In their *testimonios* they spoke of justice and equality, and especially, of an atmosphere of peace in which to raise their children. Even though the refugees were often referred to as "communists," their strong beliefs were directed against their own government, mostly in response to atrocities they had personally experienced; the women rarely spoke in terms of global conflicts, such as the Cold War. Although Mirabela, in her *testimonio*, reported that her parents had accused her of being influenced by "Cuban ideas," her reaction later to me concerning this was, "I don't need to go to Cuba for my ideas. All I have to do is open my eyes and look around me."

Having leftist leanings in Costa Rica does not necessarily categorize a person as being militant or anti-government, as it had in El Salvador, though the term "communist" is often used derogatorily. Political opinions in Costa Rica are more openly expressed; freedom of speech and the ideals of democracy allow for a wide range of theoretical beliefs.

This wide range of political thought is exemplified, though clearly an oversimplification, by the two contrasting state-run universities. The more traditional institution is the University of Costa Rica [*Universidad de Costa Rica*, or UCR] in San José, founded in 1940, to which the parents of the wealthy have usually sent their children. This university is occasionally identified by Costa Ricans as the "capitalist" one. Although theoretically anyone can attend UCR, the standards for acceptance are more stringent, the costs are greater, and the academic degree conferred is more prestigious than for the National University [*Universidad Nacional Autónoma*, or UNA], which is the other publicly funded institution. UNA was founded in Heredia in 1973 by the labor leader and priest, Padre Bénjamin Nuñez (Biesanz 1982:128), partly in protest against the elitism of UCR and partly to accommodate the children of workers and peasants who might also want a higher education. This latter institution is sometimes referred to as the "communist" one. While certain departments at both universities—such as the social sciences, fine arts, and medicine—are said to be pro-communist in their teaching (Biesanz 1982:131), the two institutions reflect the disparity in background of the young people who attend them, and their alleged political orientation.

The Costa Rican government, except for the fact that they refused employment and citizenship privileges to the refugees, encourages socialist thinking. In addition to providing health care, public education, and benefits for mothers with young children, they foster an atmosphere of caring for their citizenry. Nevertheless, capitalism on all levels is also promoted, such that a sidewalk stand selling penny candy and bubble gum can exist alongside a huge multinational corporation selling computer equipment.

In this open atmosphere of Costa Rica, the refugees became considerably more leftist in their political attitudes than they had ever been in El Salvador, or at least, had ever dared express. Their everyday existence became intertwined through communal housing, group projects, and the breakdown of traditional family ties. Their concerns about finding jobs, searching for housing, and raising children in an alien environment were issues shared by all. Although one couldn't call the Salvadoran community a "commune," cooperation among the group members was clearly a survival tactic that had made their lives easier.

The Swedes, on whom the Salvadorans depended economically, pushed the refugees into even greater cooperative behavior. Because the Swedish government provides its citizens with many basic social benefits, including education, health, extended parental leave, and generous pensions, they encouraged the refugees to have similar expectations. The Swedes saw few practical or theoretical conflicts between such socialist goals and the principles of capitalist behavior. So they pressured the women to turn their daycare center into a money-making enterprise at the same time that they sought to provide the refugees with all the basic necessities of health, education, and welfare. The Swedish "handouts" were thus linked to industrious behavior.

Even though the Salvadorans were not part of the Costa Rican "welfare" workforce, they were influenced by it, as well as by the Swedish idealism. But probably the strongest pressure toward cooperative behavior came from the refugees' own belief that if they wished to help push their government to change they had to act together, as evidenced in their agreement to collaborate with me. A single voice, when no one joins it, is lost in the realm of politics. One woman, crying out in her *testimonio* that she has been wronged—her husband has been brutally murdered, her son has mysteriously "disappeared," or her daughter has been viciously raped—is an anomaly on the landscape, a sad curiosity. But the collective voice of many women protesting such wrongdoings cannot so easily be ignored.

Carolina had come with her husband and six children to Costa Rica. Even though she had experienced the general threat against teachers in El Salvador, her family had arrived intact. Her reluctance to let me use her *testimonio* didn't prevent her from being very open in her comparisons between the two countries.

In talking about male-female relationships, Carolina expresses some emotional confusion over the differences in patterns of authority between El Salvador and Costa Rica. She is clearly troubled by the limitations placed on women in her home country, yet she sees problems in the new freedoms experienced by Costa Rican women.

Robin: And what kind of differences do you see?

Carolina: Well, I think that here there is more freedom, but young people seeking to be free are becoming decadent. And I say this because in the capital back home you won't see what you see on the streets here, young students making love everywhere. Such things you won't see at home . . . at least you wouldn't have when I left. Now I don't know. This really gets me upset.

Robin: Do you also notice differences in the relationship between, for example, husbands and wives or between parents and their children?

Carolina: More than anything I have observed a difference in the relationship between parents, between a husband and his wife. For example, back home our men are *macho* . . . *machistos*; they act like, well, "This woman is mine, and she is not free to do anything."

Robin: Just back home? Or here, too?

Carolina: Back home. Really. On the other hand, I see that here, in the families, if a woman wants to go to a party, she can. And everyone here smokes. Back home it's rare that you see a woman smoking. Much less on the street. A man can smoke, but not a woman.

Robin: What else can a woman do or not do? I'm very interested in such things.

Carolina: Women cannot go out alone without their husbands.

Robin: At night? Or anytime?

Carolina: Well, to go out during the day, she has to ask permission from her husband. At night, even if God wills it, a woman cannot go out alone. Back there, the man is . . . is, well, more dominating.
Also, during those years, a man wouldn't think of going to the market to buy things. But here I notice that it is the men who do the shopping. I think that things are more progressive here, really, because men share some of the work with the women. Back there though, a man does only "men's work," and a woman does only "women's work," such as work around the house.
In El Salvador we have a pattern of conduct that is sad for women, because she is very limited. She is viewed as having less ability. For example, if you are a peasant woman, for starters, you cannot read or write because you don't have the opportunity to learn. If, by any chance, you succeed in going to school, your father is the first to tell you, "Now you, if you only learn to read, that will be plenty. And you should learn to write your name, so that you can make your signature." This is the position that our men have taken, really.

Carolina's discussion about the relationship between women and men in El Salvador leads directly to the more pressing political issue of class. Even though a woman's family obviously contributes to her lack of equality—such as her father not encouraging her to get a good education—the harshest inequities are between higher-class *patrones* who mistreat their lower-class female employees.

Carolina: Now we have gotten to the point where a woman may work in a factory. Because she didn't used to be able to. But when a woman goes into a factory, she is chosen for the more detailed work, the fine work, because the hand of a woman is considered more docile.

But there is another thing. In order for a woman to get hired, she has to be young, without any children, and single—really, single and child-less—because if the *patrón* likes her, he will start to flirt with her, and if she doesn't agree to have sexual relations with him, she won't be hired. That is the way things are for women. Then when she gets pregnant at work, if the *patrón* says so, she is allowed a certain amount of time off, but if he doesn't say so, or if she needs more time, she loses her job. In any case, they deduct it from her pay.

That's the way it is for women who work in factories. Now, for the women that work as domestics, it is even worse. When a woman is young and pretty, the *patrón* takes advantage of her. The head of the family takes advantage of her when his wife is not at home, or whenever he can. So many things happen. And then, if the woman, or rather this young girl, gets pregnant, they throw her out into the street. Because, of course, the wife cannot tolerate the girl having a child by her husband in the house. She is thrown out into the street without even a loan, without anything at all. It doesn't matter to them how she and her child survive.

And then comes the next problem. Now that this young woman has a child and has to search for a way to feed it, she becomes a prostitute. She needs a way to feed her child, so she goes and gets pregnant with another man. This man comes, takes his pleasure, and then leaves her as well, because she has already had a child. Our men are *macho* and require that a woman be a virgin when they marry her, and if she isn't, well, she loses him. And from this point on, she goes downhill.

Another situation is this: let's say the husband respects the servant girl—it is called "respect" when he doesn't take advantage of her—if he respects her, then the son, the handsome son of the household, comes to make her pregnant. And the same results occur, since a *patrón* cannot marry a servant girl. People look upon a servant as someone of no value, the same as a slave. This has been how it is.

Regarding your pay, if they pay you, it is a salary that isn't even adequate for buying shoes, really. This has been the reason that Salvadoran women have gotten into the conflict—some have gone to the mass demonstrations in the streets, and some have even been involved in the armed conflict.

But, as Carolina goes on to say, the excesses of the upper-class *patrón* are not limited to the rape and abandonment of lower-class women; they extend to the mistreatment of lower-class men, as well. Her description of "debt peonage" shows how *patronismo* serves the *patrón* at the expense of the peasant employee.

Carolina: Because of the general conditions, there are people who don't even have enough money to buy salt. And people who work on the large farms often don't get paid on the weekend.

What happens is this. Back home it is the custom for the *patrón* of a large farm, the owner of a coffee plantation, to hire a foreman to run the place. I don't know what his real title is, but back there they call him *el capataz*. He is the one who gives the orders; he assigns all the jobs. The workers live in little shacks made out of cardboard or pieces of wood, *champitas* we call them. And on the farm, the *patrón* has a store where they sell everything, anything that a person might need. The workers just have to go there and ask for what they want—a pound of beans, or salt, or some corn. But at the end of a week or fifteen days, they already owe twice as much as they have earned. And *el capataz* uses this to threaten the workers: "Well, today you already owe this amount; now you will have to work day and night, in order to pay it back." And since the workers usually can't read or write, the *patrón* puts whatever amount he wants to collect from them on the bill. It has been this way for a long time now . . .

Robin: And these debts that arise from such a situation, are they inherited? For example, if your father has piled up debts and then dies, is the family responsible? Do his children or his wife have to assume his debts?

Carolina: Yes, when people work on one of these large farms, a man's widow is left with his debts, and if the widow dies, the debt goes to his eldest son. That's how it is. The children end up with it. And this is how the *patrón* gains control over the entire family, until all of them die there.

Costa Rica is another place where *patronismo* has traditionally been practiced. However, many Costa Ricans complain that government interference has impersonalized the once close relationship between a *patrón* and his employees (Biesanz 1982:30). The government, through laws and regulations, has taken on the role of the benevolent *patrón*, protecting citizens with numerous social and economic benefits. The regulations have been enacted under the assumption that the individual *patrón* needs to be controlled, even though Costa Rican employers have traditionally tried to lessen the disparity in wealth and prestige between themselves and their employees by mingling with them on certain social occasions, such as baptisms and feast-days (Biesanz 1982:50). The refugees, of course, view these government regulations in a more positive light, having experienced the excesses of their own system of *patronismo*. They see equity and justice in such laws, goals toward which their own government should strive.

14

Ligia

"There are limits as to what you can do."

All the women at the Center have at least a theoretical understanding of "democracy." They know that the concept involves the election of officials who enact laws and oversee the enforcement of those laws. The Salvadoran refugees are also cynics, however, and can see a sharp distinction between a government that acts in support of the majority of people who elected them and a government that acts in accordance with only a select and influential few. Their attitudes became clear to me on the morning it was announced that the democratically elected leader of El Salvador, Napoleón Duarte, had been diagnosed with terminal cancer of the liver.

"I'm sorry that Duarte has cancer," says Carmen, "but I'm not at all sad to see him go."

"Has he been a bad president?" I ask. "The Salvadoran people elected him."

Mirabela pipes up, "Duarte was chosen by your government, Doña Robin. He had no power to act on his own. He cannot do anything without the stamp of approval of the Fourteen Families."

"Were the other candidates any good?" I probe.

"No," is the general response.

"Even the revolution won't help," says Carolina. "No one in our country has any training to run a democracy. Here in Costa Rica you can see how it works. Let's say a revolutionary leader takes over the Salvadoran government. He will only become a dictator. He doesn't know how to be anything else."

At the Center there was a concerted effort to provide an experience in democracy and equality for the women. The refugees consciously worked toward this goal by setting up meetings to discuss issues openly.   They said that the daycare center operated on a cooperative basis, with input from everyone who worked there.   They also claimed that the various tasks of cleaning, cooking, and caring for the children at the Center were rotated, so that everyone could learn how to do everything.   Two basic requirements imposed on them by their Swedish benefactors set the tone for equality.   The first was that all workers at the Center were to receive the same salary, no matter what their specific duties entailed (when I was there everyone earned 12,000 *colones* [$170] a month).   The other requirement by the Swedes involved financial accountability.   The women had to keep close track of the expenses at the Center, thus reducing the chance that money could be used to enhance one person's position to the detriment of another's.

When Ligia came to work at the daycare center in 1984, a year after its founding, she was upset by what she perceived as a lack of organization.   Work schedules for the women and plans for the children were formulated on a daily basis, allowing for various contingencies in the lives of the staff members.   Since there was no single leader, the women were allowed to make decisions on their own whenever they were in charge.   Ligia saw this failure to make long-term plans as harmful to the children.   She felt compelled to reorganize the Center.   Her justification for taking over this job was that nobody else was doing it.   Also, Ligia felt that since everyone's salary at the Center was always the same amount, she could not be accused of seeking a promotion for the money.   This did not protect her, however, from insinuations that her reorganization was motivated by a desire for personal gain within the Center.

Ligia's education must have seemed impressive to the other workers.   At the time of her arrival she was the only person with a secondary degree working at the Center.   In addition, she came from a wealthy family in El Salvador and was currently married to a doctor.   Her marriage could conceivably have worked against her, but her husband was actively involved in human rights issues, thus placing Ligia on the "correct" political side.   Ligia's background gave her a higher status than the others, both in her own mind and in theirs, but her words and her actions expressed the contradictory nature of her position.

Ligia: I came to work at the Center, sometime around the month of May. I first came as a volunteer and spent a couple of months just helping out, in order to see if I could become involved.   Two months later a friend came from the Committee of Mothers.   She saw that I was here without receiving a salary.   So from the month of July on, they began to pay me.

I am now coordinator of the Center.   I think that I am doing something positive here, really.   I try to do my best for the children, to attend to their problems, to see that they are not abused.   This is one of the things I have always fought against.

I have been here since 1984. I arrived with the responsibility for the preschool children. I worked directly with the children all the time from 1984 until the end of 1985. I like working with the children. Even now, when I have time, I go and work with them. When the coordinator left, I took over the job as coordinator. The last one was a man, trained as a secondary school teacher [the same man mentioned by Alicia, the one who worked as advisor to the Center]. At the time there were other women working here, but I was the only one trained as a teacher. So I suppose that they said, "Well, she is the one who is qualified for the job." And they voted for me as coordinator.

Ever since then I've been the coordinator. It is not an easy job. People have different ideas about my work. They think it is wonderful to be in my position, but this isn't so. It is difficult. You want to be a good boss, a good friend, a good coordinator, and a good manager. But there are limits as to what you can do. And this is where you run into trouble. Well, most of the staff members approve of my work. If one of them doesn't like my work [alluding to Alicia], well, this doesn't worry me.

Alicia was unhappy with Ligia's new management techniques because she saw her own role becoming increasingly insignificant as trained teachers began to replace the original staff members. Alicia had become accustomed to making her own decisions and setting her own schedule; now she had to follow someone else's plans. While the reorganization meant more predictable work schedules and higher standards of care for the children, a certain amount of flexibility was lost. The new way of management was certainly a rejection of the earlier work that the women had accomplished.

Alicia's lack of higher education put her at a definite disadvantage with respect to Ligia. Her lower status as the daughter of a rural farmer undoubtedly did not help, either, in spite of all the talk about equality. She provided the voice of opposition at the Center, a kind of devil's advocate, but at considerable sacrifice. Her contrary opinions were followed by more unpleasant task assignments at the Center. She was not able to regain leadership charge because she was unofficially outranked.

Although Ligia does not mention Alicia's role in the founding of the Center, she makes it clear that she did not approve of the way things had been going. Moreover, Ligia told me several times that she felt "uncomfortable" with the uneducated women on the staff. She claimed that such people were uneasy when she treated them too nicely. Ligia preferred working closely together with the teachers that she herself had hired, for on some level, at least, they were her equals.

Robin: May I ask how you make decisions, for example, about the work schedule and things like that? Do you write it all up?

Ligia: These things vary. I'll explain how the daycare center functioned before, when I arrived. Well, back home you know what your work is supposed to be. I am a teacher. When you arrive at a school, you know that the school will give you a certain plan to follow. We say, "This is your plan. This is the level you will teach." Apart from the plan, you already know how to do things. You organize things, you formalize things, and you make up work schedules. You are already aware of your obligations.

But here nobody was telling anybody what to do. When I arrived at the Center, there was a Salvadoran teacher and a Swedish woman in charge. I expected them to give me some kind of a program, something that I could use as a basis for my daily lesson plans.

"Who assigns the programs?" I asked them.

And I was told, "Nobody makes plans here, Ligia. Here they don't tell you anything. You do what you can."

I felt a bit strange, because I was thinking, "How awful to work someplace where they don't plan anything!"

None of the staff had done anything to improve the work, at least in the sense of planning or formalizing it. Maybe they had done good things with the children, but without planning. I felt it was necessary to organize things.

Robin: The coordinator at that time was doing nothing?

Ligia: Nothing. The man had another job. He almost never came by here. When he did come, he would maybe greet the children and then disappear. Then I came along and began to see the problem.

Things have always been set up here so that everyone earns the same amount of money. The person who sweeps the floors at the Center gets the same salary as the person who does the coordinating. So I had no problems in trying to improve things in a professional sense. I set a goal. Whenever there was a vacancy because one of the staff had left, I would try to put a teacher in her place. And that is why we now have three teachers, four including me. As teachers, we try to work together. We would like to get more technical people—like psychologists, doctors, nutritionists—for the benefit of the Center. Anyway, little by little I started bringing in teachers.

As long as we are all in the same situation, it is no problem. There would be a problem if we had different salaries for the sweeper and the teacher. But since we don't have a difference in salary, it is easy for me to bring in qualified people.

The new management techniques introduced by Ligia certainly created a sense of professionalism and efficiency at the Center, but they also caused a certain amount of rigidity. Schedules were set up and staff duties were clearly outlined. Task assignments became more specialized when trained teachers were hired. A hierarchy of professional status began to form, headed by Ligia as director and Carmen as assistant director (even though Ligia always referred to herself as the "coordinator," the others called her the "director"). Lower on the hierarchy were the other teachers, and at the bottom were the cooks and the cleaning people. This meant that some of the initial workers, like

Alicia and Rita, were shunted aside. Instead of encouraging the training of these less educated women, Ligia pushed them into unskilled and less satisfying positions.

Since I had been told by various staff members at the Center that all the work was rotated in order to promote equality among the women, I made a point of examining the duties of each woman. My observations soon led me to understand that this "rotation" was something of a myth. It was true that some of the non-teachers assumed various tasks. Rita, for instance, occasionally took care of the babies in the morning. During naptime, she could be seen washing dishes in the kitchen, and then later, she would act as teacher's aide to the older children, sometimes out on the playground and other times in the classroom. Mirabela was another example. During the morning her tasks often included first going to the market to buy fruit and vegetables for the children's lunch, and then helping the others make tortillas in the kitchen. Those who rotated were used as teacher's aides when the more permanent teachers needed help or were absent.

On the other hand, Alicia was rarely given a chance to rotate her position; most of her time was spent cleaning and cooking. I never saw her working directly with the children, even though I expect she would have enjoyed doing so. Neither did the teachers rotate much. I never saw the teachers washing the dishes, cooking, or mopping the floors. At mealtimes they waited on the children and then sat down to eat and supervise over the table manners. After the meals they put the children down for their naps. I could see that privileges and punishments were woven into the system in a subtle way. Everyone except Alicia, however, seemed to feel the system was just.

I also made a point of examining the decision-making process at the Center, since several of the women expressed with pride the cooperative basis on which the Center was operated. Even though everyone met together to make final decisions, informal meetings between Ligia and one or two of the teachers, especially Carmen, were held to hash over matters in a preliminary way. During these informal discussions with Carmen, Ligia tended to make up her mind. Then when the more formal meetings took place, Ligia laid out her plan of action, and it was discussed by the entire Center staff. Ligia's arguments were usually well presented, and only rarely did members of the staff disagree openly with her on important issues. Alicia occasionally grumbled about things in the meetings and expressed negative opinions. Although she was allowed to talk, no one appeared to support her. Sometimes Alicia received supporting comments in whispers after the meeting, but the decision had already been reached by this time. What appeared on the surface to be a consensus in decision-making was clearly a deference to Ligia's leadership.

The system worked smoothly, however. Ligia was genuinely concerned about the children who attended the Center. She was also concerned that the Center remain open, because otherwise she and all the others would be without jobs. Steady jobs such as the ones at the Center were considered a real luxury. In addition to the monthly salary, members of the staff all received a large noonday meal and two snacks daily, and many had children at the Center who were also fed. Moreover, they enjoyed the community and positive atmosphere provided by the daycare center. The children were a great source of comfort. Any deference to Ligia was apparently perceived by most of the women as being in the best interest of the group.

Ligia: I think things are improving every day. When I came, there were 14–20 children, with about the same number on the staff. Sometimes it worries me when people say that the work load has decreased. I don't believe it. If there used to be 14–20 children and now there are 50–60, it cannot be less work for us now. It couldn't be less, since there is only one more staff person. Maybe the work is better and more professional. Before, the work was general and disorganized, not because anybody wanted it that way but because there were no qualified people. For example, the rest of the staff was uneducated. I couldn't demand that they plan things if they weren't educated.

Now that we have a group of teachers, we work together as a professional team. We meet to make decisions, to search for solutions to problems, and even to see where problems exist. Our work is never finished.

Robin: So the teachers meet. How about the rest of the staff? Does the entire staff ever meet together?

Ligia: When the issue is pedagogical, only the teachers meet. When it is something general, concerning the whole project, we all get together. But since the contributions of the rest of the staff are not . . . not as great, sometimes we decide to have just the teachers meet.

With all the pride expressed among the women about egalitarianism and democracy, I expected such ideals to become an integral part of the teaching methodology used at the Center. The teachers obviously loved the children, demonstrating much affectionate physical contact, especially with the younger ones. Any child who cried for his mother was given hugs and kisses and a comforting lap to sit on. On the other hand, during lessons and mealtime, strict discipline was enforced. Teachers severely scolded any young wiggler who refused to sit quietly on the bench listening while another child recited a poem. The teachers were the obvious authorities; I rarely saw children being encouraged to decide things or to think for themselves. I wondered as I watched their behavior if this was the best way to teach future Salvadoran citizens how to operate in a democracy.

The Swedish relief workers at DIAKONÍA expressed considerable ambivalence about their "hands-off" method of overseeing the daycare project. Tina and others spoke to me about how they wanted to let the women create their own style of organization, but the Swedes' own progressive attitudes toward the raising of children and their sense of personal freedom led them to have strong expectations about the Salvadorans. From the beginning they had supported Alicia, feeling that her independent attitude was a positive influence on the others. On the other hand, the Swedes had a harder time accepting Ligia and her more authoritarian style. Even though they could see that Ligia was reorganizing the Center in some very positive ways, they questioned the kinds of teaching methods being promoted. They were also vaguely suspicious of Ligia's wealthy family background. The Swedes could see that Ligia felt more comfortable associating with the urban-trained teachers than with the rural Salvadorans like Alicia.

In spite of their ambivalence, however, the Swedes did not interfere with the organizational process at the Center, other than to set the ground rules of equal salaries for the women and of accountability in the finances. They concentrated, instead, on indirect methods of influence, such as providing classes for the women and arranging conferences with other daycare centers, so that the women could learn about other styles of childrearing.

Because of her elitist background, Ligia probably had more trouble than most in adjusting to the relatively low standard of living available to the refugees. She was the only one of the women who had lived in a wealthy house as an adult back home. In Costa Rica she dreamed of again having an active career in education alongside her physician husband; the combined salaries of both could lead to a rich house in the suburbs—if only they were allowed to work.

Ligia: The other problem that affects us—not only us, but even the Costa Ricans—is that the housing is so difficult to find and so expensive. I was talking with Carmen about how you struggle to improve the conditions of your life in your own country, in order to get decent housing and enough food for everybody. Carmen said to me, speaking specifically about decent housing, "I never imagined that I would have to live in a dump and pay 6000 *colones* [$83] for it."

You couldn't call them houses, those places that refugees can afford to rent. Houses do exist, but nobody would be able to rent them, even with a decent salary. There are beautiful houses that cost 30,000–40,000 *colones* to rent [about $400–$550]. If you were to pay it . . . well, you never could. Never. It is a dream, really. And the houses that are more or less affordable, say 10,000–15,000 *colones* [about $150–$200], are not affordable on our salary. So even these houses are a dream. . . .

Ligia gained support and inspiration from her husband Marco though she was slow to follow his lead. Marco now worked as a medical doctor for the refugees and was heavily involved in international activities concerning issues of human rights, so he was often absent from home. This did not prevent him from appreciating the value of her work, however. Not only did he support her involvement at the Center, but he contributed his own technical expertise through workshops on nutrition and health. Moreover, his encouragement in allowing Ligia to continue her university studies in Costa Rica increased her competency as director-coordinator of the daycare center.

Ligia and her husband were fortunate in having two reliable incomes to support their family. They were also at an advantage because their two incomes followed the ideal standard for a Salvadoran household, with the husband making more money than the wife. In spite of Ligia's wistfulness about not living in a big expensive house, she and her family were a success story in comparison to the other refugees.

15

Alicia

"For the sake of our cause . . ."

There is a different atmosphere at the Center during July because the public schools are on "winter break" for two weeks of the rainy season. It is also the time of year in Costa Rica for sore throats and colds. Many of the daycare center children are staying at home with their older siblings or with mothers who are on sick leave, and most of the staff members at the Center are on vacation. Alicia is among those absent. No one discusses her absence with me, even though she does not return to work at the end of July, when everyone else comes back. I know that her baby is due fairly soon. Maybe she has had the baby. It also occurs to me that perhaps Alicia has been fired. I wait for someone to mention what has happened to her, but I hear nothing.

Then in the middle of August I run over to the Center to tell everybody that I have to make an emergency trip to the United States and will therefore not be visiting them again for two weeks. Carmen and Carolina have taken their group of two- and three-year-olds out onto the sidewalk into the sun. The children have been cooped up for too many days during the rainy season. Carolina devises a game of racing up and down on the sidewalk, while Carmen and I catch the little ones who stray into the street.

Carmen finally brings up the subject I have been waiting for. "Have you seen Alicia's new baby?"

"No," I reply, suppressing my curiosity. "When was it born?"

Carmen looks surprised that I have not yet heard the news. "He is named after two *gringos*—friends of Alicia—'Bernard' for the Swede and 'Steven' for the American."

With some bitterness, Carmen adds, "Her *gringo* friends are always sending her money."

"How much money?" I probe.

"I once saw a check for $200."

Carmen then goes on to tell me that everyone at the daycare center is going to suffer because of Alicia. Alicia's pregnancy sick leave is using up all the Center's funds saved for Christmas bonuses. All the staff members will have to give up their legal rights to an *aguinaldo* at Christmas. (By law, every worker in Costa Rica receives an extra month's salary in December; this bonus, called an *aguinaldo*, is counted on yearly by families to pay for taxes, insurance, gifts, or vacations.) I am shocked that Alicia's exercise of her legal right to two months' maternity leave will force all the others to give up their own legal rights to a Christmas bonus. It has been known for months that Alicia was going to have a baby. Why have I not heard about this problem before?

Unfortunately, I do not have time to follow up on this train of thought until two weeks later when I return from the United States. When I tell some friends outside of the Center about the sacrifice of bonuses that the women have to make for Alicia's leave of absence, they all "pooh-pooh" the idea, saying that the Center cannot let that happen—it is illegal. I argue, however, that the law may not apply in this case. This is a refugee project, after all, with only a limited amount of funding. After further discussion, I become baffled by another issue. How could the salary of one woman for two months be equivalent to the *aguinaldos* of approximately ten full-time staff members? Possibly the worst that could happen would be a small reduction in each person's bonus.

It is time to visit Alicia. I want to see her new baby and hear her side of this affair. I have been careful enough to avoid visiting her while she was on vacation, knowing that any show of favoritism would only stir up trouble. Now Alicia is in more trouble than ever, and everyone seems to assume that I have been in contact with Alicia all along anyway. Carmen could hardly believe I had not already seen the baby.

Sunday is a beautiful day. Jessica and I head for Alicia's little village in the car. I have not warned her we are coming. She has no telephone, and I did not wish to send a message through any of the other refugees. Our visit will be obvious enough to everyone in any case, since the only parking spot for the car near Alicia's house is on a widened space in the road in front of the cramped apartments where Rita and Rina live. We take our modest gift for the baby and walk up the street to Alicia's with the neighbors watching and nodding politely as we go by. Alicia's tiny livingroom is full of people. Rita is sitting on the couch chatting with Alicia's brother Pablo and her sister Julia, the two who had traveled with Alicia on the airplane from El Salvador. Although I have not met either one before, I already know that Pablo lives in the house with Alicia, and I now learn that Julia is a student living elsewhere, but who often comes to stay for the day. Alicia, however, is not at home.

She has taken her youngest children to Cartago to get the baby, Bernard Steven, baptized there.

"Why didn't Alicia have her son baptized by one of the Salvadoran priests that holds mass right here in the village?" I ask.

Julia tells me, "This is a sacred pilgrimage. Alicia made a promise to go to Cartago for the baptism if the baby was born healthy."

I now remember that the doctor had ordered Alicia's workload lightened because of constant problems with her pregnancy. She had obviously been worried.

Pablo tries to get us to stay at the house until Alicia's return. "Please sit with us. I know Alicia will feel sorry if she misses your visit."

"How long do you suppose it will be?"

"She will be back by dark," Pablo says. "She left very early this morning."

Five or six hours seems a long time to wait, so I promise that Jessica and I will return the next morning. "Please let Alicia know that we are coming," I request as we say our goodbyes.

"I know that she is anxious to see you," Pablo assures us.

The following morning Alicia is at home with her baby. She is delighted at our visit, calling us immediately into the bedroom to watch as she dresses Bernard Steven in his new clothes. He looks charming in the little knitted blue suit she puts on him—such a relaxed plump baby with beautiful long black hair. As Jessica and I admire and hold him, she tells us about the baby's Swedish namesake, Bernard.

"The clothes came from Sweden. Bernard's wife knitted them," Alicia proudly informs us.

"Who is this man 'Bernard'?" I want to know.

"Greta and Bernard are the Swedish couple who worked with the Center after we started it. They were with me when I had my baby girl. If they hadn't been here, I don't know what I would have done."

"Where was the baby's father?"

"He was here in Costa Rica, but he didn't wait around for the baby to be born."

"Was he a Salvadoran?"

"A refugee, yes."

Greta and Bernard had sympathized with Alicia in her predicament. They adored the new baby girl and gave her a crib, a stroller, and new clothes and blankets. They even talked with Alicia at length about the possibility of adopting the baby. Bernard was afflicted with a degenerative nervous disorder, so the young couple could not hope to have children of their own. Alicia seriously considered the idea of giving up her child to them. A year or two passed. Bernard's condition got considerably worse, and the couple was forced to return to Sweden for medical reasons. They still wanted to take Alicia's child, but it no longer seemed such a wonderful idea to any of them. Bernard probably would not live long enough to see the child grow up, and it would not be good for the little girl to watch him die. Besides, Alicia had become very attached to her smallest child, who was a real charmer.

Alicia says to me, "Bernard is dying. He cannot get out of bed anymore; he cannot even speak."

"Where are Greta and Bernard now?"

"Back in Sweden. They just sent me this letter. It came with baby Bernard's suit and the money."

"What money?" I ask.

"They sent me a check for $200," explains Alicia. "When they found out I had a baby boy, they were very excited. Greta told me that Bernard suddenly came alive again. He even smiled and nodded when Greta read him the letter."

"It must have been nice for them to learn that you named the little boy Bernard."

"I hope so," says Alicia.

Baby Bernard's middle name, Steven, apparently came from an American man. Carmen had told me that the American sent Alicia money too, but Alicia never talked about him. I wondered later if Steven was the reporter who had written about Alicia in the article I had translated. I did not think to ask at the time.

Bernard's knitted blue suit has been on for little more than half an hour when it is time for his bath. Alicia's nine-year-old daughter has already heated the necessary water on the electric stove, and we all troop into the kitchen to watch. Alicia bathes Bernard in the cement *pila*, carefully mixing cold water with hot to get the right temperature. She tells me that Bernard gets irritable if he does not get his bath. Sometimes she has to bathe him twice a day just to keep him happy. After the bath Bernard is dressed in a new set of clothes. Alicia slicks his hair down with oil and combs it with a part on the side. We all laugh when Jessica remarks that baby Bernard looks ready for first grade. In fact, he does.

While the children take Bernard out for a walk in the stroller, Alicia and I sit on the bed and talk.

She confides, "I'm afraid to go back to the Center. I don't know how it will be."

"What do you mean?" I ask. "You can take the baby with you to work, can't you?"

"Yes, of course. That's one good thing."

"Then what are you afraid will happen?"

"I don't know how they will treat me. The doctor ordered me to stay home another month because of the difficult birth."

"What was the problem?"

"I was hemorrhaging."

"Oh dear."

"But Ligia and the others told me they would not allow me the extra time at home. They say I have to come back to work right away. When I told the doctor what they said, he got very angry. He said, 'They have no choice in the matter; they must let you stay home.'"

"Did the doctor give you the official medical orders to show to the people at the Center?"

"Yes, but I'm afraid to ask for more time. I'm going back to work next week."

Alicia's friends have advised her to quit her job at the Center, but she feels she cannot. With five children to support, and one of them so tiny, she does not dare leave. There are no other jobs. But even if there were, she does not have permission from the Costa Rican government to work anywhere else.

"Why do the women at the Center treat you this way?" I inquire.

Alicia hesitates at first, "I don't know. Well . . . no, I don't really know." But then she tells me, "It's jealousy. I think they must be jealous of me."

Alicia has no time to elaborate. The children are bringing Bernard in from the street. Jessica comes up to me and says, "That stroller is totally useless here. It just gets caught in the ruts and the mud." I smile. My daughter is learning.

Alicia puts Bernard to bed and starts to prepare lunch. This visit she insists that we stay for a meal. I accept the invitation, saying, "We would love to stay. But you must let me take the children to school in the car afterwards. Otherwise it is too much of a rush."

Lunch consists of rice and beans, a small spicy hamburger, and a salad of cabbage and tomatoes. The drink is made from fresh blackberries blended with milk. During the meal, Alicia talks about nutrition, telling me that Coca-Cola is bad for you, but rice, beans, and vegetables are good. I am impressed. At the Center Ligia has emphasized good nutrition for the children and their mothers. The experts she has called in have obviously done some good.

"Did you eat this kind of food back in El Salvador?" I ask.

"No. This is Costa Rican food. Salvadorans do not eat rice; they eat tortillas."

"Tortillas are good for you, too." I say.

"I know. But Costa Rican tortillas are terrible, so thin and tasteless. If I had time to make my own, I would. I don't, though, so we eat Costa Rican rice."

The conversation shifts to focus on the children. I ask Alicia how the children manage by themselves when she is away at work for the day. I know that her youngest girl is in kindergarten during the mornings and her eldest three children go to grade school twice a week in the mornings and three times a week in the afternoons. The cultural assumption is that there is a family member or a servant at home to take care of the children, but such luxuries are impossible in this case. Alicia says that twice a week the five-year-old goes to school alone in the morning, walking the kilometer to the bus stop, riding the local bus for twenty minutes to Heredia, and finally walking the few remaining blocks to school. She makes the return trip alone again at noon. Her older brother and sisters make this same trip in the afternoons. Before they leave the house, though, the nine-year-old cooks the noonday meal for all of them, leaving a plateful for the kindergartner when she arrives home alone. The children seem amazingly independent to me, a lot like Alicia herself.

The time has come for me to take the older children to school. It is raining again, and we rush out to the car. Alicia waves to us as we drive away, saying she hopes to see me next week at the Center. She looks radiant with her little baby in her arms. It is hard for me to imagine why she is so despised at the daycare center. Her explanation must be right. Jealousy is the only possible reason for such resentment. Alicia has youth and beauty and is blessed with a lovely new baby. Her wit and intelligence make her a dramatic storyteller. Ligia's claim that Alicia lures foreigners into her house and takes advantage of them is only a half-truth.   Outsiders are attracted by her natural charm, they sympathize with her in her predicament, and they give to her willingly.

That evening I visit my Swedish friend Tina. I tell her the story of Greta and Bernard and their relationship with Alicia.

"Yes, I have heard about this Swedish couple. But I didn't realize they had become so close to Alicia. I'm a little disturbed; they are not supposed to do that."

"What do you mean—not supposed to do that? Do what?" I ask. Now I am confused. "They weren't supposed to be friends with Alicia?"

"Not just Alicia, Robin. Our volunteers are not allowed to form close personal relationships with particular refugees. We are trained to treat everyone equally and avoid giving special help to anyone."

"You mean Greta and Bernard overstepped their boundaries in the case of Alicia?"

"Yes." Tina pauses and then continues, "You know those ads in American magazines for adopting a child in some underdeveloped country . . . where you send in $10 once a month and become the child's sponsor?"

"Oh, yes. When I was a kid I always wanted my family to do that."

"Well, our training tells us that this kind of help causes friction and jealousy in the community. Just imagine giving one little girl in a poor village extra food and clothing, and even enough money for school. Suddenly she is the only one on the street wearing new shoes and a pretty dress. How do you think this makes the other children feel? Or their parents? And how does it make the little girl herself feel?"

"So you are saying that Alicia's situation is analogous?"

"Yes."

I begin to fear for Alicia's future and that of her five children.

Alicia returns to work the Monday following my visit to her house. She is back doing the cleaning, against the doctor's orders, but she has decided not to fight the issue. Bernard Steven has been given a special place to sleep underneath a table in Ligia's office. It is the only spot where a baby will be safe from being stepped on by another child. Alicia looks happy during those first few weeks. Her worst fears have not been realized, and she is allowed to give her baby all the attention he needs.

Carmen makes a point of coming up to me soon after Alicia's arrival. She says, "Things are better with Alicia now. She doesn't seem to cause so much trouble."

I still notice some tension, however. I feel the others watching me nervously whenever I get into a conversation with Alicia. No such tension arises when I speak to any of the others.

One morning the women, including Alicia, get into a lively discussion in the kitchen. They are talking about something that happened in one of the refugee families. Apparently a thirteen-year-old girl was left in charge of her younger brothers and sisters, while her parents were out. The girl became distracted by a male visitor, and the two went for a short walk. During her absence, one of the smaller children was seriously injured. The women at the Center are now discussing what should have been done to prevent the incident from happening. Most of the women agree that the older child should have been more carefully supervised by her parents. The parents should not have put her in charge of her younger siblings, and they should not have allowed her the opportunity to go out walking with a young man. Alicia takes her usual role of maverick. She feels that the young girl is to blame. She is old enough to be responsible and should not have chosen this particular time to go out wandering with her young man. (I remember that Alicia went to San Salvador alone at about this same age to earn her own living.) The curious thing about this discussion is the strange tension and silence created by Alicia's dissenting opinion. Is it that Alicia is not allowed to have a different voice? Or does Alicia's opinion reflect a morality that varies significantly from that of the others?

As tensions between Alicia and the other women seem to ease, I seriously consider gathering more in-depth cultural data from the women in order to follow up on my original research plans. From what

I have gathered informally there is material for a variety of interesting studies. But I am loathe to upset the delicate balance of emotions that is finally being achieved. Do I have the right to disturb that balance by continuing my interviews? I consider this question for many days and slowly come to the conclusion that I do not have the right, nor even the need. The women themselves have already chosen the focus of my research and given me all the necessary information.

I continue to visit the Center for several months after Alicia's return. By the time I leave Costa Rica, Bernard Steven is six months old and has joined the babies' group. Alicia has become subdued. She and I often talk at the Center, but she is no longer as aggressive about seeking me out. Maybe she understands that the others may treat her better if she does not demand special attention from me. I appreciate her self-control, if that is indeed what it is, but I feel sorry.

The week of my departure, a general meeting is held at the Center, at which we discuss the final plans for my research. I tell the refugees that I hope to incorporate some of their *testimonios* into a book, and I ask who would like to be included. The response surprises me. Everyone at the meeting wants to participate in any public document, even Carolina and Eduardo, who were so reluctant at first. Then I notice that Alicia is not at the meeting. So only her *testimonio* is in question. I decide to speak with her privately later to make sure what it is that she wants. At the general meeting, however, I go on to remind everyone about the potential dangers of making their stories available for others to read. They hardly needed such grim reminders. The consensus nevertheless is that they want the stories made public—for the future benefit of the daycare center and for the benefit of all their children.

After the meeting I look for Alicia. When I find her sweeping out Doña Ligia's office, I ask her, "Why didn't you come to the meeting?"

"I wasn't invited," she says. "I didn't even know about it."

"I am planning to make a book based on the *testimonios*. Do you want yours to be included? It would be a public document."

Alicia's response is slow and deliberate. "For the sake of the solidarity of the Center, for the sake of our cause, I want my *testimonio* to appear along with all the others. . . ."

Epilogue

"That is the way life is."

When I left Costa Rica, I was worried that the demise of the Center would mean increasing poverty and a dismal future for the Salvadoran refugee women. However, this turned out not to be the case. The women had created the daycare project for their own financial and emotional security, and the project had served them well. Their salaries, while minimal, had allowed them to rent small houses and accumulate basic furnishings. Upon leaving the Center, their severance pay, equivalent to one month's salary for each year of service, helped the women to pass easily onto the next phase of their lives, even giving them the luxury of making some choices. In addition, the Center had given them a supportive community where they could share their joys and sorrows, as well as raise their children. Thus, while the daycare center failed as an economic enterprise, in other ways—as a social experiment, as a grass roots project designed to help people—it was a great success.

During the year I was in Costa Rica, the Swedes who were funding the project had slowed their normal process of financial withdrawal, to allow the women to come up with more innovative ways of raising money. The people at DIAKONÍA were well aware that the care of children is rarely profitable. While I was there, the Center conducted fundraisers to sell food, send local vacationers to the beach, and collect secondhand donations for resale. All of these efforts brought in money, but not enough to save the Center. The only way to make the project self-sustaining, which was the ultimate requirement for the Swedish funding of grass root projects, would have been to collect tuition from the parents. Since one of the purposes of the Center was to provide free daycare for refugee children whose parents were struggling to survive, this solution was considered unacceptable.

Swedish funding finally ran out at the end of 1989, though the Center was able to remain open for another year by begging from friends and using some of the project's savings. After a six month's closure in 1991, a Dutch agency agreed to support the daycare center, but only if the Center undertook the care of all needy children, not just Salvadoran refugee children. By 1993 the Center served mostly Costa Rican children (70%); the remaining children (30%) were from Nicaragua, El Salvador, and other neighboring countries. The goals and focus of the original grass roots project had clearly changed. However, by then most of the women had gone on to other things.

During these same years I received scattered letters from the women, each telling me she had left the Center. None of them mentioned that she had been "let go," but I imagined this to be the reason in every case. The women were entitled to collect severance pay from the Center, but only if they had been "fired" or were ready for retirement. Leaving the job voluntarily would have meant forfeiting this money. The legal requirements for severance pay are established by the Costa Rican government; organizations like the Center are under obligation to set aside such money for their workers. From the perspective of the women who worked at the Center, the severance pay was an absolute necessity for tiding them over to their next job. However, from the perspective of the Center, the severance pay requirement was an obvious drain on the organization's meager resources.

In July of 1993 I returned to Costa Rica for a visit. Much had happened since I had last seen the women at the Center. On New Year's Eve of 1991 the Salvadoran Peace Accords were signed, in which the guerrillas agreed to give up their arms, and the Salvadoran government pledged to purge the army of its terrorist tactics and of the officials directly involved in acts of atrocity.

Following the six month's closure of the Center in 1991, only Doña Ligia, Eduardo, and María came back to work there under the newly established, though minimal, funding by the Dutch. María soon had to be dismissed for lack of money, however, so by the time I arrived in Costa Rica, Ligia and Eduardo were the two remaining employees of the ones I had originally known.

Mirabela, Carmen, and Carolina had repatriated to El Salvador in 1990–1991, and Rina had earlier left for Canada. The rest of the women—Ligia, María, Rita, and Alicia—had remained in Costa Rica. The goal of my visit to Costa Rica in 1993 was to piece together the women's lives and to see to what extent they still existed as a community. For the ones who had returned to El Salvador, this meant reexamining their letters and gathering what information about them I could through hearsay. For those who had remained in Costa Rica, it meant visiting them once again and reinterpreting their letters in light of their current lives.

LIGIA

The first thing I did during my visit to Costa Rica was go to see what had become of the daycare center. I had only received letters from women who had eventually left the Center. Since Ligia had not written to me, I was not sure what had happened to her.

I found Ligia still running the daycare project, but the only other worker I recognized was Eduardo. Ligia and I sat down in her office to talk. She told me then about the loss of Swedish funding and about the modest continuation of the project under support from the Dutch. I could see that she was discouraged about the changes that were taking place at the Center. She even spoke of quitting her job as director. She said she could no longer travel daily from across San José to get to work; it was simply too exhausting. She had fought hard for the daycare center as a place for Salvadoran children to learn about their cultural heritage, but her goals of making the Center self-sustaining had remained beyond her reach. The knowledge she had gained from her university classes in preschool education and administration would have to be put to use somewhere else.

MIRABELA

Until recently, I received a letter every year from Mirabela following my departure, the first two from Costa Rica and all the others from El Salvador. Mirabela left the Center in 1990, after the Swedish funding was cut off. Getting a job in a clothes factory, she decided to leave Costa Rica at the end of the school year in November. She returned to El Salvador to live in her native village in her family's old house (her sister had inherited the house upon her mother's death).

Back in El Salvador, Mirabela's three children began to attend school in the nearby town, riding the bus back and forth every day. Since army recruitment often takes place by force, many times from among the young male passengers on a bus, her eldest son moved to the town to avoid recruitment. In her latest letters, Mirabela told me that this same son was living and working in the United States, in Los Angeles, because the family could no longer afford to send him to school. The son moved there to join one of Mirabela's brothers, who had escaped from El Salvador earlier.

Mirabela's dream had been to teach sewing to poor rural women in order to help improve their existence, but so far she had not been able to achieve this modest goal. Her sisters, for one thing, did not approve of her getting politically "involved," as this would be perceived to be, and Mirabela could not afford to leave the family home. Mirabela's political opinions remained strong; she complained in a letter to me about those members of her family who seemed to "live their lives and that's it."

My latest letters to Mirabela have remained unanswered.

CARMEN

Carmen wrote me two letters, one in 1989 inviting me to the sixth anniversary of the Center (as usual Carmen took it upon herself to invite me to activities) and the other in 1990, six months after she had returned to El Salvador. According to Alicia, Carmen had gone back to El Salvador because her mother had to undergo an operation. Carmen had other reasons for returning, as well. Her husband Federico felt pressured to leave Costa Rica; his lack of a steady job and the government's reluctance to give him permanent status as a refugee both contributed to his restlessness.

Carmen's second letter was primarily a description of her new job as a teacher in a Salvadoran school. The children in the school were from "displaced" families, refugees within their own country. Carmen wrote of these students:

"I am teaching reading and writing to poor children, the poorest of the poor. They live under the worst possible conditions, eating from the garbage dumps and writing in used notebooks. Their lack of food doesn't allow them to withstand more than three hours of classes a day."

I wrote letters to Carmen's address in El Salvador, but I received no answer. My most recent card (1993) was returned to me by the Salvadoran post office.

CAROLINA

On the occasion of the Salvadoran Mother's Day celebration at the Center on May 10, 1989, Carolina wrote me an optimistic letter, but by July of 1990, her outlook was not so positive. Although she was still working in Costa Rica, it was clear that the Center would have to close down soon, due to lack of funding. Worse yet, as she described, thieves had entered her house and had stolen everything she and her family had worked so hard during the past ten years to acquire. Carolina spoke of returning to El Salvador, but she was not sure how to manage the move because, as she said, "There is no money." By 1993, when I visited Costa Rica, she had found a way to go back to her homeland. I was not able to obtain an address for her, however, and she hasn't written to me again.

RINA

Soon after I left Costa Rica in 1988, Rina moved to Canada with her children and her new husband. She wrote me that while English was difficult for her to learn, her children were having no problems communicating. The family was living in an apartment, and the children were attending Canadian schools. She missed the people at the daycare center and her life in Costa Rica, but as she said, "I had to leave; that's the way life is."

My most recent letter to Rina in Canada was returned, stamped "Addressee Unknown."

MARÍA

María had been rehired at the Center following the brief closure in 1991, but due to lack of project funds she was dismissed again in 1992. Ligia was unhappy about María's demands for severance pay; from Ligia's perspective María was forcing the Center to go bankrupt. María, however, obviously needed the money to survive.

When I saw María in 1993, she was still living in the tiny lean-to shack where she and her family had lived before. Her brother was still making shoes, although with much greater success now. María no longer had to provide a steady income for the family; she could concentrate on raising her children and taking domestic care of her brother.

María looked happy. Her vague talk of returning home to her native village in El Salvador was counterbalanced by her children's animated discussion of their busy lives in Costa Rica. The younger ones had adjusted well, and María, in spite of her words, was not likely to uproot them and go back to an uncertain existence in El Salvador, where she had such terrifying memories of rape and murder.

RITA

Rita wrote me two letters in 1990, the year after she had been dismissed from the Center. In her writing Rita sounded much more cheerful than I remembered her. She was no longer focusing on how tired she was and how her life was almost over. She even expressed an interest in international affairs, requesting that I send her information about the Persian Gulf War (as I recall, not one of the women had discussed world events unrelated to El Salvador during the entire year I was there).

When I saw Rita in 1993, I found her living in a small country house surrounded by vegetation. She had passed along her small apartment to her daughter's young family. Rita looked wonderfully healthy—color in her face and a lively smile (with a whole new set of teeth). She said she still had backaches, but not as often or as severe. She was glad not to be working at the Center any longer. Her husband had maintained a job as night watchman for a financial institution for two years already, allowing Rita a much needed rest from supporting the family.

ALICIA

I received letters from Alicia, saying she thought the Center would lose its funding and she would lose her job. She began planning ways to buy a lot and build a small house. She wrote that because of the constantly rising rents, she needed a place of her own to raise her five children. The new house would serve as an investment. Should she decide to return home to El Salvador, she could sell it and buy a new place back home. Somewhat later she wrote that she had moved to a rural village in the Department of Limón and was living in her new house. In this letter she enclosed a photo of her sixth baby, born of yet another Costa Rican father. In addition to expressing great joy in having a new baby, Alicia also says of this event: "I am still alone. This appears to be my destiny."

Thus, when I arrived in Costa Rica I was pleasantly surprised to discover from the other Salvadoran women that Alicia was finally married. Her new Costa Rican husband enjoyed her six children; I was told he could not have any of his own. The couple lived on a farm near the Guápiles highway going down to Puerto Limón.

I visited Alicia on her farm. This was not the house she had bought with her severance pay; her father had come from El Salvador and was residing in her "investment." She was living across the highway with her husband on a farm he rented from his brother. The farmland was spectacular, right at the edge of the rainforest. Toucans lived in the trees beyond the stream, and occasional monkeys howled from the rainforest. The farm was apparently productive as well; they were raising chickens, horses, cattle, and fruit trees. In the back of the house they had built a small nursery, where they were starting new fruit trees and house plants for sale. Much of the food and potential income needed for the family was right here on the farm. The stream that ran through the land brought clean fresh water from the rainforest. The farmhouse was rustic, but it had running water and electricity. The family had a television, a stereo, and a radio—no refrigerator. Alicia, with her six children and low hopes of finding a "male companion," had discovered an idyllic little corner of the world and a man to share it with.

Thinking back on my experiences with the Salvadoran refugee women in Costa Rica, I realize I had known them during a crucial transition period in their lives. While they all hoped that the daycare center would remain a permanent economic support, they also dreamed of other things. For instance, Mirabela felt her future life lay in assuming an active political role in the formation of a postwar El Salvador. She knew that, in order to do this, she needed to go back home. Alicia, on the other hand, wanted to focus on completing her family by finding a father for her children. Whether she accomplished this in Costa Rica or in El Salvador was not an issue. Rina wanted to go off to Canada to begin a new life for herself and her children. She hoped to join her mother and siblings who had already settled up north. Others, like Rita, María, Carmen, and Carolina, simply wished for a peaceful existence—preferably in El Salvador, though Costa Rica seemed acceptable, too. Doña Ligia was the only one who had invested her personal dreams in the Center. The university courses she took were intended to help her as director of the daycare center. Her energies and emotions were devoted to keeping the project afloat: she wrote appeals for funding, she fussed over the accounts, and she worried about giving out money for severance pay. In the long run, although she remained employed at the Center, she was perhaps the most disappointed of all the women by the changes that were taking place. She hoped to create a safe and healthy haven for Salvadoran refugee children, a permanent place that they could go to learn about their own cultural roots. Her dreams had to be changed to adjust to the reality of the funding situation.

For all the women, then, their years at the daycare center were simply a stage in the transition to a new life. I hope that their future lives will be fruitful and satisfying; my own life has truly been enriched by theirs.

Works Cited

Alas, Higinio. *El Salvador: Por Qué la Insurrección?* San José, Costa Rica: Comisión para la Defensa de los Derechos Humanos en Centroamérica, 1982.

Anderson, Thomas P. *Matanza.* Lincoln: University of Nebraska, 1971.

Armstrong, Robert, and Janet Shenk. *El Salvador: The Face of Revolution.* Boston: South End, 1982.

Baloyra, Enrique A. *El Salvador in Transition.* Chapel Hill: University of North Carolina, 1982.

Bethell, Leslie, ed. *Colonial Spanish America.* New York: Cambridge University, 1987.

Beverley, John. "The Margin at the Center: On *Testimonio.*" In *De-Colonizing the Subject*, edited by Sidonie Smith and Julia Watson, 91–114. Minneapolis: University of Minnesota, 1992.

Biesanz, Richard, et al. *The Costa Ricans.* Prospect Heights, Ill.: Waveland, 1982.

Booth, John A., and Thomas W. Walker. *Understanding Central America.* Boulder, Colo.: Westview, 1989.

Bricker, Victoria Reifler. *Ritual Humor in Highland Chiapas.* Austin: University of Texas, 1973.

Brown, Peter. *The Cult of the Saints: Its Rise and Function in Latin Christianity.* Chicago: University of Chicago, 1981.

Browning, David. *El Salvador: Landscape and Society.* Oxford: Clarendon, 1971.

Broyles-Gonzalez, Yolanda. "The Living Legacy of Chicana Performers: Preserving History through Oral Testimony." *Frontiers* 11:1 (1990): 46–52.

Bunster-Burotto, Ximena. "Surviving Beyond Fear." In *Women and Change in Latin America*, edited by June Nash and Helen Safa, 297–325. South Hadley, Mass.: Bergin & Garvey, 1986.

Burgos-Debray, Elisabeth, ed. and trans. *I . . . Rigoberta Menchú: An Indian Woman in Guatemala.* New York: Verso, 1984.

Burkholder, Mark A., and Lyman L. Johnson. *Colonial Latin America.* New York: Oxford University, 1990.

Byrne, Hugh. *El Salvador's Civil War: A Study of Revolution.* Boulder, Colo.: Lynne Rienner, 1996.

CEDAL. *Los Refugiados en Centroamérica: Soluciones Políticas Jurídicas.* Heredia, Costa Rica: CEDAL, 1986.

Cott, Nancy F. *The Grounding of Modern Feminism.* New Haven, Conn.: Yale University, 1987.

Eckstein, S., ed. *Power and Popular Protest: Latin American Social Movements.* Berkeley: University of California, 1986.

Facts on File 33.1708 (1973): 629.

Golden, Renny. *The Hour of the Poor, The Hour of Women: Salvadoran Women Speak.* New York: Crossroad, 1991.

Gonzalez Casanova, Pablo, ed. *Historia Política de los Campesinos Latinoamericanos.* México, D.F.: Siglo Veintiuno, 1985.

Harlow, Barbara. *Resistance Literature.* New York: Methuen, 1987.

Jaquette, Jane S., ed. *The Women's Movement in Latin America: Feminism and the Transition to Democracy.* Boston: Unwin Hyman, 1989.

Kaplan, Caren. "Resisting Autobiography: Outlaw Genres and Transnational Feminist Subjects." In *De-Colonizing the Subject,* edited by Sidonie Smith and Julia Watson, 115–38. Minneapolis: University of Minnesota, 1992.

Mainwaring, Scott, and Alexander Wilde, eds. *The Progressive Church in Latin America.* Notre Dame, Ind.: University of Notre Dame, 1989.

Molineu, Harold. *U.S. Policy Toward Latin America: From Regionalism to Globalism.* Boulder, Colo.: Westview, 1986.

Montgomery, Tommie Sue. *Revolution in El Salvador: Origins and Evolution.* Boulder, Colo.: Westview, 1982.

Nash, June, and Helen Safa, eds. *Women and Change in Latin America.* South Hadley, Mass.: Bergin & Garvey, 1986.

New Americas Press, ed. *A Dream Compels Us: Voices of Salvadoran Women.* Boston: South End, 1989.

New York Times. 18 March (1981) 13:5; 12 April (1981) 21:1.

North, Liisa. *Bitter Grounds: Roots of Revolt in El Salvador.* 2nd ed. Toronto, Ontario: Between the Lines, 1985.

Perez-Brignoli, Hector. *A Brief History of Central America.* Trans. Ricardo B. Sawrey A. and Susana Stettri de Sawrey. Berkeley: University of California, 1989.

Pescatello, Ann M., ed. *Female and Male in Latin America.* Pittsburgh: University of Pittsburgh, 1973.

Petras, James, and Morris Morley. *U.S. Hegemony Under Siege: Class, Politics and Development in Latin America.* New York: Verso, 1990.

Radcliffe, Sarah A., and Sallie Westwood, eds. *VIVA: Women and Popular Protest in Latin America.* New York: Routledge, 1993.

Rodriguez, Francisco. *Life for Those Who Come After.* Trans. Jennifer Tucker. San José, Costa Rica: La Jomada, 1993.

Russell, Philip L. *El Salvador in Crisis.* Austin, Texas: Colorado River, 1984.

Sheets, Payson. *The Cerén Site: A Prehistoric Village Buried by Volcanic Ash in Central America.* Fort Worth: Harcourt Brace Jovanovich, 1992.

Skidmore, Thomas E., and Peter H. Smith. *Modern Latin America.* New York: Oxford University, 1984.

Smith, Sidonie, and Julia Watson, eds. *De-Colonizing the Subject.* Minneapolis: University of Minnesota, 1992.

Stevens, E. P. "*Marianismo*: The Other Face of *Machismo* in Latin America." In *Female and Male in Latin America*, edited by Ann M. Pescatello, 89–101. Pittsburgh: University of Pittsburgh, 1973.

Thomson, M. *Women of El Salvador.* Philadelphia: Institute for the Study of Human Issues, 1986.

Todorov, Tzvetan. *The Conquest of America: The Question of the Other.* Trans. Richard Howard. New York: Harper, 1987.

Universidad para la Paz and Universidad Nacional, eds. *Los Refugiados Centroamericanos.* Heredia, Costa Rica: Dept. Publicaciones, 1987.

Van der Veer, Guus. *Counseling and Therapy with Refugees.* New York: John Wiley, 1992.

Water Power 25.9 (1973): 321.

Webre, Stephen. *Jose Napoleón Duarte and the Christian Democratic Party in San Salvador Politics, 1960–72.* Baton Rouge: Louisiana State University, 1979.

Westwood, Sallie, and Sarah A. Radcliffe. "Gender, Racism and the Politics of Identities in Latin America." In *VIVA: Women and Popular Protest in Latin America*, edited by Sarah A. Radcliffe and Sallie Westwood, 1–29. New York: Routledge, 1993.

White, Alastair. *El Salvador.* New York: Praeger, 1973.

Yundt, Keith W. *Latin American States and Political Refugees.* New York: Praeger, 1988.

Index

ACNUR (*Alto Comisionado de las Naciones Unidas para los Refugiados*, United Nations High Commission for the Refugees), 95–96

Agrarian reform, "transformation," 42, 53

Aguinaldo, 168

Alas, Higinio (Father Higinio), 98, 101, 126–28

Alliance for Progress, 58

Amparo, 149

ANDES (*Asociación Nacional de Educadores Salvadoreños*, National Association of Salvadoran Educators), 41, 43

ANSESAL (*Agencia Nacional de Seguridad Salvadoreña*, Salvadoran National Security Agency), 52

Apastepeque, 20

Archeological data, 20

Arias, Óscar, 9

Army: arrest, 18, 33; attack, 13, 29–30, 43, 142; control, 31–32; execution, 29; loss of men to, 147; National, 31; nightmares about, 110; not targeted by, 85; Popular Revolutionary, 53; Press Office, 55; quarters, 28; recruitment, 54, 177; search, 23, 25, 29, 34; spying, 13, 30; terrorist tactics, 176; threat to, 23; torture by, 96

Authoritarianism, 26, 80, 141, 155, 164–65

Aztecs, 20

Bachillerato, 41, 62

Birth certificate, 135

Birth control, 150–51

BPR (Popular Revolutionary Bloc), 53

Cabrones, 5

Cacao, 20–21

Canada: emigration to, 17–18, 35, 112, 147–49, 176, 181; jobs, 18; life, 179

Canadian Embassy, 17, 149

Cantón, 40–41, 69
El capataz, 158
Capitalism, 154–55
Carlos Aguero Echeverría
    Command, 101
Cartago, 169
Carter administration, 58–59
Casanova, Eugenio Vides
    (Salvadoran Minister of
    Defense), 56
Castillo, Chato, 56
Catholicism: contraception, 150;
    human rights, 54, 58;
    liberation theology, 49, 64,
    118; Marian cult, 146;
    mass, 118, 124; Popular
    Church, 55, 64, 150;
    rector (Higinio Alas), 126;
    refugee center, 98–99;
    sanctity of church, 14, 63;
    social activism, 53, 64;
    Spanish colonial, 26–27;
    teachings, 64
Catholics, persecution of, 5, 133
Cecamuresa (branch of
    DIAKONÍA), 129
Cerén Site, 54
Cerrón Grande (dam), 19, 22, 69,
    113
Chalatenango, 19, 68, 70, 77, 79
Champitas, 158
Chicano political activism. *See* El
    Teatro Campesina
Childrearing, 165
Church. *See* Catholicism; Catholics
Class (socioeconomic): classless
    society, 87–89;
    distinctions, 85, 89–90,
    157; lower, 42, 58, 146,
    157–58; middle, 4, 27,
    38, 42, 60, 89–90, 105,
    146; upper, 63, 146, 157
CNK. *See* NCK
Coffee: industry, 22, 32, 38, 44, 88,

158; picking, 97, 121–23,
    125, 153
Coffee barons, 31, 38, 42, 53,
    57–58, 88. *See also*
    Oligarchy
Cofradía, 27
Cojutepeque, 20
Cold War, 154
Collaboration: at daycare center,
    107, 154; with
    ethnographer, 8, 132; with
    men, 105
Collective action, 88, 100, 121, 155
Colónes: Costa Rica, 29, 98,
    124–25, 128, 133, 160,
    165; El Salvador, 29,
    68–70
Colonialism: modern, 57, 60, 64;
    Spanish, 20–22, 25–27
Committee of Mothers
    (COMADRES): Costa Rica,
    111, 126; daycare center,
    111–12, 127, 160;
    founding, 56; El Salva-
    dor, 61, 80, 126, 135
Communism: global struggle, 53,
    57–58; idealism, 64
"Communist" label, 34, 42, 51, 53,
    64, 85, 153–54
Compañero, 129, 147–48, 150, 180
Conquest, Spanish, 20–22, 25–27
Contraception, 150
Cooperative behavior, 8, 13, 39–40,
    42, 155, 160, 163. *See also*
    Collaboration
Cooperatives, 35, 42–43, 103–104,
    111
Coordinator, daycare center,
    160–62, 166
COPREFA (Army Press Office), 55
Costa Rican Embassy, 95
Cuba, 57, 61, 64, 154
Cultural expectations: drama, 48,
    131; gender roles, 104,

141, 145–46; *machismo*, 13, 141, 145–46; *marianismo*, 13–15, 146; servants, 172; social invitations, 119, 138
Cuscatlán, 18, 25

D'Aubuissón, Roberto, 53, 55, 63
Death Squad, 23, 33, 43, 53, 59, 64
Debt peonage, 21, 57, 158
Decision-making process (daycare center), 160–61, 163–64
Democracy: Costa Rica, 86–87, 154; daycare center, 90, 159, 164; El Salvador, 42, 159; idealism, 64; resistance to, 53; U.S. promotion, 57–58
Demonstrations, 41–45, 56, 88–89, 157
Derechos Humanos en Centroamérica (periodical *Human Rights in Central America*), 98
DIAKONÍA, 104, 129, 145, 165, 175
Director (daycare center). *See* Coordinator
"Disappeared," 55, 65, 70, 155; family members, 18, 28, 33, 54, 57, 61, 136; martyrdom, 65; prejudice about, 133; search for, 56, 135
Disease, 21, 26
"Displaced" families, 178
Documentation (legal). *See* Identification papers
"Dollar diplomacy," 57
Doña, 91–92
Drama, 48–50, 132, 138
Duarte, José Napoleón, 53–54, 59, 159
Dutch, 111, 126–27, 176–77

Education: for better jobs, 38, 44, 60, 62, 150–51; degree in, 39, 41, 165, 177; expenses, 113; identification with social problems, 40–42, 44, 49; jobs in, 38, 40; lack of, 161, 163–64; public, 87, 90, 113; refugee programs in, 6, 145; refusal to recognize, 87; university, 90, 104, 154, 160–61
Educational materials (daycare center), 11, 48
Educators, unskilled, 39–40
Educators' union (ANDES), 41–42
Egalitarianism, 58, 88, 90, 164
El Asentamiento, 69
Electoral fraud, 53, 58
Elitism, 26–27, 42, 44, 90, 154, 165
El Murciélago, 95
El Salvador (book), 98
El Teatro Campesina, 131
Embargo, 103
Emergency aid, 95–97, 111, 142. *See also* Relief aid
Encomienda, 21, 31
English (language), 8, 10, 17–18, 129–30, 179
Episcopal Church, 96
Equality: fight for, 60; ideals of, 64, 154; lack of, 92, 157; promotion of (at daycare center), 159–61, 163, 165; training in (for Swedes), 172. *See also* Egalitarianism
Ereguayquín, 52, 62
ERP (Popular Revolutionary Army), 53

Family planning, 150
FAPU (United Popular Action

Front), 53
FARN (Armed Forces of National
    Resistance), 53
Fátima Refugee Center, 95, 98–99,
    110, 124, 126
Feminism, 145
Fertilizer, 5, 13, 23, 41
Financial accountability, 160
Financial support, 85, 104, 111,
    127–28, 143, 175. *See also*
    Funding
FMLN (Farabundo Martí National
    Liberation Front), 53–54,
    124
Founding (daycare center), 111–12,
    126–28, 160–61
Fourteen Families, 31, 56, 159
FPL-FM (Popular Forces of
    Liberation-Farabundo
    Martí), 53
Freedom, 154, 156
Funding: Dutch, 111, 126, 129,
    176–77; international, 97,
    111, 121; loss of, 178–81;
    reduction of, 12, 143, 175,
    177; Swedish, 11, 111,
    129, 175–77. *See also*
    Emergency aid; Relief aid
Fundraising: community, 40;
    daycare center, 12, 139,
    175

García-Villas, Marianella, 54–55,
    63
Gender equality, 145–46, 157
Gender roles. *See* Feminism
Gold, 20
"Good neighbor" policy, 57
Grass roots projects, 6, 111,
    175–76; funding, 35, 111,
    176
Gringo, 13, 18–19, 67, 167
Guanacaste, 95
Guápiles highway, 180

Guatemala, 118, 131
"Guerrilla" label, 126, 133
Guerrillas: association with, 5;
    attack by, 101; combat-
    ting, 59; enlistment in,
    147; identification as, 30,
    32, 44, 64, 134; recruit-
    ment by, 54; surrender of
    arms, 176; women as, 65
Guilt, 12, 64

Hacienda, 21–22, 31, 95
Health care: center, 99; children,
    38, 103; community,
    40–42, 56, 87, 154–55;
    problems, 6, 35, 60, 75,
    134, 171–72; workshops,
    166. *See also* Medical care
Heredia, 6, 95, 98, 123–24, 126,
    138, 154, 172
Hijos naturales, 149
Houses: communal 95, 98–101,
    110, 123, 155; of
    ethnographer, 132–33;
    individual, 3–4, 117, 125,
    133, 138, 168, 175,
    179–80; resettlement, 19,
    23, 69, 148
Housing: conditions, 40–41, 68,
    136, 138, 165; daycare
    center, 4, 7, 112, 127;
    emergency, 95; rent, 5,
    41, 87, 142, 165
Human rights, 10, 54–55, 57–58,
    85, 87, 160, 166
Human Rights Commission in Costa
    Rica, 98
Human Rights Commission of El
    Salvador (CDHES,
    *Comisión de Derechos
    Humanos de El Salvador*),
    28, 54–55, 57, 96

Identification papers, El Salvador,

44, 72, 76–78. *See also*
Refugee papers; Visas;
Work, permission
Illegitimate children, 149–50
Ilopango, 52
Immigration, 95, 101–2, 149
Imperialist aggression, 22–23, 59,
64
Income, 21–22, 56, 89, 111, 166,
179–80. *See also* Salary;
Wages
Indian. *See* Indigenous people
Indigenous people, 10, 20–22,
26–27, 31
Indigo, 21–22
Inter-American Committee on
Human Rights, 54
International, agencies and funding.
See Funding
International relief organizations.
See Relief aid
Izalco, 20

Jealousy, 68, 81, 171–72
Juan Santamaría airport, 121

Kennedy administration, 58

Land: confiscation, 20–22, 38;
communally-owned, 20,
22, 26, 31, 64; fertilization,
41, 69; private ownership,
20; reform, 42, 58–59;
refugee farm, 6; refugee
ownership, 111, 121, 180;
resettlement, 19, 22–23,
27, 69, 113; spiritual
relationship to, 20; tenure
(Costa Rica), 88; tenure
(El Salvador), 20–21, 31,
38, 42, 62–63, 141
Landowners (El Salvador), 13, 19,
38; colonial, 26, 31;
military, 32

Lenca, 20
Ley de Orden (Law of Public
Order), 52, 54, 58
Liberation theology, 49, 64, 118
Los Ángeles (agricultural project),
95

Machismo, 13, 104, 141, 145–47,
156–57
Maize, 20
Majagual, 62
Male authority, 141, 155–56
Malnutrition. *See* Nutrition
Management techniques, 161–62
Managua, 103
Manhood, 141
Manzana, 19, 47
Marian cult, 146
Marianismo, 13–14, 146
Marriage: birth control, 150;
common law, 79, 129,
147–48, 150; decisions
about, 32–33, 63, 103,
148–49; effect on parents,
33, 35, 63, 114–15, 134;
expectations, 87; moral
code, 149; new household,
46, 52, 69; problems, 33,
70, 105, 114, 147; rate,
147; relationships, 136;
secrecy about, 76, 78–79
Martínez, General Maximiliano
Hernández, 31, 55, 58
Martyrdom, 63–65, 90
Marxism, 42
Mass (church). *See* Catholic Church
Matanza (of 1932), 31, 42, 58
Maternity leave, 146, 168
Mayan, 20
Medical care: anti-malaria, 62;
birth control, 150;
emergency, 95, 120;
orders from doctors, 171;
for refugees, 166;

services, 41, 90, 97, 99;
for "subversives," 85, 130.
See also Health care
Mejicano, 75
Menchú, Rigoberta, 131
Menstruation, 63
Men's work, 156
Mexico, 91, 102, 146
Military: aid, 58–59, 64; associ-
ation with oligarchy, 32,
53; control of elections,
54; forces, 14, 43, 53,
58–59, 64, 75, 96, 134,
141; reaction to opposition,
32; rule, 13–14, 31–32,
42, 53–54, 57–58, 109.
See also Paramilitary groups
Ministerio de Trabajo (Ministry of
Labor), 149
Molina, Colonel Arturo Armando,
52–54, 58, 69
Monroe Doctrine, 57
Monte Carmelo, 71
Motherhood, 14, 146
Mother's Day (*Día de la Madre*),
37, 65, 91, 178

National Anthem, 39, 91
National Campaign Against Malaria,
62
National Guard: activity, 29,
44–45, 47, 52–53, 73–75,
78–79, 96; director, 56;
forces, 31, 52–53, 73–74
National Police, 31–32, 43
Native communities. *See* Indigenous
people
NCK (Dutch relief agency), 126,
129
New Laws of 1542, 21
Nicaragua, 59, 89, 95, 102–4, 127,
176
Nicaraguan Embassy, 101
Nightmares, 96, 110

Nobel Peace Prize. *See* Menchú,
Rigoberta
Nuñez, Padre Bénjamin, 154
Nutrition, 90, 112, 145, 162, 166,
171

OAR-CASPRE (relief agencies),
142
OAS (Organization of American
States), 57
Ochoa, Colonel Sigifredo
(Commander of the Fourth
Brigade), 56
Oligarchy, 31–32, 42, 53, 57–58.
See also Coffee barons.
Oral literature, 15, 121, 131–32
ORDEN (*Organización Democrática
Nacionalista,* Democratic
Nationalist Organization),
43, 53
Otera, 55
"Outlaw genre," 132

Panama, 59, 91
Papal bull of 1537, 21
Paramilitary groups, 43, 53, 59, 64.
See also Military
Parental leave, 155
Paternalism, 11, 42, 141. *See also*
Patrón
Patrón, 11, 157–58. *See also*
Paternalism
Patron saint of El Salvador, 49
Pensions, 155
Pila, 3–4, 170
Pilgrimage, 169
Pipil, 20
Pneumonia, 26
"Poema de Amor" ("Love Poem"),
91
Pokomam, 20
Policía de Hacienda. See Treasury
Police
Popular Church, 49, 55, 64, 150.

See also Liberation theology
Population, 20–21, 25–26, 42, 150
Potonico, 68, 78
Pregnancy: attitudes, 150; lack of
    knowledge, 63; medical
    orders, 137; problems,
    84, 91, 127, 137–38, 169;
    sick leave, 168; in young
    girls, 149
Pregnant women: abandonment of,
    147–48, 157; marriage of,
    63; poverty of, 57; rape
    of, 5–6, 14; seizure of,
    33; unmarried, 127, 138,
    148–49
Prisoners (political), 52–53, 55–56,
    60–61, 64–65; amnesty,
    55; in Costa Rica, 102;
    dramatic portrayal, 49;
    female, 13; gaining
    freedom for, 55–56;
    rebellion leaders, 32;
    torture, 13, 52–53
Private army, 31
Private ownership of land, 20, 22
Propagandizing, 47, 52
Protest, 27, 41–42, 101–2,
    154–55. *See also*
    Demonstrations
Prostitutes, 157
Pseudonyms, 8
Psychological care, 105, 109, 162
Psychological therapy, 109–10, 143
Psychological torture, 13–14, 53
Psychological wounds, 109, 137,
    142
Puerto Limón, 180
Pupusas, 3, 84

Rape: in church, 5–6, 14; by
    employers, 157; gang, 13;
    memories of, 140–41, 179;
    of pregnant women, 5–6,
    14; protest of, 155

Rapists, forgiveness of, 15, 140–41
Reagan, President Ronald, 9
Reagan administration, 59
Red Cross, 71, 96, 125, 128
Refugee camp (Los Ángeles), 95
Refugee centers: Fátima Church,
    95, 98–99, 109–10, 153;
    Nicaragua, 102; El
    Salvador, 6–7, 34–35;
Refugee farm, 6–7
Refugee papers, 95, 97, 101–2,
    104, 107, 148–49. *See also*
    Identification papers;
    Visas; Work
Relief aid: agencies, 6, 97, 111,
    131, 139, 142; Dutch
    (NCK), 126–27; emer-
    gency, 142; funds, 100,
    120–21; Red Cross, 125;
    United Nations, 99, 121;
    work, 12; workers, 6, 10,
    68, 165. *See also*
    Emergency aid
Rent: control, 87, 142; funds for,
    100, 127; rising, 180
Renting: houses, 3, 95, 133, 165,
    175, 180; land, 111, 180;
    problems, 133, 142
Reorganization (of the Center),
    160–61
Repartimiento, 21, 31, 57
Reporters, 6, 10, 68, 130–31, 139,
    170
Research: conclusion, 173–74;
    obligations, 9, 11;
    preparation, 6–12;
    problems, 68, 81, 84–85,
    118–20; refugee control,
    9–10, 84–85, 91–92, 131,
    146; resentment about, 7
Resettlement, 17, 19, 22–23,
    27–28, 69, 113, 148
"Resistance literature," 132
"Respect," 140, 157

Reubicación, 69. *See also* Resettlement
Richard Nixon (school), 128
Roadblock, 43, 76–78
Romero, Archbishop Óscar Arnulfo, 4–5, 13, 37, 53
Romero, General Carlos Humberto, 45, 52–54, 56, 58–59
Roosevelt, President Franklin D., 57
Rosales Hospital, 71

Sabana, 126
Sacred Family, 6
Salary: Christmas bonus, 168; daycare center, 35, 111, 127, 133, 160, 162, 164–65; equality in, 160, 162, 165; servant girls, 157; severance pay, 175; sex discrimination, 145; teachers (El Salvador), 41–42, 44, 91; women, 105. *See also* Income; Wages
Salvadoran Peace Accords, 176
Sandinistas, 103
San José, 6, 98, 101, 104, 125, 154, 177
San Miguel, 52
Santa Tecla, 53, 55
Santa Teresa, 68–69
Santibáñez, 56
Searches (for "disappeared"), 28, 56, 61, 70–71, 80
Searches (for "subversives"), 45, 75, 78–79; blocks of houses, 47; Costa Rica, 101; resettlement communities, 23, 32–34; teachers, 43–44; union leaders, 52
Servants, 38, 85, 87–89, 97, 153, 157, 172
Settlement. *See* Resettlement
Severance pay, 175–76, 179–81

Sex discrimination, 145
Sexual relationship, 138, 140–41, 157
Shifting agriculture, 22
Sick leave, 137, 167–68
Silver, 20
Single parent, 84
SIT (secret police of the Interior Department), 52
Slavery, 21, 57, 157
Smallpox, 26
"Social activism," 23, 49
Socialism, 154–55
Solidarity, 174
Somoza, 95
Song of Salvation, 25
Soviet Union, 57
Soyapango, 71–72
Spanish clergy, 26–27
Spanish colonists, 20–22, 25–27
Spanish Empire, 21
Storytelling: content, 6, 10, 12, 14–15, 18, 80, 85, 119, 131–32, 134, 138; purpose, 121; repetition, 132; style, 6, 51–52, 68, 119, 131–32, 134, 138, 172; unrecorded, 134
Strikes, 28, 42, 44, 70, 88–89
"Subversive" activity: definition, 54; lack of evidence, 32; propagandizing, 47; searching for "disappeared," 28–29; working with unions, 42
"Subversive" label, 64, 133
"Subversives": Church influence on, 14; imprisonment of, 55; peasants, 27; physicians, 130; political activists, 15; searching for, 49; seizure of, 33; teachers, 43–44, 47; torture of, 55
Surveillance, 22, 27, 44

Swallow, 12
Swedes, namesake, 167, 169–70, 172
Swedish international funding, 111
Swedish Peace Corps, 12
Swedish sponsors: classes for refugees, 145; DIAKONÍA, 104, 129, 145; idealism, 155, 160, 165; reduction of funding, 11–12, 175–77
"Switzerland of the Americas," 86–87

Tape recording (of interviews), 6, 8–11, 50–51, 67, 100, 118, 132–34, 140
Teaching methology, 164–65
Testimonios: "authorship" of, 121; choreography of, 9, 85; commodity, 83–85, 118, 120; control, 10, 120–21, 131, 138; drama, 68, 80; oral literature, 121, 131–32; political rhetoric, 63–64, 134, 138, 154; rights over, 81, 83–84, 119, 130; therapy, 109
Theater. *See* Drama
Tonantzin (Mexican goddess "Our Mother"), 146
Torrijos-Carter treaty, 59
Torture, 44, 52–53, 72–73, 96; children, 14; female prisoners, 13–14, 141, 143; peasants, 31; pregnant women, 14, 141, 143; propagandizers, 52; union leaders, 52–53, 64, 72
Transcription (of tapes), 6, 10–11, 132–33
Translation, 8, 10, 129–30, 132, 170

Treasury Police (*Policía de Hacienda*), 31
Tribute, 21–22, 26, 31
Trichinosis, 60
Tropical Bottling Company, 70, 76, 79
Tuition, 175
Typhus, 26

UCA (*Universidad Centro-americana*, Central American University), 41, 70
UCR (*Universidad de Costa Rica*, University of Costa Rica), 154
UNA (*Universidad Nacional Autónoma*, National University), 154
United Nations, 80, 95, 99–100, 102, 121
Union: activity, 42; leaders' wives, 55, 69–70, 80, 134, 138; meetings, 55, 70; members' rights, 57
Unions, 53, 55, 63; bottling company, 69–70; crayon factory, 52; students, 44; teachers (ANDES), 41, 43–44; utilities, 52
U.S. Embassy, 11, 101
U.S. involvement. *See* Colonialism, modern; Imperialist aggression; Military
Usulután, 52

Viceroyalty of New Spain, 26
Village councils, 26
Virginity, 14, 149, 157
Virgin Mary, 14, 146
Visas: Canadian, 17; resident (Costa Rica), 97. *See* Identification papers; Refugee papers; Work

Wage earners, 27; agriculture,
        21–22, 38, 44; children,
        113; factory, 52; men,
        141
Wages, 42, 52, 64, 97, 150. *See
        also* Income; Salary
Welfare system, 41, 88, 141, 155
"White Hand," 43
Widows, 48, 76, 130, 138, 158
Women, legal status of, 145–46
Women's liberation, 145–46
Women's work, 156
Work, permission, 97, 148–49, 171
Work schedules, 160–62, 163
World War II, 53

Zafier (factory owner), 52

About the Author

ROBIN ORMES QUIZAR is Associate Professor in the English Department at Metro State College of Denver. In Costa Rica she held a Fulbright Senior Lectureship in linguistics at the National University in Heredia, and while there she conducted research among both Salvadoran and Guatemalan refugees.